Chicken Soup for the Soul®

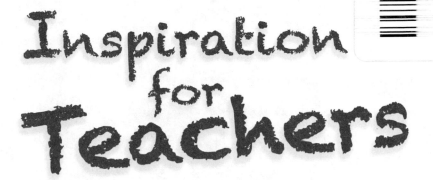

Inspiration for Teachers

101 Stories about How You Make a Difference

Amy Newmark
Alex Kajitani

CSS

Chicken Soup for the Soul, LLC
Cos Cob, CT

Changing lives one story at a time®
www.chickensoup.com

Table of Contents

❸
~The Teacher Who Taught Me to Teach~

❹
~Making a Difference~

❺
~That First Year~

❻
~My Teacher Changed My Life~

❼
~Lessons from Non-Traditional Classrooms~

8

~Breaking Through~

9

~Learning from the Students~

❿
~The Quiet Ones~

Introduction

My very first day of high school, I nervously walked into my first period class, made my way to the back of the classroom and sat down. As the other students began filling in the seats around me, I looked up and noticed a poster hanging on the wall. It was a photo of a surfer riding a huge wave in Hawaii (my ultimate dream at that point). The caption above the photo said, "Success consists of getting up just one more time than you fall."

What I might today simply dismiss as a "cheesy inspirational poster" deeply stirred something inside my fourteen-year-old self. Then and there, I adopted that line as my mantra. As I stumbled my way through high school, then college — and even through my later travels around the world (where I got to live my dream of surfing some big waves in Hawaii) — each time things got hard or went badly, that darn poster would pop into my head.

But never did it make more sense than when I started teaching. There are days when things go badly. Very badly. And there are days when things go great. Really great. And somehow, it often seems like the best days I've had teaching have come right on the heels of the worst days. Success, it seems, actually does consist of getting up just one more time than you fall.

People often ask me why I teach. My answer is simple: I want to live forever. Machines fall apart, money runs out and beauty fades. Our ideas, our lessons and our stories are all that can truly be passed down from one generation to the next.

Chicken Soup for the Soul: Inspiration for Teachers is proof that when we teach, we live forever. This book is not a collection of stories where everything always works out perfectly in the end. Rather, it is a collection of real-life stories, each thoughtfully and beautifully told, about the moments that matter the most and that live on in our hearts.

They are stories that make us laugh out loud at the wonderful and funny things kids do and say, like Cindy Jolley's experience with a second grader "giving her the finger." They are heart-wrenching, tear-inducing stories like Julie Rine's, about the impact on her school of the death of three former students — which remind us of the fragility of life and the importance of community. And they are the stories that make us stop and reflect on the sometimes simple, sometimes epic, actions that teachers like Carrie Malinowski take when they choose to see students not just as they are, but also as they can be.

This book is a testament to the fact that there is no one way to teach or one type of teacher. Sometimes, teachers pop up in the wildest places, when we least expect them. Ginny Huff Conahan shares what she learns from an enlightened former student, who teaches her the true meaning of being present in the moment. When Jeanne Kraus just can't seem to reach a challenging student, she learns that a puppy can. And Mike McCrobie's story is a fitting reminder that even as adults playing softball with friends, our teachers never stop showing up to encourage us to look past what is easy and instead do what is right.

There is no doubt that the past few years have not been easy for those of us who have chosen teaching as a profession. As someone who travels the country speaking to and motivating teachers at conferences and conducting professional development in everything from district offices to school cafeterias, I am well aware of the issues teachers face on a daily basis. Staff lounges everywhere are filled with passionate educators who often feel belittled by politicians, public perception, or their own paychecks. But we keep coming back. Why? Because of the stories you will read in this book.

Working on this book with Amy Newmark and the team at Chicken Soup for the Soul is more than an honor. It is an obligation. An obligation to make sure that these stories about teachers get told, are shared, and are used to inspire all teachers to keep doing the incredible work we do each day to ensure a better future for our students and for our world.

This book is also an opportunity. An opportunity to inspire a future generation of teachers to live a life of significance, one in which someone else's life is better because of something you did or said. Or maybe you didn't say or do anything—you just made a commitment to show up every day, be your authentic self, and believe that every one of your students could be more than they ever dreamed possible.

And this book is a celebration. Not just a celebration of the moments when we were victorious. It is a celebration of the moments when we felt the pain of our students or when they felt ours. A celebration of the moments when we thought we had it all figured out, only to realize that we weren't even close. And a celebration of the moments when success consists of getting up just one more time than we fall.

Teaching is not just what we do, teaching is what we are. Through our work as teachers — and through these shared stories — we will live forever.

Happy Teaching,
Alex Kajitani

California Teacher of the Year
Top-4 Finalist, National Teacher of the Year

Chapter 1

Inspiration for Teachers

The Power of Each Other

Students don't care how much you know
until they know how much you care.
~Author Unknown

After the Silence

What we have once enjoyed deeply we can never lose.
All that we love deeply becomes a part of us.
~Helen Keller

irst, there is the cacophony of noise and action. The Facebook posts, ambiguous requests for prayer with no details.

Then the texts and personal Facebook messages: "Did you hear?" "Is it true?" "Do you know?" "Is it her?" "Was he with them?"

Then the confirmations. The phone calls. The breaking of the news to friends. The gasps, the cries, the denial.

Then the planning: "Will we do this?" "Should we do that?" "What would be best?" "When is it?" "Vigil tomorrow night?" "Counselors at school on Monday?" "Calling hours Wednesday for all three of them?"

And then comes the silence. The phone stops buzzing; the texts stop coming. Everyone knows. And there is nothing to say.

And there I was, in the shower, trying to wash it all away. My quiet tears started falling, and suddenly I jumped at a scream, a keening sound that came from deep within me. "NOT MY KIDS!" Please God, no.

But it *was* my kids. Three beautiful, vibrant, funny kids. A junior in my class this year, a quiet and gorgeous blonde who loved pink. A senior boy who had been in my class last year, the star of the football team, a boy I had seen out playing pool with his friends a few weeks ago on a Friday night to celebrate his nineteenth birthday. And a girl who was a student in my class a few years ago, who was loving her first year of college at West Virginia University where she was the women's basketball team manager. Gone in a tragic car accident less than a mile from my house, their car sliding into a school bus traveling in the opposite direction.

The ice storm had hit in an instant. The roads had turned from wet to ice in no time. It was no one's fault. It was just a regular Saturday morning in November, but it was one that changed everything in our town forever.

The silence persisted. The next night, a vigil was held. Our school gym had never been entered so quietly, and it was packed. There was the sniffling, the quiet tears of disbelief. After the speaker finished, he told us we could stay as long as we wanted.

The formal part of the night was over, but no one moved. No one spoke. We all just sat there, tightly squeezed together in the gym where Storm had played basketball, where A'liyah had walked across the floor at the Promenade, where Savannah had sat with her friends for pep rallies.

The superintendent reiterated that we were free to go when we wanted, but we sat still, not moving, not talking. Not wanting to break free of the comfort of shared pain and strength.

Finally, some of the kids stood up and started hugging each other. Maybe kids are wiser than we give them credit for. The gym floor was soon filled with adults and kids, crying and hugging one another.

One of my freshman students walked up to people and said, "You don't know me. I'm Morgan. Let's hug." I saw her do that at least three times. Several of my older students sobbed in my arms and asked, "Why?" I sobbed, too. "I don't know," I said.

Teachers are used to having the answers. They expect to have some wisdom to impart, whether it's about how to pass a standardized test, write a college application essay, or get over your first broken heart. But this? There were no answers.

The silence was back on Monday. Have you ever heard kids go to their lockers and then to first period in complete silence? When the bell rang for class to start, they stared at me, silently, expectantly. "Fix this," they seemed to be saying. "Make sense of this for us," they silently begged. I couldn't. Instead, I opened my mouth to speak… and lost my composure. I cried. I said I didn't know what to do. Or how to move forward. In the end, we decided on hugs.

Today was better. We pretended to care a little about what school is about and did some lessons. One girl left in the middle of class. I sat on the floor outside my room with her, and we cried for a few minutes. In fifth period, a boy passed gas, loudly, near another boy who was on the floor watching *Tuesdays with Morrie* with him. They laughed and ended up rolling around on the floor, half-hugging and half-wrestling with each other.

I turned away to hide my tears. These are teenagers. They should only be full of laughter. The laughter should not have to make room for grief and pain. They shouldn't have to go to calling hours tomorrow night for three of their friends. There should not be three coffins in a school gym and a long snaking line that consists of an entire town of mourning people waiting to pay their respects.

I don't know if the calling hours tomorrow night will be silent. But I know that silence visits when there is nothing to say. And sometimes, there are just no words. Only heartbreak and unity. But after that? Then comes the healing.

~Julie Rine

That Clinging Love

How mutable are our feelings, and how strange
is that clinging love we have of life even in
the excess of misery!
~Mary Shelley, Frankenstein

y mother's two weeks in Intensive Care kept death at bay temporarily, but the Stage 4 cancer that had invaded her bones necessitated interventions that seemed like science fiction. I was teaching *Frankenstein* to my tenth grade classes at the same time that we were keeping Mom alive by pushing the edges of science.

As my students grappled with Mary Shelley's vocabulary, I had my own learning curve in the hospital. Each school day for those two weeks, I discussed the scientific morality of *Frankenstein*, while I took notes in the hospital on the new language of transfusions, chemotherapy, scans, and acronym after acronym. No teacher likes to admit that she's distracted past the point of effective education, but I was. In class, I'd start pondering CAT scans and lose track of which topic we were covering.

To comfort my mother, I drove to the hospital during my off period, which backed up to lunch, and returned for sixth. Since I'd just given birth six weeks prior, I had no sick days left to take off from school, and we were so broke I couldn't afford to take an unpaid day.

One Thursday, however, my mother clung to me. She wanted me to stay for the next round of poisons they would run through her veins.

"Don't go." Mom squeezed my hand.

"I'll come after school," I said. "I'll just stop home and feed the baby first."

"Bye, Kristie," a nurse said, adjusting the morphine above Mom's IV. Since I spent more waking hours at the hospital than I did at home with my new baby—and almost as many as I did with the teenagers at school—they knew me here. When I glanced at the clock above the nurse's head, I cursed. I was going to be late for my next class.

I drove ten miles over the speed limit and parked in a spot reserved for guests. When I pushed open the school doors, I heard only muffled noise from classrooms, while the hallways buzzed only with fluorescent light. That meant the final bell had rung at least five minutes ago.

I could be fired for being so irresponsible. Teachers had been sued for leaving classrooms unattended. I ran up the concrete stairs, cursing my post-pregnancy weight gain beneath each out-of-shape breath.

"Yeah, but is it Victor Frankenstein's fault?" A popular slacker wearing skater-tight jeans stood in front of my British Literature class, writing his classmates' answers on the whiteboard. He couldn't have cared less about academics, but he liked poetry because he wanted to be a rock star. He wrote music about having to leave his whole world behind when floodwaters forced his family out of New Orleans.

I stood in the doorway, panting, and let him continue. In an understated but effective style, this young musician continued the conversation about how society creates monsters in Mary Shelley's *Frankenstein*.

The rest of the students, who could have been lighting fires or getting each other pregnant during this unsupervised time, listened intently.

Bless them.

I've never tried to play the superhero in my classroom. I grade papers; I maintain discipline; I solve problems. But I don't do superhero. My kids know that I lose my train of thought even when my mother isn't dying nearby. They know I can't help but laugh at inappropriate teenage jokes. (I try not to laugh, I swear.) They know I cry every time we read the last chapter of *The Things They Carried*.

"I got this," my student said.

"Well, then I'm heading back to the hospital," I said. My class laughed. They could handle dark humor, not to mention frank discussions of life and death, science and responsibility. They could access compassion.

Thankfully.

I clung to their loving understanding.

~Kristie Betts Letter

Doing Something Right

*When you see that many people with a smile on their
face, then you must be doing something right.*
~Greg Norman

The last bell rang and I sank immediately into the chair behind my desk, defeated. I mumbled a few goodbyes to my students as they shuffled out of the classroom, too exhausted to do more. Everything hurt: my legs, my head, my heart, my pride. I had been on autopilot all day, and now that the day was over, I had no choice but to confront my feelings.

I was so unhappy.

The realization hit me like a wave. I watched students talking in the hallway, pulling backpacks out of lockers, leaving school with their friends, and I tried to pinpoint exactly why I was so miserable. It had been a tough couple of weeks. Two students had been killed in gang-related shootings; one of my twelfth graders had left the state to protect himself; and no one would tell the teachers what was going on with these gang wars.

I had noticed a sudden change in my students as a result of these events, even in those who had no direct ties to the gangs. They were all angry, restless, and full of despair. Tamara blew up in class over the D on her essay. Markus sat at his desk with a blank look in his eyes, refusing to do any work. Asia burst into tears and had to leave the room. The delicate atmosphere I had worked so hard to create all year had been shattered, and I was starting to feel hopeless.

What had made me think that I could teach on the west side of Chicago? Here I was, a twenty-three-year-old white girl in her second year of teaching, thinking that I could make a difference. I wanted to laugh at myself, and I would have, had it not been for the lump hardening like cement in the back of my throat.

I may have covered up my frustration with a smile, but I couldn't cover up the dark circles under my eyes, no matter how much make-up I used. I may have pretended to be older than I was, to assert some sort of authority, but I couldn't pretend to understand the hardships that my kids faced every day. I may have lied to my family about how completely fine I was, but I couldn't keep lying to myself.

Maybe I wasn't cut out to be a teacher.

The thought brought tears to my eyes. Just then, one of the tenth graders walked into the room with a smile stretched across his face. I stared at my computer screen and blinked back the tears as quickly as I could.

"Hi, Ms. Raicu," he said, not noticing my red eyes. I had gotten very good at hiding my emotions lately.

"Hi, honey," I said, smiling back. "How was your day?"

Lamar wasn't one of my students, but he had made a habit of coming to check in with me every day. I don't remember how it started, but I always looked forward to his visits. It took my mind off other things, and I genuinely enjoyed our conversations.

"It was fine," he said. "Mr. D brought in his turtles today."

We talked about the turtles, the awful burgers that had been served for lunch, and the upcoming field trip to the zoo. Still, for some reason, I couldn't shake my sadness.

There was a knock at my door, and John walked in. He worked at a neighboring school and had gone through teacher training with me.

"John!" I exclaimed, jumping out of my seat. "How are you? I haven't seen you in forever!" I gave him a hug and introduced him to Lamar.

"Nice to meet you," said John. "I'm just visiting."

He looked around my room and smiled.

"Your classroom's great, Laura," he said. "Very bright and welcoming." He took a moment to look at the quotes on the door, the posters on the wall, my students' projects on the bulletin board, and the thank-you notes I had received from my kids over the course of the year.

"Looks like you're doing something right," he said, tapping the notes.

"How's teaching been?" I asked, and he gave me a look that I understood all too well.

"This teaching thing is not what we were expecting, huh?" he asked, and we both laughed. I felt an overwhelming sense of relief being in the presence of someone who completely understood what this crazy field was all about.

John suddenly turned to look at Lamar, who was silently taking in our conversation.

"So, Lamar," said John, "what do you like most about Ms. Raicu?"

I blushed at the unexpected question, but Lamar took it seriously. He thought about it for a few seconds before formulating his response.

"Sometimes," he said slowly, "the only reason I come to school is because of Ms. Raicu. She's always here for me."

That was all he needed to say.

I held in my tears until we said our goodbyes. Then, like a waterfall, I let them run down my cheeks and chin. They were tears of pain, joy, and relief. I stood like that for a few minutes, staring at the bulletin board full of thank-yous, letting myself cry.

Ms. Raicu, thank you for being the best teacher ever, said Britney's note. *Even when you're hard on me, I know you love me,* said Camron's note. *I'm going to miss you so much when I graduate,* said Mikayla's note.

I read every single note, all twenty-four of them. Then I wiped my eyes, took a deep breath, and smiled the first real smile in three weeks. John's words rang in my head: "Looks like you're doing something right."

Maybe I was.

~Laura Raicu

Saving Daniel

Alone we can do so little, together we can do so much.
~Helen Keller

irst graders literally hung from the light fixtures as I stepped into the room on that first day. A row of angry mothers lined the back wall with frowns on their faces and belts in their hands. The aide ran a carpet sweeper over spilled cereal while chaos erupted all around her in this inner-city classroom.

It was the thirteenth day of school, and the class had already gone through fifteen teachers. I was lucky sixteen, and this was my first day of teaching — ever.

Over the previous weeks, the classroom had been stripped bare save for a tub of broken crayons, a ream of newsprint, and a handful of chewed-up pencils. No books, no supplies and, I was told, *no* budget to buy any.

A third of my students spoke only Spanish; I only spoke English. My aide knew ten basic Spanish commands, and that was it.

But I was young, energetic and determined. So, we began.

I started by using my salary to buy supplies for the classroom. I could live on beans; my kids needed pencils. I got donations of used books from libraries, bought crackers and cheese spread for hungry tummies, and searched Goodwill for sweaters and jackets for the students who came to school on cold days in flip-flops and shorts.

Many of my English-speaking students had never been past their own block. Some had not stepped out their front doors before they entered school, and had never interacted with other kids. Many of my Spanish speakers were new arrivals to this country. It was like English was a second language for everyone.

So, I went to the universal language — music. We sang.

We sang our good-morning song. We sang our days of the week, our numbers and our colors. We sang about the seasons and our body parts and how to move. We sang about how to line up and how to sit down. And we danced. We danced our way to lunch, to our seats, to our stations. We danced the water cycle and our addition facts. We jumped, we skipped, we twisted and froze, and then we bowed and sat.

And we laughed.

Don't get me wrong… there were many days I cried. The job felt impossible. I barely slept, hardly ate, and never had enough time. The students entered first grade at least three years behind the kids at most other schools, and while some parents were very supportive, others were downright hostile. I'd go home drained, exhausted, and ready to give up.

Except, there was Daniel. I couldn't give up on Daniel. None of us could.

A full head shorter than all the other students, Daniel's yellow hue showed through his dark skin. The whites of his eyes were the color of egg yolks, and his trembling body was clearly ill and stressed.

And yet, despite his limited English, the child would shine like the sun whenever we'd sing and dance. He'd kick and twist and clap until he had to find the beanbag chair to sit and catch his breath. Even there, panting for breath, his smile would beam while his eyes followed his classmates as they marched and galloped and twirled.

Unfortunately, each day Daniel danced for shorter and shorter periods and then fell asleep for hours. His mom came to me with an interpreter. He had kidney failure. He was on the list for a transplant, but no one knew if he would get it in time. He might not be able to do schoolwork — but he loved the music. They lived right across the street from school. She wanted to know if she could bring him whenever we were singing, and then take him home after. He was dying, and his mother believed that the music was giving him a reason to go on.

With Administration's approval, we made a plan: Whenever Daniel was awake and strong enough to come to school, his mom would bring him. I'd arrange our classroom schedule so that we'd do music when Daniel came into the room, and since we sang ten times a day, adding in a few songs on whatever topics we were working on would be easy.

And it changed everything.

Students who believed they had nothing and offered nothing were suddenly empowered — to save Daniel.

They might have been fidgety or naughty before he showed up, but as soon as Daniel entered the room, everyone was single-minded in purpose. They sat up straight, included Daniel in the circle, and listened. They performed their hearts out until they could elicit a smile from the fragile boy. Each day when they were done, they'd walk Daniel to the beanbag chair, cover him with a blanket, and let him sleep until his mom came to pick him up.

We became a family — a loving, caring family. We had a common cause — to save Daniel — and to do so, we sang our hearts out.

Each week, I brought new songs as we learned new subjects. Each week, our motley band bonded more and more in our common cause. Nevertheless, Daniel's strength waned.

Soon, he could not dance with us. He could no longer walk into the room. He couldn't stand. He couldn't sit up. Finally, his mother had to carry him in and lay him on the beanbag chair. She'd prop up his head and cover him, but he had stopped opening his eyes. When she lay him down, we'd quietly get up and begin a song. Softly, slowly, we'd start, then let the volume build as we began to dance and keep the rhythm. The students seemed to pour their wills and determination into giving their all for Daniel. And when they did, sometimes Daniel's lips would make the smallest smile, and we would all break into cheers.

Then Daniel didn't come.

I went over to Daniel's house at recess, but no one was home. That night, I cried myself to sleep.

But there was no need to mourn. Daniel was gone because he was to get a kidney.

We'd done our job and helped him stay alive until that could happen.

Last I heard, Daniel had graduated from high school. He'd gone on to live the life of a normal child and teen. He was into video games — and loved music.

I've moved away from that school and teaching, but the lessons of that year changed who I am. I understand the power of song, hope, and giving. I understand the determination of the human heart. I know that the least of us can be empowered to change the world, and that Daniel did as much to save us as we did to save Daniel.

~Susan Traugh

Consequences

A man sooner or later discovers that he is the master-gardener of his soul, the director of his life.
~James Allen

I leaned against Susie's open door. "If I have to grade another paper right now, I'm gonna lose it. I really need a break." I dragged myself into her classroom and plopped down at the closest student's desk.

"Tell me about it." Susie, my friend and mentor, put down her red pen and pushed away from her crowded desk.

I slouched farther down. "I'm overworked, overloaded, and just over it. Final projects, exams, grades, parent conferences, paperwork, graduation, cleanup, checkout. I'm exhausted. I won't relax till we walk out of this building next week."

"Then we'll have the whole summer."

I glanced out the door. "I know, but — " *Oh, my God. Was that Kelly White coming up the hall?* Seeing Kelly silenced my tirade. *What was he doing here?* I sat up straight.

Even though I was a fairly young teacher, I didn't remember all my former students' names and faces. But I'd never forget Kelly. He'd taken my public-speaking class several years earlier when he was a senior. When he failed and didn't graduate on time, he was furious.

Kelly stopped at the door.

I forced a smile. "Hi, Kelly… What are you doin' here?"

"I came to find you," he said.

"Oh?" I shifted my position and held my breath. *Why did he need to find me? Why now?*

A recent event had put me on edge. A senior had threatened an English teacher because he hadn't passed her class. He'd told her, "I'll get you."

The next day, as she left work, he was waiting in the teachers' parking lot with his dog. He walked toward her. She went back inside the school, called the police, and pressed charges against him.

Kelly stepped inside the room. "I've needed to do something for a long time."

I looked over to Susie. She had gone back to grading papers and probably thought nothing of a former student dropping by to see me.

All the events surrounding his failure came rushing back to me. Kelly wasn't a behavior problem. He never put much effort into the class, but did enough to get by and pass first semester. Second semester was a different story. He didn't do any classwork and blew off the exam. Even with my liberal grading scale, his average was below 50. He had no chance of passing, but he needed that elective credit to graduate.

A gifted athlete, Kelly had won a state championship in track. He ranked as one of the school's all-time stars. A large photograph of him in his uniform was prominently displayed in the gym foyer. The coaches held high expectations for him. His athletic skills had earned him a scholarship.

His track coach approached me and asked me to change his grade. Then the head guidance counselor came. Finally, an assistant principal tried to pressure me to pass Kelly. They played all the typical cards — pity, guilt, race.

I just couldn't do it. If his average had been higher and closer to passing, I might have been swayed. But it wasn't, and I wasn't.

If I changed Kelly's grade, why shouldn't I change every other student's failing grade? Why should he be treated differently because he was blessed with athletic talents?

These men were upset and frustrated with me for not giving in.

The whole stressful ordeal had been tense and disheartening. I resented being questioned about a student's grade. *Didn't we have standards? Weren't we supposed to prepare students for the real world — not give them a pass? How could this successful coach and these administrators want me to do something unethical?* I lost respect for them for asking me.

At the center of this firestorm, Kelly blamed me because he didn't graduate with his class and had to go to summer school to earn that last required credit.

My stomach tightened as Kelly stepped farther into the room.

"You know, in my whole life, you were the first obstacle I ever encountered. Because of sports, I kind of slid by. I got away with things," he said. "Even with my mother. But not you. No one ever held me responsible for my actions. I blamed you for failing me and keeping me from graduating on time." Kelly shook his head. "But I learned an important lesson from you. I learned that I have to be responsible for my own actions."

He paused and then grinned broadly. "I needed to come back to thank you."

Did I hear that right? I began to breathe normally again.

He stepped closer to me. "You didn't fail me. *I* failed," he said, putting his hand to his chest. "You did the right thing."

Tears streamed down my face.

Kelly sat on the desk next to me. "I wanted you to know that I did go on to college. I competed in track there, too."

Still trim and fit, he was doing well. We talked for a few more minutes.

"Well, I know you must have a lot to do, so I better go." Kelly stood.

"Wait." I got up and hugged him. "Thank you for coming to see me. It really means a lot."

As he was leaving, he stopped and turned. "I know you don't think I learned anything about public speaking, but I really did."

"Well, the short speech you just gave was wonderful," I said.

He smiled and nodded before walking out the door.

I stood in the doorway and watched him walk down the hall.

Susie sighed and put down her pen. "One class down and two to go. What was that all about?"

"Closure. You know, sometimes we're completely unaware of our impact on people."

I was proud of Kelly. I was proud of myself, too.

~Linda Carol Cobb

Generation to Generation

A healthy community is one in which the elderly
protect, care for, love and assist the younger
ones to provide continuity and hope.
~Maggie Kuhn

A stack of construction paper cards covered with bright drawings caught my eye as I entered Dad's assisted living apartment. I picked up the top card. "What's this?"

Dad glanced up. "Oh, those are from my pen pals."

"Pen pals?" A medical condition made his hands so numb he could barely sign his name. How could he write to pen pals?

"It's all Barbara's fault. She got me into this."

Barbara coordinated activities for the elderly residents at the facility. A group of teachers from the local primary school had contacted her and asked if their first grade classes could write to the residents and have them write back. She agreed and recruited several she thought would participate, my dad among them.

How she convinced Dad to join in I'll never know. When he first moved into the facility, I was thrilled they offered such a variety of activities. Maybe they would help keep him occupied after losing my mom. I knew some of the pastimes would not interest him — you'd never catch him painting birdhouses — but they offered a lot of other choices. Dad joined the weekly bingo games for a while, but tired of them. I encouraged him to stay fit with exercise classes, but he considered them silly. Being outnumbered by women six to one didn't help. He eventually withdrew to his room where he read and watched TV, coming out only for meals and weekly trips to Walmart. The staff expressed concern that he seemed depressed, but I knew my dad. He'd always been a solitary soul, happy with his sedentary ways.

And now he was going to write to first graders?

The teacher who chose my dad for her class wisely found a connection from the start. Her last name was Kirk, the same as my dad's. To start things off, Barbara had Dad dictate a letter about himself. Then the children's letters started coming. Their questions were sweet and insightful. *What is your favorite book? What do you like to carve?* (My dad had been a whittler with a wild imagination.) *Do you like the "nursing home?"* Individual letters required individual responses, and Dad dictated twenty-five replies to poor Barbara.

Christmas brought a bundle of red and green cards. The kids wanted to know what their pen pal was getting for Christmas and told him what they wanted. Many mentioned their elves and the mischief they'd been up to. Dad had never heard of Elf on the Shelf and wondered at the sudden fascination with Santa's helpers.

I looked through the cards and smiled at the crooked writing and occasional misspelled words — *"What cind of wood do you carv?"* — but it amazed me how well they wrote for first graders. Some filled their cards with artwork, but others wrote long missives and tackled big words — *"I play dynasty warriors. Do you?"*

Then February rolled around, and the teachers invited their classes' pen pals from the assisted living facility to a Valentine's Day party.

Dad didn't exactly jump up and down at the news. "What am I supposed to say to them? I'm eighty-eight, and they're six. I don't even get along that well with kids."

I wondered what the children's reactions would be. I remembered instances at that age of being afraid of "old" people. They have all those wrinkles and hair in funny places. They don't see well or hear what you say. They're just… different. At 6'7", my dad was already an intimidating guy. Add a motorized chair, and I could see him terrifying first graders.

I needn't have worried about the kids accepting Dad. They had a great time. But no one was prepared for Dad's reaction.

"I didn't know what to expect," he told me the next day. "I took some of my carvings with me just to have something to show them. On the ride over, two of the women complained about going. They said things like 'I wish I'd never agreed to this!' That was about how I felt."

"So how did it go?" I asked.

Intensity I'd seldom seen since we lost Mom shone in his eyes. "I... I can't tell you what it meant to me."

The kids came up one at a time to hug Dad and present him with Valentine's cards. He read each one. Reed's card pictured a "hrat filled with joy!" One little girl's card said, "I have a big smile," but she looked sad. Dad soon had her laughing. Luke drew pictures of his school and wrote about the video games he liked to play. His card ended with "P.S. I love you!" But the child who impressed Dad the most was a tiny girl with an innocent face and big brown eyes. Her expectant look melted his heart. She wanted not one hug... but two.

"Those children made me feel popular, like a hero or something." My normally reserved father paused, his eyes filling with tears. "When I left there, I felt full of love."

I wasn't the only one touched by Dad's story.

"If I don't accomplish anything else the rest of the year," Barbara said, "your dad's reaction was worth it all."

Dad later learned that three of his fellow seniors refused to go for the school visit. Their classes cried when they didn't show up. Dad shook his head. "I'm sure glad I didn't poop out on them!"

So am I.

Little did we know that a month later, Dad would be gone. This time, it was his pen pals who cried, along with the faculty.

I'm not sure a group of primary school teachers knew what they were starting when they invited elderly people to become pen pals with their classes. Or maybe they did. The bond the kids and my dad formed through writing back and forth overcame any differences in age or race or ethnicity. It linked the generations in a way nothing else could.

Teachers teach their students many things, but this may have been the most valuable lesson of all.

~Tracy Kirk Crump

A Shooting Star

There is no footprint too small to leave
an imprint on this world.
~Author Unknown

n the Friday before a long President's Day weekend, the school secretary came to my fifth grade classroom just before the close of school. She asked if I could meet with the principal as soon as I dismissed my class. At 3:00 p.m., I said goodbye to my excited students, who were anxious to begin their extended holiday weekend, and then went to my principal's office. She asked me to take a seat and then, with tears in her eyes, informed me that one of my students—a boy who had left earlier that very day for a family vacation—died in a car accident.

I returned to my classroom and went to Weston's desk. There I cried new tears, as well as some that were many years old. The news took me back many years to the death of my brother, who had also died in an accident when he was eleven years old. I remembered the loss my family felt over my brother Robert. I thought about the way my classmates and teachers had initially offered words of comfort, and about how these were eventually followed by awkward glances and silences.

Weston had not only been part of our tightly knit community since kindergarten, but he also held a very special place in my heart. He was a leader among his peers. He was a star athlete, and he treated his classmates with kindness and compassion. I will always remember the day a new boy with special needs sat longingly watching Weston and his friends playing a game. Weston walked over to the child and asked him to join their group. The child was shy and nervous, but Weston's encouragement and engaging smile welcomed him into the game and into our class.

When school reopened after the long weekend, students entered the room with their moms and dads. Each child's eyes turned to look at the desk, now separated slightly from the group and topped with a bouquet of flowers and Weston's class photo.

After everyone arrived, I met my pupils' gazes with much trepidation. I asked his friends and their parents to share some of their favorite memories of Weston. Some of the stories brought smiles, some tears, and a few even brought gentle laughter.

After a short while, the counselors rounded up the parents and took them to the conference room. It was then that my plan began to unfold. As I stood by Weston's desk, I slid a note I had written to his parents inside. I told my students that they could do the same. They could bring photos, notes, and various mementos and place them in his desk anytime. I would collect them in a box each night to be given to his parents at a later date.

Then we brainstormed about things we could do to help us remember our friend and classmate. After several class meetings, we had made a decision: We were going to make a memory book for his parents, as well as look into replacing the basketball hoop and placing a plaque on it in memory of our star athlete. This would take money, so we agreed to hold a bake sale to help cover the costs.

When we had the bake sale, some of my better math students realized that we might not make enough money. I tried not to smile as they began splitting brownies and other treats in half before placing them in small plastic bags. As children lined up outside the lunchroom, several adults also waited in line with five- and ten-dollar bills requiring "no change." By the end of the day, we had met our goal.

I was pleased to see that Weston's best friend, most devastated by the loss, was beginning to take a leadership role in the process. His mother and several others purchased an album and supplies for the memory book. Each child had a page to himself for a collage of memories. They would rush through their lunches to meet with parent volunteers to begin their "gift" of memories.

The following month, on what would have been Weston's twelfth birthday, his family came to join us. I remember the sadness in his parents' eyes as they looked upon Weston's desk, empty except for his framed class photo. His best friend walked up to his mother and handed her their gift of memories. Their sadness turned to joy as they turned the pages of this treasure. I studied the proud looks on each of my students' faces.

We had one month to complete our second goal: installing the basketball hoop. I put in a request to the district to purchase a new net and hoop. A week later, a man from the district office stood outside my classroom door. He apologized for the interruption and asked if this was the class that wanted to fix the broken basketball hoop. When I replied that we were, he explained that after inspecting the cracked backboard, he feared that it would not support the repair. Upon hearing this, I explained the reason behind the request. After a moment, the man coughed, cleared his throat, and said that the backboard was probably a safety violation. In fact, he would see to it that a new one was ordered and delivered with a new hoop and net.

Several weeks later, we heard a truck pull up to the basketball court outside our classroom door. Three men unloaded a new backboard. We went outside and sat on the lawn to watch the excitement unfold. After the men replaced the backboard and installed the plaque honoring Weston, they bowed, jumped back into their truck, and bounced over the hilly field to the road to the cheers and applause of my boys and girls.

The last week of school is a time of celebrations, some bittersweet. The last Friday of the school year is traditionally a time to honor children for their academic achievements. This year, a special recognition was added: Weston's Shooting Star Award. This honored a child who truly exemplified the spirit of Weston through sportsmanship and leadership. Joining us at the ceremony were his family, aunts, and grandmother. My class stood proudly as the award honoring Weston was bestowed upon his longtime friend and classmate.

After everyone had left except my class and Weston's family, his dad pulled a new basketball from a sack and signaled for us to join him. Then I watched with a heavy heart as everyone, including Weston's grandmother, came up to the basketball hoop and made a shot in memory of our Shooting Star.

~Catherine Kopp

It Takes a Village

*A mentor is someone who allows you
to see the hope inside yourself.*
~Oprah Winfrey

The downward spiral began the summer before my daughter's senior year of high school, when her boyfriend experienced his first overdose. Then there was a second overdose. She cried, and he made promises he couldn't keep. Time passed without any visible signs of focus or drive. Instead, there was a plethora of denials and lies.

I paced the floor, wept in bed, confided in her high-school guidance counselor and trusted teachers, and sought every therapist and support group in a thirty-mile radius. My daughter and her high-school sweetheart had dated for well over a year, so when he went down the ominous road of drug use, her emotional investment in him was established and strong. My fear was that she would follow his lead into the dark world of addiction. And to be honest, I painfully acknowledge catapulting her deeper into his drug-damaged arms, making my fear even more of a distinct possibility.

"Julia, he's lying to you! I know he's just saying what you want to hear. It's time you wake up. You're either on this dark road with him, or you are completely naïve regarding the warning signs and lies. But let's just set the drug issue aside for a moment; he is also emotionally abusing you with controlling behavior. He's manipulating you by playing on your sympathy. You need to get off this crazy train. Now!"

Parenting Teen Daughters 101 says that if there are red flags regarding a boyfriend, you should strategically ask questions to get your daughter to open up so you can guide her down a healthy path. Never blatantly criticize the boyfriend. It will backfire, as it did for me. For the next year, my daughter's sole mission was to change this young man and prove me wrong.

As her senior year moved forward, it was nothing like we had envisioned. Julia rarely hung out with her girlfriends; she chose not to go to school dances; and she withdrew from all of her loved ones. I continued to seek guidance from those experienced in handling this type of situation, fully disclosing the error of my ways. It broke our hearts to watch this young man, so full of promise, sink deeper into addiction and refuse all help. And our greatest fear was that Jules would adopt the mindset, "If I can't change him, I'll join him." So our family continued to rally behind her, showing love and support at all times. Still, she continued to pull away. It was obvious to everyone, so much so that her teachers voiced deep concern on a number of occasions.

"Hey, Julia, have a minute?" Mrs. Poster called from across the hallway as students hustled to their next class. It was now springtime, and while Julia's four years at the high school were coming to an end, their paths had never really crossed. Julia had been at the top of her class, taking advanced classes, and this teacher taught troubled students in jeopardy of not graduating. My other daughter, Anna, watched her sister walk over to Mrs. Poster. Within moments, Jules was crying uncontrollably. Seeing her sister cry had been the norm for months, but Anna felt something was different this time.

I was unaware at the time, but the tribe of teachers I had been confiding in had talked among themselves and devised a plan. Mrs. Poster was actually the most experienced at handling situations like Julia's, and because they did not know each other well, the group of teachers agreed that Julia might open up to her. Just as they suspected, Julia poured out her heart to Mrs. P. They continued to meet numerous times over the coming months. I don't know what was shared and discussed, but what I do know is that her timing, skill, and grace were nothing short of incredible. And the relationships among Jules and the entire group of teachers strengthened; she genuinely looked to them for support and guidance, and remains good friends with one of them to this day.

Mostly, I know that what my daughter learned from Mrs. Poster and this special family of teachers — outside an academic classroom — will have more meaning in her life than algebraic equations or chemistry properties. I know this because there was a distinct change in my daughter once she started confiding in this team of educators. Her unhealthy relationship ended, as did other unhealthy behaviors. She slowly began to laugh and smile again, and spent time with her family and friends. It was nothing short of beautiful to see this young lady go from being withdrawn every moment of the day to reciting the Serenity Prayer and acknowledging that she *couldn't* change someone. Most of all, my greatest fear, that she would use drugs, became a thing of the past.

Jules went off to college and, ironically, majored in psychology. She learned how to channel her kind heart down a healthy and productive path, and is now positively impacting the lives of others. If it weren't for that team of teachers, Julia's senior year and beyond might have had a very different narrative, and the people she now helps wouldn't have her.

That old saying — It takes a village to raise a child — is so true. I embrace every person who has positively impacted my children, but especially Mrs. P and the group of teachers whose divine intervention — which went far beyond their job description — came just when it was needed most. I hope they realize just how much they changed a life.

~Mara Somerset

My Students, My Angels

We are all dependent on one another,
every soul of us on earth.
~George Bernard Shaw

I had two aspirations growing up: to be a teacher and a mom. I achieved the first within a year of marrying the love of my life, Joe, but the latter took a while. A long, long, long while.

My plan was to get pregnant with my first child right after graduation, then to go on to have three more children by the time I was thirty years old. I thought this was completely doable since I got married at twenty-two, and big families were *my* norm. (I'm one of ten children.) In a perfect world, I was going to return to teaching when my youngest child was school-age and live happily ever after on the same work/school schedule as my children.

But the world is not perfect, and God had other plans.

Month after month (eventually turning into year after year), I didn't get pregnant. While I immersed myself in teaching, the ugly reality of infertility crept into my daily life. Thank goodness I had my students to help me reset my emotions.

As I launched my teaching career and marriage, I also launched an investigation into my infertility. As a result, I had to miss school periodically for doctors' appointments. One spring morning, I went to see yet another fertility specialist. His "sage" medical advice was, "Relax and take a vacation because you're too young to worry about not getting pregnant." Apparently, I hadn't relaxed or vacationed enough during the first few years of our marriage.

Driving out of the doctor's office parking lot, I felt depressed, discouraged, and defeated. *How was it possible that I could love children so much, yet not be able to have any?* When I arrived at school, I dried my eyes and put on my teacher face. As I entered my second grade classroom, I was embraced, first by the familiar comforting scent, then by multiple short arms squeezing my waist, and finally by a chorus of tiny voices filling my heart with joy.

"We're so glad you're back, Ms. Magee! The sub didn't read the story the right way — the way *you* do," Jared chimed. (Unfortunately, the sub was standing right next to me when Jared said this.)

"Please don't be absent anymore, Ms. Magee. I miss you when you are gone," Dante pleaded.

On that day in that classroom, surrounded by children who loved me and accepted me exactly how I was, I made a decision. I realized that what I really wanted was to be a parent, not just to get pregnant. I was going to adopt.

Joe and I researched foreign adoptions, domestic adoptions, open adoptions, closed adoptions, adoptions via private agencies, adoptions via county agencies, and foster adoptions. We hadn't settled on the approach we were going to take when, through a series of unexpected events, we became foster parents to two girls — a three-and-a-half-year-old and a six-month-old — with the promise that we could adopt them.

My students and their families rallied around our newly formed family, lending us strollers and swings, toddler toys and a tricycle. They embraced me as a new mom in my new version of my perfect world.

But, as I mentioned earlier, the world is not perfect, and God had other plans.

The reunification process for our foster daughters' birthmother was farther along than the social worker originally disclosed. In fact, the reality of adoption laws and the court system caused us to advocate for the birthmother to reunite with her children. Eventually, the girls were returned, and my husband and I were once again childless. Thank goodness I still had my students, my angels, to help me reset my emotions.

One afternoon after dismissal, a few days after we had said goodbye to our foster daughters, one of my second graders found me with my head in my hands, crying at my desk.

"It's okay, Ms. Magee. My mom said you can keep the toddler toys to play with since you have extra time now," Chelsea whispered.

This struck me as being so sweet (the joy of playing with toys as a cure for sadness) and so funny (with my extra time?) that I burst out laughing. I was going to be okay.

The following school year, hoping to put my energy into something other than building a family, I changed grade levels. Kindergarten became my focus. In August, when I was setting up my classroom, I received a surprising phone call from a neighboring county's Department of Social Services Adoption Unit. The social worker asked if we'd like to be put on their adoption waiting list. Immediately, I responded, "No way." When the social worker asked why I reacted in such a way, I relayed our painful previous experience. She assured me that she wouldn't call us with a placement unless the situation was a "sure thing." Even though, intellectually, I knew that nothing was a "sure thing," I believed her. A small voice deep inside me told me to trust her. Joe and I took another leap of faith in an effort to build our family.

To prepare for our "sure thing," we took parenting classes, completed our home study, renewed our foster license, and filled out mountains of paperwork—all while I taught my rambunctious kindergarteners.

"Ms. Magee, watch this!" called Tony from the sensory table right before he poured his water bottle into a tub full of rice.

"Ms. Magee, I'm reading!" shouted Mari as she recited the story I read to the class earlier in the day—her words a page or two off the text in the book.

These little people occupied my mind, body, and spirit until the following April. At eight o'clock on a Monday morning, our social worker called my husband and said, "An Asian baby girl was born Saturday night. What do you and Bridget want to do?" That's all the information he got.

Immediately, he tried to get in touch with me, but my kindergarten class was in a temporary building with an intercom system, but no phone.

After shoes were tied and snacks were found, with two sweaty palms in mine I walked my students out to morning recess. When I got to the office, I found a stack of messages from Joe in my box. He picked up the phone on the first ring and relayed what the social worker had told him.

A sense of calm came over me. "Let's go pick up our daughter," I said. And that's what we did. With four hours' notice, we picked up our thirty-six-hour-old daughter, Colleen, and never looked back. We were parents. Finally.

And then God had one more surprise for us. Six years later, I got pregnant with our daughter, Maureen. Go figure. Our family was finally complete.

In hindsight, I realized that my world was perfect throughout our journey. God knew what He was doing; I just had to be open to His plans. And have a nice long warm-up with my students — my angels.

~Bridget Magee

Our Tiny Dancer

Sometimes even to live is an act of courage.
~Lucius Annaeus Seneca

I didn't meet Tammy until the last four weeks of my final student-teaching semester. I looked up from my reading group one morning and saw a porcelain doll of a child standing in the doorway. Except for her hairless head, she looked like the ballerina that adorned my childhood music box. In seconds, this fragile girl was surrounded by a gaggle of second graders competing for her hugs. Then, the sea of children parted, and this tiny dancer in her pink tutu and sparkly purple headband struggled to move toward her desk.

The children often spoke of Tammy, the gifted girl who had been out of school for several months. They missed her and couldn't wait for her return. My master teacher, Mrs. C., told me that Tammy had recently survived her second operation in New York to halt the spread of a cancerous brain tumor. It was a rare condition, one that required the aid of the best neurosurgeon in the country — the same doctor who had been the subject of a *Nova* special on PBS the previous year.

The children prepared me for Tammy's arrival by showing me her picture and telling me that she was the smartest and sweetest girl in the second grade. They said that I should treat her as I would any of the other healthy children.

Little did I know that one fiercely brave little girl would teach me far more than I could ever teach her. With each step, Tammy fought for balance, but no one rushed to her side. We must have stood in silence for five minutes as Tammy walked five feet to her seat. A roar of approval burst out of thirty second-grade students as soon as Tammy sat down. With a toothless smile as big and bright as the Manhattan skyline, she looked around the room as if to say, "I'm home."

After Tammy's first day back, the lessons continued as usual, but I had a new star to brighten my days. It was Tammy who raised her hand for every question; it was Tammy who volunteered for every leadership role; it was Tammy who took all of our hearts and held them hostage under her spell. She taught us so many things that spring: the patience to wait for her labored answers; the intelligence to decode her garbled speech; and, the pride we felt every time she struggled to be normal. But it was one kickball game that changed me forever.

I directed all of the children in Mrs. C's class to their positions on the field one afternoon after quickly teaching them the rules of the game. When the bases were loaded, and the students had proven their adequate knowledge of kickball, it was Tammy's turn. I held my breath. Like a wounded gazelle, she held her head high and limped to the ball. With the effort and concentration of an Olympic athlete, Tammy kicked her better leg out from under her. The ball barely rolled. Simultaneously, the whole field of players moved in slow motion as if they were one highly trained troupe of ballerinas. Within minutes, I became a silent spectator to the most beautiful dance I had ever seen.

The pitcher slowly undulated toward the ball as Tammy loped to first base. In a graceful, methodical arc, he threw the ball to first. Even the ball moved in slow motion. Tammy limped to second base as the first baseman took an eternity to wind up her throw. When Tammy struggled to reach third base, the outfielder held the ball in an arabesque pose on tiptoes, releasing it only after Tammy tagged in. I don't know how long I had been holding my breath by the time Tammy tripped into home base, but when the catcher caught her just before she fell, I was choking on my tears.

I have never seen anything more perfectly choreographed in kindness than that kickball game.

Tammy did not live long after that school year, but she faced cancer with extraordinary wisdom and a superhuman will to survive. Even now, after thirty-six years of teaching in the California public schools where many, many lives have honored my work and touched my heart, not many days pass between the times I think about our tiny dancer in Mrs. C's second grade class.

~Jeaninne Escallier Kato

Embracing Colors

We need to give each other the space to grow, to be
ourselves, to exercise our diversity.
~Max De Pree

I had been teaching for two years in a small rural community, but my new husband and I wanted to move to an area with greater business opportunities for him. I also wanted to teach in a private Christian school where I could openly pray with, and for, my students. After searching the Internet and putting out applications, I received one call for an interview, in Michigan.

I was picked up at the airport by the school's health and physical education teacher. As he listened to me nervously babbling he didn't say much, but what he said remains in my memory: "You have to be tough to work here." Little did I know then how true this would be.

The interview was amazing. I loved sharing my passion and enthusiasm for English and for my students, and hearing about the mission of the school. I was given a tour by a freshman who beamed with pride as she led me down the hallway. As I followed her, asking questions and looking at the pictures of the alumni, I wondered, *Could I fit here? Could I make a difference? Could this be home? Would others be able to see past the color of my skin?*

"They'll never hire me!" I told my husband while waiting for my flight back to Omaha, Nebraska. "The entire school is black, teachers included. I wouldn't fit in. I'm definitely not what they're looking for."

And so I was completely surprised a few days later when a call came from the academy superintendent with the job offer. Not being one to back away from a challenge, I accepted. When I tearfully told my current students and co-workers goodbye, several of my students were positive it was not safe. From the way the media had portrayed the Detroit area, they were certain I would be mugged, shot, or even worse. Many of my peers were also concerned. They knew about Detroit's economic situation and weren't sure my husband would find a job once we got there.

It was initially a culture shock. I had never been the minority before. I remember going to church with my students and co-workers, being a dinner guest at people's houses, and attending various school events, always feeling different, like I didn't quite fit in.

As often occurs with teaching, it was my students who taught *me*, and it was my new school family that helped me fit in. They showed me how to get past these obstacles and loosen up. I vividly remember meeting some of my students for the first time. It was clear they were all wondering what my agenda was… Why was I really there? I admit I wondered myself. I later found out many had wagered how long I would last, some giving me as little as a month. And yet, it was one of these same students who helped break the ice.

One day, I was struggling to get my seventh and eighth grade students to focus. Which seemed to be a daily battle. I think I had gotten angry and lost my patience, which caused my face to turn bright red. A brave seventh grade boy with a wide smile and big heart raised his hand and caught me off guard. "Why do people call *us* colored? You turn more colors than anyone. You're red when you're angry, and you're pale white or green when you're sick." I didn't know what to say, and it seemed as if all the students were waiting for my reaction. Finally, I just laughed, and it was this laughter that helped me break through.

As a result, I found myself embracing the cultural differences between my students and myself. What used to feel like a barrier became multiple opportunities to learn, grow, and change.

And I learned from my school family. I learned that church will not end at noon, but can keep going until two or three in the afternoon. I learned about greens, sweet potato pie, soul, and "swag." I learned not just about Dr. Martin Luther King, Jr. and Rosa Parks, but also about Thurgood Marshall and Bessie Coleman. And I learned that when my students and co-workers said they had my back, they meant it.

Likewise, I grew with my students. We learned together, both inside and outside the classroom. We cried together. We laughed together over things others just wouldn't understand. We worked together on various projects for the betterment of our school. We also succeeded together, reaching goals we carefully set for ourselves.

Finally, I changed… for the better. Looking back after six years there, I realize now how limited my perspective had been and how much clearer it is now. As I have watched the news, with story after story of racial tensions and prejudice in our country, I realize how limited the perspective of others still is.

My teaching experience there wasn't easy. If it had been, I don't think it would mean as much to me as it does.

Before I left my school, while reading the writer's journal of one of my seniors (that same brave seventh grader with the wide smile and big heart), I was touched to read the following:

> *I was in the 7th grade and this year was a new new year. Now the reason why I said new twice, well duh! It was a new year, but something new was coming. A New Teacher! Mrs. Harsany was not just a teacher; she was a very special teacher. How could this teacher be special when I had no clue about her? Well, she was white! Mrs. Harsany was our first white teacher here that I know of. As the years have come, she has been the best teacher and unexpected mom.*

It was students like this who taught me more than I probably taught them. Though we all are various shades of color, what matters is what is in our hearts — and what was in the hearts of my school family was pure gold.

~Elizabeth Ann Harsany

12

A Returned Reward

A friend is one of the nicest things you can have,
and one of the best things you can be.
~Douglas Pagels

She sat at the picnic table alone. Her shoulders were slumped. Recess was in full swing, and while the rest of the third- and fourth-graders were racing around with unabashed freedom, the new girl was once again excluding herself from the mid-day celebration.

Even though school had been in session for several weeks already, and the opportunity to make friends had presented itself many times, she remained awkward around her classmates. She seemed unsure of what to do or say, yet I could see her eyes pleading for acceptance. Many students had already decided that her friendship would not be worth the energy required to overcome the awkwardness. Others teased her. Most ignored her—except for one.

Brianna, the class clown, was standing near the playground making the other students laugh, as usual. So, when I interrupted her fun with a finger motioning for her to come speak with me, her irritation was understandable.

"Yes, Mrs. D?"

"Brianna, do you see Molly down there?"

I pointed. She nodded. I continued.

"She looks awfully lonely. Would you mind walking down there and inviting her to come up here with the rest of us?"

Brianna sighed. I could tell she didn't want to sacrifice precious minutes of her own recess to do what I was asking of her, but I also knew her heart. She was sweet and kind, and often thought of others before herself — a rare trait for anyone, much less a kid. I had specifically selected her for this task, and she knew it. She looked at her friends, then at Molly.

Knowing this choice was paining her, I reached into my pocket and pulled out a D-buck, our class currency. Though bribery was not the ideal way to handle this situation, I was the only teacher on duty and unable to venture far from the other kids. I needed to ensure her cooperation.

"Here, I'll pay you for your time."

She offered an insincere smile, grasped the green paper, and headed down the hill.

As the rest of the children screamed and laughed, my eyes locked on Brianna as she neared the picnic table. I hoped I hadn't just sent her on an impossible mission. Molly could be difficult, and I wouldn't have been surprised if she sent Brianna back alone, refusing her invitation.

I watched closely as they talked. Molly rocked back and forth awkwardly as she sat. When she propelled herself to a standing position, I sighed with relief.

The girls walked back up the hill together, and I turned my attention back to the other students.

A minute later, I felt a tap on my shoulder. I turned to see who it was.

Brianna.

"Here, Mrs. D." She handed me the D-buck.

"What's this for?" I asked.

"I shouldn't keep this." Her eyes fell to her feet, guilt radiating from her quiet voice. "I don't want Molly to think I only went to get her so I could earn a D-buck." She lifted her big brown eyes to mine. "She's my friend."

She's my friend. Her sweet voice echoed through me as I slid the D-buck back into my pocket. Brianna skipped back to her group, ready to resume her place as their comedic ringleader. A moment later, they were all laughing hysterically again, and who should I see amongst them, laughing for the first time that week? Molly.

~Stephanie A. Delorme

Chapter 2

Inspiration for Teachers

Teaching with Heart

*Too often we underestimate the power of a touch,
a smile, a kind word, a listening ear, an honest
compliment, or the smallest act of caring, all of
which have the potential to turn a life around.*
~Leo Buscaglia

13

Paying It Forward

No person was ever honored for what he
received, but for what he gave.
~Calvin Coolidge

I t seemed like the semester was dragging by at the middle school where I taught English as a Second Language (ESL). One particular sixth grader, Pablo, was struggling with fluency in reading, so after class I suggested that he get extra practice by reading aloud to his mom while she prepared dinner each evening. This was something I routinely encouraged my struggling students to do. I explained that it didn't matter if she understood enough English to know what he was reading; he would still benefit from the extra practice.

Imagine my surprise when Pablo responded by starting to cry. He exclaimed, "My mom can't cook dinner!" Then he sobbed long and hard, like I had never heard before. Eventually, he calmed down enough to tell me, through his tears, that his mom was only able to "cry in her bed" when he got home every afternoon. He said that he was caring for his six-month-old baby brother by himself from the time he got home each day. His mother, it seemed, had an abscessed tooth and was in excruciating pain. He proclaimed that his father "didn't have enough money to get it fixed," and that there was no insurance and no way for her to go to a dentist. This child's heart was broken for his mom.

I was speechless! He was still crying when he left me that day, and I promised him I would try to help. As I taught my afternoon classes, I kept asking myself how I could help this student who was hurting so badly because his mother was hurting. How could I help his mother when we didn't even speak the same language? I realized it was no wonder he couldn't focus on reading with all that was going on in his young life.

The next day, I sent a note, which a friend helped me translate, to Pablo's mother asking if she would like me to find someone to help her. The following day, Pablo, grinning from ear to ear, brought me a note from his mom accepting my offer to help.

Meanwhile, I had been doing some networking among my friends, asking if anyone knew a dentist who might do some pro bono work for this lady. At the time, I was not able to pay for the work to be done myself. Several friends suggested a dental office that had recently opened up in the area, thinking that they might be willing to provide the services. I didn't want to waste a lot of time going to several dentists, so I prayed that this would be the one.

Stopping by the dental office one afternoon, I told the receptionist the gist of my need. She smiled at me and said, "Wait right here for just a minute." She returned and took me back to the beautifully decorated office of one of the dentists, who asked for more details. I told him the story. I was awestruck at his response! He told me that he was once an English as a Second Language student. He had immigrated from Iran, first to Canada, at seven years old, and later to the United States. He stated that he saw this as an excellent opportunity to "pay it forward" and help another ESL student.

Dr. N. said that he would remove her tooth, provide her antibiotics, and if she needed an oral surgeon, he would pay for that as well. It turned out that Pablo's mom didn't need oral surgery, and Dr. N. was able to take care of the tooth himself. When we went to have the tooth removed, Pablo went back with her and translated the conversation between the patient and the dentist. She was soon able to return to her role as Mom, and Pablo to his role as a child.

That experience taught me that I don't have a clue what may be going on in the lives of the students I teach. Each one has a story, and each one has family dynamics and issues that I might have difficulty even comprehending. Since then, I have always tried to pause and listen with my heart.

~Carolyn Lee

14

Lunch Mentor

If we all did the things we are capable of doing,
we would literally astound ourselves.
~Thomas Alva Edison

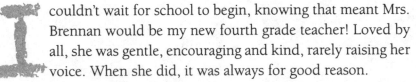

I couldn't wait for school to begin, knowing that meant Mrs. Brennan would be my new fourth grade teacher! Loved by all, she was gentle, encouraging and kind, rarely raising her voice. When she did, it was always for good reason.

I adored her from the first day I attended elementary school. She always greeted me with a warm hug when no one was around to witness her favoritism, addressing me as "Little Mary," a nickname that made me smile.

Like many others in our impoverished neighborhood, both my parents worked out of necessity. Mama started cleaning houses the year before. She couldn't afford to have someone watch me at lunchtime, so I became a latchkey kid. Because I was scared to be alone at home, I would eat quickly and run back to hide in an outside stairwell in the schoolyard to wait until afternoon classes resumed.

No one had ever found me there, but a week into that September, Mrs. Brennan did while retrieving her sweater that had fallen out a window. That same afternoon, she sent a message to Mama requesting that I stay at school every lunchtime to help with some small chores, instead of going home for lunch. The note stated that she would provide a meal for me as "payment." Relieved that I'd be under adult supervision, Mama signed the permission slip.

My duties started the next afternoon. One minute before the dismissal bell rang, I would quietly leave my seat in the back row and exit the room. No one noticed me leaving as they slammed books into their desks, restlessly waiting to leave.

I would race up to the third-floor teachers' room and pull out a paper bag with Mrs. Brennan's initials on it from the fridge. I knew that it held at least two delicious sliced-meat sandwiches garnished with fresh tomatoes and lettuce, along with a large piece of cheese, some cake or cookies, and a small container of milk. Although Mama was an excellent cook, deli meat was a rarity in our home. Cheese was almost unheard of. There was never enough money.

As we ate, Mrs. Brennan listened intently to my trivial childish chatter, drawing me out of my timid shell with her genuine interest. After lunch, I would tidy up, wipe the blackboard and chalk tray, and take the erasers to the central vacuum to clean in preparation for afternoon class. Then I would sneak out the side door and join the other students as if I was coming from home myself. My "job" was over, but never without a tight hug and a whispered "You're a good girl, Little Mary."

That year, we were introduced to creative writing, and I loved it. Mrs. Brennan quickly noticed my aptitude for writing, urging me to do more of it during our meal, and supplying me with extra notebooks to jot down my thoughts and stories. Over time, she encouraged me to try poetry, raving over my crude, silly rhymes as if I were Emily Dickinson.

While I scribbled down my dreams and verses, time seemed to stop. It was only when I heard Mrs. Brennan at the vacuum, cleaning her own brushes, that I realized I was neglecting my duties. Instead of scolding me, she merely grinned.

"It was never about the blackboards, Little Mary," she told me softly. "It was about making you feel safe."

In fifth and sixth grade, Mama made arrangements to send me elsewhere for lunch, but I continued to see Mrs. Brennan and share my creative writing with her every chance I could, never tiring of her excited praise and warm embraces. On the last day of sixth grade, she hugged me as always, but her grip was tighter, longer and somehow more desperate. When we broke apart, I was stunned to see she was crying.

"Are you okay, Mrs. Brennan?" I asked worriedly.

"Don't worry about me, Little Mary," she soothed, wiping her eyes. "I'm just saying goodbye. You have a good holiday and remember to keep writing."

Summer vacation flew by. That September, I rushed to school, eager to see her again, but when the bell rang, a stranger stood in the schoolyard facing the line of fourth grade students. Mrs. Brennan was nowhere to be seen. I asked my new teacher, Mrs. Kondracki, where she was.

"Marya, I know how close the two of you were, so I'll be honest. Mrs. Brennan had cancer in the past, and it's come back. She's dying, dear. I'm sorry."

I had subconsciously known something was terribly wrong but this was still a shock. I swallowed back tears and tried to find my voice.

"C-can I visit her?"

"I'm afraid not. No one under eighteen is allowed, but I see her at least once a week. I'll tell her you asked about her."

"Thank you," I whispered, turning to go back to my desk in a haze. Mrs. Kondracki was considerate and did not call on me for any answers for the rest of the day.

A week later, I approached her again, this time with a meticulously folded piece of paper I'd carefully torn out of my copybook. In my best penmanship, I'd written Mrs. Brennan a poem, telling her how much I missed her, loved her, and wished she was well again.

"Could you give her this?" I asked, my eyes tearing up. "It's something I wrote for her."

"Of course," she replied, tucking it into her purse. "I'll make sure she gets it."

Mrs. Brennan died several months later. I was finally allowed to see her. There was no age limit at funeral parlors.

I stood at the casket, hating that my last memory of her would be this still, lifeless, pale shell of the vibrant woman I'd known.

"Are you Marya?" a voice asked behind me, and I turned around to see a woman about Mrs. Brennan's age.

"Yes," I choked.

"My sister talked about you. She cared about you very much. I want you to know how happy she was that you sent her that poem. She loved it. She asked me to give you this if you came," she added, handing me a note and a little bottle of cheap hand lotion I'd given Mrs. Brennan one Christmas when I had nothing else to offer in return for her kindness. I grinned through my tears at the memory.

"She also said to tell you something else."

"What?" I croaked.

She said, "Remember to keep writing, Little Mary."

I nodded my thanks. I couldn't speak anymore. I placed the little bottle in my pocket, turned back toward the coffin, and said my last goodbye before leaving.

Outside, I looked up at the stars. One seemed brighter than the rest for some reason. I like to think it was her spirit suspended in the heavens, free from pain and at peace.

"Thank you for making me feel special and safe," I whispered into the night sky. "And I promise — I'll never stop writing."

I kept my word.

~Marya Morin

15

Close Encounters in a Classroom

*I learned that courage was not the absence of fear, but
the triumph over it. The brave man is not he who does
not feel afraid, but he who conquers that fear.*
~Nelson Mandela

Beethoven's Fifth blared from the speaker as students called out the feelings the music evoked: thunder, dancing, traffic. I wrote their responses on the board so they could weave them into poetry. Because Elizabeth was quiet, I didn't notice her among the boisterous students in the classroom.

That was the fall of 1999, when I volunteered every Friday in a twelfth grade English classroom at East Side Community High School in Manhattan, a school which admitted students who showed promise but whose grades had fallen short of their ability. The teacher I was assisting, Ms. Martin, was barely thirty and she dressed in jeans like her students.

Ms. Martin knew that I had published dozens of personal essays, so she asked if I would help the students with their college essays. I readily agreed, and she showed me Elizabeth's and said, "I'd like your opinion."

Elizabeth and I sat together as Beethoven bounced off the walls. She was petite, barely five feet tall, and weighed less than ninety pounds. She was feminine and appeared fragile, as if someone could break her.

Her essay explained that she couldn't concentrate at the beginning of high school. Her grades were low, but had really improved since coming to this school in tenth grade. A page later, she described walking home one afternoon in ninth grade when a man jumped her, dragged her into an alley, and raped her.

No wonder she couldn't concentrate. I was shaken. I didn't even know what to say. I feared blurting out words meant to comfort, only to injure her again in some unwitting way. Yet Elizabeth was serene, sitting there in a fuzzy sweater. I looked into her brown eyes. "I'm so sorry," I croaked.

"It's not your fault," she said.

I wanted to hug her, but we'd just met. "Are you okay?" I asked. "I mean…"

"It changed my life." She fidgeted with a pen. "I moped around for months. I think I was depressed." She sounded as if she were telling someone else's story.

I wished to do the impossible — make the rape go away.

"My mother knew something was wrong, but I wouldn't tell her. I was so ashamed. We're Puerto Rican, and I didn't think my family could take it."

I listened, spellbound and flummoxed.

"My advisor said I'd changed. She kept asking me why. Finally, I told her. She got me into this school. She saved me."

"You're brave to write your story," I said.

We sat in silence for a moment. I picked up her essay.

"Is it any good?" she asked.

"It's outstanding. It's everything a personal essay should be — it's honest and thought provoking. You revealed your character and showed growth."

Ms. Martin zoomed toward us. "Isn't she a marvelous writer?"

"I'm impressed with her depth," I said.

"But can I make my essay better?" Elizabeth asked.

I paused. I didn't know how to express what I was thinking without sounding insensitive. But I took a risk. "Would you consider starting the essay with the rape?"

"That's where I wrote it in my first draft," Elizabeth said.

"It's true. I suggested she move it to the middle of the essay," said Ms. Martin. "I thought it was too upsetting for the opening."

"It's heartbreaking wherever it appears," I said. "But it sets up the essay's theme. With a new lead, admissions people will notice Elizabeth's essay."

"You're right," she said. "I tell my students to open with a grabber."

Elizabeth and I tweaked her essay before she submitted it with her application and a request for financial aid to the State University of New York. For weeks, I worked with her classmates, honing their essays, too.

One Friday in April as the trees started budding, Elizabeth ran over. "I got in!" she said. "With a scholarship. I can't believe it — I'm going to college!"

"Congratulations!" I said, hugging her. "I'm thrilled for you!"

She was excited about the future. "I want to be a teacher," she gushed. "To help kids with problems… the way so many teachers, like you, have helped me."

"You'll be a wonderful teacher," I said.

She grew pensive. "I'm the first person in my family to go to college. I don't know what to expect."

I tried explaining what college was like. Living in a dorm with roommates. Enjoying freedom but taking responsibility for yourself.

Over the next few weeks, she had more questions. "I don't even know what to bring to college."

I gave her an article I'd published called "In Gear for College," which listed every item students need, including a door stopper.

"Wow, some of this stuff is expensive," she said.

I crossed out items that weren't necessary.

"How will I get everything to college? My parents don't own a car. We're going there by bus."

"You can buy most of it on campus or nearby," I said.

In June, I hugged her again when we said goodbye. "Listen," I said. "There'll be parties at school. Watch how much you drink."

"I know," she said. "I don't want any more bad things to happen."

"Just be careful and use your head," I said. "You'll be fine."

My relationship with Elizabeth left me yearning to teach again. That fall as she started college, I began working for Teachers & Writers Collaborative, a nonprofit that sends writers into public schools to teach writing alongside classroom teachers. Since then, I've been nurturing the magic inside hundreds of students.

One third grader wrote exclusively about her father, who had died of cancer. I welled up reading her stories. She was working out her sorrow, while keeping his memory alive.

There was a girl in a special-education class who wouldn't speak. Her teacher told me she'd been abused. The day I taught the persuasive essay, I asked students what they'd like to change in this world.

"Screaming," she whispered.

"I know how you feel," I said. "My mother was a screamer."

I coaxed her to put her thoughts on paper. "Stop screaming," she wrote. "It is mean. It makes me scared."

A fifth grader wrote a poem about an ancestor in slavery, describing lashings and his bloody back. She desperately wanted it published in the annual anthology. When administrators worried it was too violent, I convinced them it was powerful.

"Thank you, thank you, thank you," the girl said when she saw it in print.

Over the sixteen years I've taught writing in classrooms throughout New York City, there are countless students I remember vividly. I carry their poems and stories in my heart, the way I cherish Elizabeth's.

She's now in her thirties. I picture her in a classroom of sad-eyed students, rescuing kids who've lost their way. I regret not staying in touch with her. But I was too green. I had no idea how much she'd mean to me.

I wish I could tell her she unleashed a talent I never knew I possessed — inspiring students to spin their lives into art. As much as I encouraged her, she gave me a gift, not the other way around.

~Linda Morel

16

Erasing the Lines

Tomorrow is fresh, with no mistakes in it.
~L. M. Montgomery

"I can't believe you drove from Florida to Tennessee to attend my wedding today," said Kyle, as tears filled his eyes. We embraced and talked in a private room in the church while groomsmen paced outside the open door and checked their watches. In a few minutes, the marriage ceremony would change Kyle's life. It was a milestone for me, too, because I had been his second grade teacher and mentor for the past twenty years.

It had started when Kyle was assigned to my second grade classroom. "Too bad you have Kyle in your second grade class this year," remarked his first grade teacher as she scanned my roster. "He won't do a thing for you."

The first day of class, I approached the thin, sad-looking boy with messy blond hair, slumped at a desk labeled with his name. "Welcome to my class, Kyle," I said. He looked at the floor and didn't respond. When I helped him with his assignments during the week, I noticed he didn't finish his work and his writing was messy. He attempted some lessons, but as soon as he penciled in his wrong answers, he changed them by erasing the lines again and again. The black marks on his papers seemed to underscore his failures.

During a conference with his grandmother, who was raising Kyle and his brother, she confided that his parents had family problems.

She added, "I thank the Lord he got you for a teacher. He never liked his teacher before, and he adores you." Unfortunately, several months later Kyle's brother became involved with the wrong crowd and the grandmother moved the boys to Tennessee.

Years later, I responded to a knock on my front door and discovered a tall teenager balancing on a skateboard. "Remember me? Kyle?" he inquired. Suddenly, I remembered that struggling student in my second grade class. He said he'd traveled to Florida to see his father… and *me*.

After that, Kyle began to visit me when he was in town each summer, and we talked about his life, the importance of making good choices, and the reasons I was proud of him. He graduated from high school, started his own landscaping business, bought a new red truck, and moved into his own apartment.

And now he was getting married.

Organ music signaled the beginning of the wedding ceremony, and a man in a tuxedo leaned into the open door of the private room and announced, "Time to go, Kyle."

The groom wiped away his tears, took my hand and looked into my eyes. He said, "I didn't have a good family, but I was lucky my grandmother and you influenced my life. I'm grateful God gave you to me." Then, as he was leaving, he said, "By the way, Mrs. Hill, I don't make those black marks from erasing the lines anymore."

I wiped away my tears.

~Miriam Hill

17

To Whom It May Concern

*Anyone who does anything to help
a child is a hero to me.*
~Fred Rogers

I still remember looking at my daughter for the first time. My heart just melted from the overwhelming love I felt for her, and I knew I would do anything to help her grow and learn. Then, before she was even of school age, I noticed she was learning at a slower pace than the other kids.

She was still the happiest girl I had ever seen, but when she started first grade, I asked the school if she could be tested for learning disabilities. They said they didn't do that type of testing until third grade. I was devastated because I knew that third grade would be too long of a wait. She needed help right away.

I kept praying and working with her at home, and then I was faced with a hard decision about moving out of state in order to live in a town with a better school system. All I could think about was how hard this move would be on my daughter, having to make new friends and get to know new teachers in the middle of first grade.

I had no idea that the move would be the answer to my prayers.

We made the move, and I went to school the first day to meet my daughter's teacher. She was so welcoming, and the way my daughter looked up at her and smiled was confirmation that I had made the

HELLO....

This book just jumped off the shelf as I strolled by. Imagine my surprise (and delight) when it whispered your name!

That being said, who was I to argue? 😊

Any book that has the "good sense" to want to spend time with you should most certainly be assisted!

Enjoy the stories....

Love,
Cath

right decision. I felt the heaviness of worry lift off my chest.

After a few months, I went to the school for a meeting with my daughter's teacher. During the meeting, I expressed my concern about her learning difficulties, and the teacher agreed with most of my concerns. I explained to her that the prior school would not test her for any learning disabilities until she was in third grade, and I felt that was wasting time. Her teacher agreed, but she was not sure if they would be able to do any testing in first grade either.

I remember quickly finishing the meeting so I could go out to my car and cry. I knew the only chance my daughter had at getting the extra help she needed was from me, but being a single mom there was no way I could homeschool and work full-time. Therefore, all I could do was cry and pray, and do the best I could to work with her at home.

I woke up the next morning and started writing a letter "to whom it may concern." In the letter, I explained how every time my daughter and I would read together, we would both end up in tears. I didn't have the proper training to teach her, and I wanted reading to be a joyful time for us. I poured all of my feelings, emotions and fears into the letter, and then shared my hope of helping her succeed. I begged for help in the letter from anyone who would listen, sealed it and gave it to my daughter's teacher. Later that day, I received an e-mail from her. She said that my letter had her in tears, and she asked if she could share the letter at the school board meeting that night. She added, "I will help you fight for your daughter."

I was so thankful that my daughter had a caring and compassionate teacher. All my daughter ever talked about was her teacher, and how she never made her read in front of the class. I was so grateful that we had made the move.

A few days later, I received a phone call from her teacher. The school board had agreed to go ahead with the testing right away. I could not thank her enough for caring so much and helping me fight for what my daughter needed. I asked for my daughter to be held back in the first grade with the agreement that she would be able to repeat with the same teacher. The school agreed.

The tests revealed that my daughter needed special education in reading and math for dyslexia and ADD. Her teacher and I worked hard to get her caught up to her grade level. By the time she was in fifth grade, she was taking all her regular classes with special accommodations that gave her a few extra tools and time limits she needed to succeed. By seventh grade, she was being pinned at a ceremony for the National Junior Honor Society as a straight A student.

If it weren't for her teacher in first grade, my daughter would not be who she is today. Every time we see her first grade teacher, Mrs. Freeman, I am reminded of the impact teachers have on our children's futures.

~Marie Ellen

Soaked Alive

You can move a lot of water with a thimble.
~Martin H. Fischer

The summer was over, and I was pulling supplies and teaching tools out of cupboards, preparing for the new school term. Books, charts, rulers, pencils, and chalk appeared. So did a bone-dry potted violet I thought a child had taken home.

Before throwing it out, I decided to soak it to see what would happen. I set it in a dish on a counter. When the class came in, they scoffed at the dead thing I was displaying. I said, "It hasn't had any water all summer. Let's see what happens if we give it a good soaking." Some of the children had hope, while others said it would never do anything.

The next day, its leaves started to green up. Day by day, it came alive. It produced more leaves, and then flowers. It was more than just alive; it was thriving!

That violet became our special secret — the plant that was dead was alive and growing. Later in the year, a colleague remarked, "What a beautiful violet. You just have a way with plants."

I told her, "This is my proof that a student who seems hopeless on the first day of school may come alive and, little by little, become a child who excels. Maybe he or she will do something wonderful in the world. It is my job to soak them in as much good instruction as possible and see what miracles can happen."

The violet had appeared dead. If I bent a twig, it was so brittle and dried out that it broke. There was no life in it. But when I gave it what it had lacked all summer, life reappeared. I like to think that we can use education the same way, to create new excitement, enthusiasm, enlightenment — new life.

~Beverly Anderson

No Excuses

*The most basic of all human needs is the need to
understand and be understood. The best way
to understand people is to listen to them.*
~Ralph Nichols

Early in my teaching career, I heard countless excuses — most of them fabricated, many of them amusing — for why students didn't have their homework. And, yes, "the dog ate it" was one of them. As time passed and I grew less gullible, I grew weary of hearing "I don't have my homework because…"

And so I quit accepting any excuse other than a verifiable death in the family.

When I was transferred to an inner-city middle school, I took my no-nonsense attitude with me. "No excuses, no extensions!" I warned my eighth graders on the first day of school. I collected homework at the beginning of each class. When a student didn't have it, I never asked why. Instead, I sighed loudly, shook my head in dramatic disgust and — with the student looking on — recorded a zero in the grade book. I soon gained the reputation I thought I wanted.

Then, one afternoon, shortly after the dismissal bell rang, Anthony approached me. "Could I talk to you a minute?" he asked shyly, not taking his eyes off the floor. "I know you said it doesn't matter why we don't have our lessons done, but I don't want you to think I'm a slacker because I come to school without mine so often."

Anthony looked up at me for the first time, and I could see that his lower lip was quivering. "It's just that… well, my dad moved out, and my mom waits tables at night, so I have to take care of my little brothers. Sometimes they cry a lot, and it makes it hard to concentrate."

I put my hand on Anthony's thin shoulder. "Why are you just now telling me…?" I stopped in mid-sentence. I knew why. So I changed the question. "Would it help if you stayed here in my classroom after school and worked on it before you go home?"

He swallowed hard and nodded.

The next day, I announced to all my students that I'd be offering an after-school study hall Monday through Friday. Anthony was the first student to show up. A couple of days later, Terrell joined him. Then Carmen, followed by twins Sandy and Randy. Before long, I had a room full of eighth graders who sometimes stayed until five o'clock to work on their lessons. I never asked why any of them were there, but I soon had a large collection of "I don't have my homework because…" stories. All were very real. None were amusing. Among the most poignant:

- *The power company cut off our lights because my dad couldn't pay the bill.*
- *We had to go get my sister out of jail again.*
- *My mom's boyfriend locked me out of the house so I spent the night in the car.*
- *My dad says schoolwork is just a waste of time.*
- *We don't have any paper in the house.*

The things I learned that year weren't taught in the education classes I'd taken in college. I discovered that not all kids come from homes that are safe and warm and dry. Not all kids have a quiet bedroom with a desk and study light and plenty of school supplies. Some don't have a home where a parent is even around. And some kids really do go to bed hungry.

Most importantly, I learned that "I'll listen" works a whole lot better than "No excuses!"

~Jennie Ivey

20

The Hot-Lunch Table

How beautiful a day can be when kindness touches it!
~George Elliston

I grew up in a large family of twelve siblings. We weren't poor by most standards, but things were definitely stretched for us. My parents never shared their financial worries, choosing instead to let us have a carefree childhood. But despite their discretion, I knew, as children often do, that there were times they went without and that certain things my friends had wouldn't be available to me.

Back in those days, hot lunch was a luxury for the wealthier kids, and hot-lunch buyers sat separately from the students who brought cold lunch. My siblings and I brought lunch from home every day: thick slices of homemade bread hiding one scant slice of bologna, three oatmeal cookies, and a small apple. We would look on longingly as the rich kids proudly sat down with their steaming plates of fried chicken or fish sticks and potato puffs, cartons of cold milk, chilled peaches and a slice of cake.

I never said anything, but my first grade teacher, Mrs. Caruso, must have seen the yearning in my eyes. One day she quietly pressed a note into my hand and whispered, "Give this to your mother."

I skipped home and gave my mom the note. She read it and smiled. "Well, Mrs. Caruso said because of all your hard work, she wants to buy your lunch tomorrow." The next day, I proudly carried my tray of chicken fricassee across the cafeteria and took my seat at the hot-lunch table. Honestly, the food wasn't as great as I had imagined, but I was pleased to be there and felt honored to be a part of the group.

One rainy day, Mrs. Caruso asked me to stay after school. My stomach instantly dropped to the floor. *Surely, I must be in trouble! Did she know I hadn't finished my math sheet? Did she see me teasing Billy on the playground?*

After the other students had left, Mrs. Caruso said she was going to finish her work and then drive me home. It was raining, and she knew I had a long walk. We pulled up to my house and she got out, depositing a few bags on the porch. "Tell your mom I had a few extra things she might want," she said. Then she drove away. Inside the bags were clothes, toys, and books.

That summer, Mrs. Caruso invited us all to her home. She gave us lemonade and sugar cookies, and we marveled at the fancy koi pond in her back yard.

I don't know why Mrs. Caruso took a shine to my family. Maybe she also grew up in a family that struggled. Maybe she knew what it was like to feel just a little less than everyone else. Somehow, even with her quiet charity, she never made me feel ashamed. She just made me feel loved and important. Thanks to her, I learned that I had just as much right as anyone to sit at the hot-lunch table.

I don't remember what Mrs. Caruso looked like anymore, but I sure do remember how she made me feel. I've never lost that feeling—of being important to someone and being protected by her. After all these years, I'm still grateful to that wonderful teacher.

~Anne Cavanaugh Sawan

21

Glory

A warm smile is the universal language of kindness.
~William Arthur Ward

efore volunteering to teach in Tanzania, I bought a travel guide to help prepare me for my journey. I learned the pronunciation of basic greetings in Swahili and facts about the town I would be teaching in.

I thought I was prepared, but then I stepped into my first classroom. My Form IV students, the equivalent of high-school seniors, stared at me as I walked through the door. They saw a smiling, white, twenty-seven-year-old, blond woman eager to teach them biology and English. As I introduced myself, nine out of the ten students continued to stare at me, but one student smiled. That student was Glory.

Back in Maine, I prided myself on quickly learning my students' names. I would come up with mnemonics to help. Tyler, his shirt is neon orange, it hurts my head and makes me want Tylenol. Cam, he has Justin Bieber hair, Justin Bieber used a camcorder to record himself singing. It was silly, but it worked. In my Form IV class, as the students said their names — Floriana, Lily, Nipaely, Innocent, Sarah, Ummy, Alphonce, Lillian, Eva, and Glory — I quickly realized that wordplay would not work. All of my students had the same shaved haircut, similar skin color, brown eyes, and the same blue-and-white uniform. I only learned Glory's name on the first day because her constant smile and deep-set dimples made her face glow in a "glorious" way.

In the United States, students had a range of personalities. Here, the students blended in with one another. It wasn't just their matching haircuts and uniforms. It was how they acted in the classroom. Much of their school experience was focused on passing their end-of-year exams. My Form IV students were constantly reminded of the pressure they were under. While their class had ten students, my Form III class (juniors) had twenty students. My Form II class (sophomores) had thirty-five students, and my Form I class (freshmen) was hot and crowded, with almost fifty students in one small classroom. The class sizes were so different because, in Tanzania, only the students who are the most apt and able to pay tuition advance to the next grade level.

After two weeks of struggling to connect with my students, I realized that I had to find a balance between what they needed as students and who I needed to be as a teacher. I was not just in Tanzania to teach biology and English; I wanted my students to learn from me, and I wanted to learn from them.

One day, I went shopping in the village and saw stationery. I purchased every package and came up with a plan to help build a connection with my students. I gave out pieces of stationery and told my Form IV students that their homework was to write me a letter that answered various prompts. Some prompts asked about their families, others about what occupation they would like to have or what school topics interested them. Their letters were due on Friday, and I would write each of them a letter in response by Monday. Week after week, we would repeat this assignment.

Through these letters, I became like a diary to my students. I learned that Alphonce wanted to be a journalist and that Ummy's faith in God was the driving force in her life. I also learned that Glory, who always had a smile, was mourning the loss of her mother. She wrote about how much she missed her mom and that she believed someday she'd see her again in heaven. As students opened up to me, I incorporated their interests into my lessons. Despite these efforts, I still couldn't get my students, who had poured their fears and dreams out to me on paper, to ask questions or take part in class discussions. I was constantly frustrated by my inability to inspire these students in the way that I had hoped to.

Then, one day, everything changed. I wish I could say that I had planned this lesson, but I hadn't. We were learning about genetics, and I had called Glory up in front of the class simply because she was my friendliest student. In retrospect, my blue eyes would have been a perfect device for our lesson about dominant and recessive traits. Instead, we focused on Glory.

I drew a Punnett square on the blackboard with bright white chalk. Glory nervously smiled, revealing her deep-set dimples. I told the class that because dimples are dominant, I knew the odds were that one of Glory's parents had dimples. I stood at the board, ready to plot out uppercase and lowercase D's. Without thinking, I asked Glory if one of her parents had dimples.

Glory's eyes welled up with tears as she softly said, "My mother had dimples."

The class, which had already been quiet, became totally silent. My mind flashed to the letters she had written me. For weeks, she wrote about her loss and her grief. In my letters back, I tried to comfort her and tell her how proud her mom would be of the person she was growing up to be.

Glory wiped her tears and looked at the chart on the chalkboard.

I silently begged for her answer to my next question to be "no." I asked, "Does your father have dimples, too?"

Glory shook her head, indicating that he did not.

I put down the chalk and stood close to her. I continued speaking, not as a science teacher, but as someone who truly cared about my student.

"Glory, you have your mother's dimples. That means every time you smile, your mom is with you."

She looked at me, scrutinizing my face for any trace of dishonesty, but wanting to believe. I nodded as tears filled both of our eyes. Glory smiled, then reached up and felt her dimples.

"Really?" she asked.

"Yes. And someday your children may have those dimples, too."

She continued to touch her cheeks.

I spoke slowly to make sure Glory would understand what I

was saying. "Even though your mom is gone, she will always be with you, not only in your memories and the person you are, but in those dimples."

Still touching her face, Glory began to weep. Her best friend, Eva, rose from her desk and hugged her tightly. As they returned to their seats, I stood in front of the class, trying to wrap my brain around what had happened and to decide if or how I should proceed with the lesson. Perhaps it was to help Glory not feel like everyone was looking at her, or maybe they were curious about the topic, but one hand rose in the air, then another. Students began to ask questions about dominant and recessive traits.

Even though I had been waiting for weeks for my students to ask questions, I don't remember what was said in the moments that followed. But what I will never forget is Glory wiping away her tears, then looking up to the ceiling and smiling. She put a hand to each dimple and closed her eyes. When she opened them, she looked at me and smiled.

~Katie Coppens

The Teacher with a Mother's Touch

I have learned that there is more power in a good
strong hug than in a thousand meaningful words.
~Ann Hood

As a sixth grader, I never could have imagined losing the one person I knew loved me more than I loved myself. My father contracted a disease called Acquired Immunodeficiency Syndrome (AIDS), which caused his immune system to shut down. He got really sick. The illness caused him to lose a lot of weight, and his body slowly deteriorated. When he died, all I could think about was that I had lost my best friend.

I knew that I had to continue to work hard in school. I wanted my father to be proud of me more than anything else in the world, but I went to school every day feeling depressed. I even attempted suicide. I had completely given up and I was an emotional train wreck. No one knew the pain and the frustration I felt. No one knew that I cried myself to sleep every night after my father died.

After I was released from the hospital, I was told that I had to see a psychiatrist, but talking about how I was feeling inside wasn't working. I still had an empty void that no one could fill. I was lost, and my frustration quickly turned into anger. I couldn't understand how an eleven-year-old deserved to be hurt in this way.

When I returned to school, I was greeted by my classmates, who expressed great concern about how I was doing. I assured them that I was okay, even though it took everything in me not to break down. I would sit at my desk and see the kids' mouths moving, but I wasn't hearing anything they were saying. I had completely become numb to my reality.

While sitting at my desk one day, I couldn't help but notice the beautiful smile Ms. Brown had on her face. She was always happy, and the love she possessed for her students was genuine. She would often tell the class stories about her three daughters, which expressed how she enjoyed being a mom.

She would stand outside the door and greet each student with a warm hug. For me, it wasn't just a hug. It made me feel safe again, like someone loved me.

I went to school every day looking forward to a hug from Ms. Brown. I would sometimes close my eyes and imagine that they were my mother's arms around me. My mother had died when I was a baby, so I never had an opportunity to hug her or tell her that I love her.

Ms. Brown constantly motivated and encouraged me. She not only believed in me, but she believed in every student in her class. I felt like there wasn't anything I could not conquer. I started smiling again, and for the first time I started to believe in myself.

Teaching was not just a job to Ms. Brown. She enjoyed interacting and challenging her students to reach for the stars. She instilled in us that failure was not an option, and that if we worked hard we would gain success.

I know that one day I want to offer kids the same thing that Ms. Brown offered me. Not only do I want to educate them, but I want to motivate and inspire in a positive way. I want to be a role model for the hundreds of kids who are motherless and fatherless.

Thanks to Ms. Brown, I went from being a scared and depressed eleven-year-old girl to being an OVERCOMER! No matter what challenges and obstacles come my way, I know that if I stay positive and persevere, I will win in the end.

~Sharika R. Reeves

School Mama

Mama was my greatest teacher, a teacher of
compassion, love and fearlessness.
~Stevie Wonder

Every day, I hear the word "Mama" more than I hear my own name.
My students are all learning to speak for the first time.
Many say "Mama" before any other language emerges.
And no wonder, as vital as she is—
The first time it happened, I almost corrected the child.
But I've since found all that Mama can mean.
A simple word, Mama is a noun, and Mama is a verb.
Mama is their comfort, their mantra.
"Ma mamamama…"
They babble throughout our daily rhythm.
Mama is the calm amidst chaos.
Sometimes "Mama" slips out when they are asking me for help
tying their shoes
or when I am tucking them in for their nap.
Mama isn't one person but code for so many comforts—
a special blanket
a preferred animal
a naptime movie
or even a teacher, honored to be caring for these tiny friends.

While I may never hear "Mama" from a child of my own
I am blessed to be a school mama —
a giver,
a comfort,
a friend.

~Naomi Townsend

Chapter 3

Inspiration for Teachers

The Teacher Who Taught Me to Teach

Education is the key to success in life, and teachers make a lasting impact in the lives of their students.
~Solomon Ortiz

24

The Highest Mountain

A teacher takes a hand, opens a
mind, and touches a heart.
~Author Unknown

I arrived that first fall morning an awkward, out-of-place ten-year-old. I had suffered a serious head injury as a toddler when I'd fallen from a twenty-foot wall, which led to constant struggling in school. Now in fifth grade, I'd been separated from my friends and tossed into a special reading class. Quickly, I tried to blend into the walls, longing to sit at the back of the room unnoticed, like I had done in so many other classrooms. However, this one was different. The room was so small that I couldn't sit unnoticed, let alone blend in. One full wall held hundreds of books. A large window along another overlooked the front of the school. Across the back there were no desks — just two long tables with only enough room for about eight students.

Six of us shared the same look of horror on our faces when we met our teacher for the first time. She had a big smile, kind eyes, and brown hair pulled back into a ponytail. She was young — only thirty-one years old. But she was in a wheelchair. I was shocked to learn that she could not move her legs at all and her arms only a little. One partially limp hand had a pencil attached to it by a metal device so that she could write.

I had never known anyone who was paralyzed before, and seeing her that first day, honestly, terrified me. I kept my head down most of the morning, feeling both fear and shame.

We were all afraid to ask our new teacher what had happened to her, except for one brave student named Jon. To our horror, he bluntly asked, "Why can't you walk?"

The question didn't seem to bother her at all. She answered it with honesty and dignity. "In my teens, I was a skier. While qualifying for the Olympics, I fell during a giant slalom race and injured my spinal cord."

My first reaction was, "Wow!" It surprised me that she didn't brag about making it to the Olympic tryouts or talk about how much her life had changed since the accident. In fact, she never dwelled on her situation or acted like she felt sorry for herself. Instead, she greeted us with a big smile every day. I later learned that she was considered a sure bet to be on the U.S. Olympics team, and that she had been featured on the cover of *Sports Illustrated* the day before her accident.

No matter what bad stuff was happening in the world, our teacher provided a safe place for us to go. It was a turbulent but important time in history as the Vietnam War raged on, astronauts prepared to walk on the moon for the first time, and Martin Luther King, Jr. fought for equal rights. Prejudice, protest, and violence were part of our world. We children didn't understand much of what was happening at the time, but we did understand that something special was happening in our classroom.

Our teacher, Jill Kinmont, nurtured our young minds with persistence, dedication, and love. She took us patiently through reading cards, spelling lessons, writing assignments, and then whole books, praising our efforts with every step. I was a very slow reader, but she showed me that it was okay to take my time. Speed-reading was never a part of our curriculum. Our focus was on the details of a story and its message. Each day, we arrived to the comforting smell of sharpened pencils in the air, and soon became enveloped in these stories, appreciating the effect of words.

She made each of our birthdays special by celebrating with cards and small gifts. During one of these celebrations, Danny announced that he had written a little children's book, and it was to be published. Miss Kinmont was thrilled. "That's wonderful! I'm so proud of you!"

The boy's face beamed with joy. His book earned him $25 — a large sum at the time.

We shared special bonds and formed friendships in class. It was during this time that I found my best friend, Debbie. We became nearly inseparable, both in and out of school, anxiously awaiting our special reading class each day. We looked up to our teacher for her courage and kindness. It didn't take long for us to forget that she was in a wheelchair. She was simply the teacher who made learning a "reachable goal" for us. Her classroom provided a safe place of acceptance, a place we didn't want to leave.

I remember the day I was "intellectually" ready to leave. I was eleven and a half and had just passed a series of rigorous reading and spelling tests. To other teachers, spelling the word "furniture" might be a small matter, but my teacher treated it as a monumental accomplishment.

"You did it, Sandy!" she marveled with a big smile. "You spelled a very difficult word and passed the tests. Now you can return to a regular classroom!"

A part of me was proud and happy — I had worked hard to get to this point — yet another part of me didn't want to leave that welcoming, accepting teacher.

When an article featuring Miss Kinmont for her talent as a special reading teacher appeared in the local newspaper, I was very pleased. It was a great honor to be photographed beside her as one of her students.

There was a book about her, and then a hit movie called *The Other Side of the Mountain.* As I watched the movie with so many others, my heart swelled. This was about *my* teacher, the bravest person I knew, who believed in *me*! She had taken an awkward ten-year-old, barely able to read and write, and changed her world forever. Looking back, I wish I had thanked her for making such a big difference in my life.

I went on to become a published author and a teacher of young children, too. I'll always remember the most important thing my teacher taught me: With persistence and love, no mountain is too high to climb.

~Sandra J. Lansing

25

The Teacher's Kid

What the teacher is, is more important
than what he teaches.
~Karl Menninger

The living room was dark, lit only by the soft light of our small Christmas tree. Everyone else, including my two children, was asleep upstairs. I tiptoed around the couch where my dad was sleeping. I knelt down to touch the presents while tears softly rolled down my cheeks.

"What's the matter, Baby Doll?" I heard my dad's voice call out to me.

"I'm just thankful, but I'm also afraid that this will be the last Christmas I'll have with my family. No one understands what this is like."

"I can't tell you that I know how you feel, Baby Doll, but I can tell you what it feels like to watch your child have cancer, and it's the worst thing I can think of. I've asked the Lord to take me instead of you."

He was good at that. It was the teacher in him. He could always help me see things from a different perspective. And what an amazing teacher he was.

Almost every memory of my childhood involves a classroom. My dad grew up in a poor family in northern Ohio, where the other kids called him "Encyclopedia Brain." He was brilliant and worked his way through college at the University of Kentucky in only three years, sometimes going hungry or sleeping in his car. He could have been anything, but he chose to be a teacher because knowledge was so important to him. And so he became a History teacher in the foothills of the Appalachian Mountains in eastern Kentucky where he met my mother.

We never had much, but Dad was a wonderful teacher, beloved by his students. He stood at the front of his classroom, talking about the history of the world without ever opening a textbook or using notes. When I was a young child, he would read to me, and I would watch him with wonder. I truly believed he knew everything about anything. Other kids felt the same way and followed him around. I craved his attention and spent many years angry and jealous of those students.

Back then, I didn't like being a teacher's kid. He was always coaching, studying, preparing a lesson, grading papers or spending long hours in the evening, weekends and summers preparing for his students. I watched as the high school students he taught called him "Dad," and it made me very angry. It wasn't until I was older that I realized that some of these children didn't have fathers of their own or the kind of father I had.

Dad was strict but kind. He expected me to work hard, get good grades, and show compassion for everyone regardless of status. His fairness-across-the-board ideals weren't always well accepted by those who thought they were entitled to special treatment, but it made him a hero to me. I used to pretend I was asleep just so I could feel his strong arms lift me up and carry me to my room. And when I was sick, I'd feel his big hands check my forehead all night long to make sure my fever was going down. He had an answer to every question and could solve any problem, but I could never completely understand why he would choose a job that paid so little. On cold winter mornings, I would wake up to watch him through my window. He would leave at 5:00 a.m. for his second job as a school-bus driver before the school day even began.

As I got older, I resisted his high standards. My grades and behavior were expected to be perfect. But when I was a sophomore in high school, I got my very first B, in Algebra. As a result, I was grounded for six months. I had never been angrier at him. Other kids I knew were allowed to date and stay out late. They didn't have to worry about studying. But I was a teacher's kid and had to set an example. I stopped talking to him, and his appendix ruptured a week later. When I finally got to see him, he could barely speak. He could have said anything, but he looked up at me with tears in his eyes and said, "I'm sorry, Baby Doll. You aren't grounded anymore."

I graduated high school and went on to college. I chose the University of Kentucky because it was where Dad went, but I told myself I would never be a teacher. I didn't want to be poor and work long hours. So, I remained undeclared while I worked two jobs to survive on a campus full of other girls who never worked at all. Boys became interested in me. I made some pretty bad decisions and found myself in the kind of relationship that requires sunglasses on a not-so-sunny day. I never told Dad what was happening, but he would always pick up the phone and offer me his ear and his very best advice. No matter what kind of mess I was in, I always had my "North Star" to guide me home.

In 2012, I was going into my third year of teaching (yes, I became a teacher) and had two small children of my own. I was married to a wonderful man, and life was good. But I found myself feeling very tired, more tired than usual. My worries were brushed aside by doctor after doctor. Finally, at the urging of my parents, I got another opinion. I was diagnosed with Stage IIB cervical cancer.

I called my dad, terrified. He told me that everything would be okay. The very next morning, my parents were on my doorstep, and we went to the Cleveland Clinic. The next few months were very difficult, and I felt sorry for myself. At my lowest, I called my dad. He read to me from the Bible and gave me passages to study. He was the pastor of a small church by then, and was, of course, excellent in yet another kind of teaching role. When he was able to be with me in the hospital, I noticed that he was falling asleep a lot. I asked him what was wrong, but he always brushed it off and turned his attention to me.

That Christmas, I found myself seeking the wisdom of my life's greatest teacher once again. I had completed my cancer treatments, and he and my mother were staying with us as I recovered from months of radiation and chemotherapy. And in the light of that Christmas tree, he reminded me of the love and understanding he'd always given me throughout my life. Although I didn't always appreciate it, I could see how truly blessed I was to be a teacher's kid.

Two weeks later, he was diagnosed with Stage IV kidney cancer. I was devastated, and I started to wonder if maybe God had taken Dad's offer to trade his life for mine. Since then, we have supported each other, and I've been able to teach *him* a few things — about living with cancer. But as my health reports have gotten better, his have gotten worse. My heart breaks at the thought of losing him. Sometimes, I wonder, "How will I navigate the world without my North Star?" But then I remember whose daughter I am. I'm a teacher's kid. I can do anything because he taught me how.

~E.M. Slone

The Ripple Effect

While it may seem small, the ripple effect
of small things is extraordinary.
~Matt Bevin

I stood in a rambunctious group of sixth grade students, waiting in suspense for the answer to our burning question: *What type of crazy tie would Mr. Miller be showcasing today?*

Our teacher careened around the corner with a… drum roll, please… GREEN ELEPHANT TIE that matched his rather large elephant coffee mug! Oh, the satisfaction in our young hearts — a green elephant tie!

As his glasses hung on for dear life at the tip of his nose, he gave us a silly grin and greeted us with a cheerful, "Good morning, folks!" Whether sunshine or hurricane, he always started out our day with a joyful salutation. He was eccentric and unique and he brightened every day for us.

I loved music, so I remember how excited I was when he said he was going to give us music lessons. But when he turned on the music, my minority, low-income classmates and I slowly turned our heads toward the sound of… Peter Paul and Mary singing "If I Had a Hammer."

Snickers filled the room. If it wasn't rap or hip hop, we didn't recognize it. What were these people singing about? My classmates were not into this at all. But for me, it was a discovery. An awakening.

Our white, eccentric teacher opened up a whole new world for me. No longer trapped within the confines of what we were expected to listen to, I learned to love John Denver, Joan Baez, and the many other artists who were hiding behind the doors of cultural stereotypes. Mr. Miller took those chances with us.

From introducing the graceful art of calligraphy to getting filthy reenacting the Gold Rush of the 1840s, he was not afraid to go out on a limb, to give all of himself in his teaching, no matter our backgrounds. He was the most innovative and creative teacher I have ever known.

Fast-forward twenty years, and now there are forty little eyes staring at my wild musical-note shirts or weird treble-clef earrings as I greet them with a joyful, "Good morning, class!" I wonder, *Do my students wait and wonder what crazy music clothes I will wear each day?*

I am blessed to teach music to English Language Learning students who happen to reside on the lower rungs of the socioeconomic ladder. Nevertheless, I go out on a limb with them, take chances, and give all of myself to teaching them. And they've developed a hunger to dance to Beethoven's Fifth, to watch Gustavo Dudamel of the Los Angeles Philharmonic conduct the Simón Bolívar Symphony Orchestra of Venezuela, and to create while Duke Ellington mixes his instrumental sounds like a painter on a canvas.

I glance at my 2015 Teacher of the Year Award, which I received for being a dynamic, innovative, and somewhat... eccentric teacher. And I chuckle to myself, wondering which child in front of me will carry this on — as I've carried on the legacy of Mr. Miller.

One teacher, who dared to be different and open new worlds to kids like me, tossed the pivotal pebble into the pond of my life. I pray the ripples never end.

~Genein M. Letford

27

Prepositions

*A philosopher once said, "Half of good
philosophy is good grammar."*
~Aloysius Martinich

I was in eighth grade and a reluctant student at St. Anne School in Fair Lawn, New Jersey. One day, Sister Joan announced that we were going to learn about prepositional phrases. Yawn. She explained that prepositional phrases start with a preposition and end with a noun or pronoun. Yawn. "There are only forty-plus commonly used prepositions," she continued. Double yawn. "And everyone must memorize them." What? Memorize prepositions? That sure captured everyone's attention. The class collectively groaned. This would make learning the eight parts of speech easier, she promised.

Sister Joan recited the forty-plus prepositions as easily as saying the days of the week. She wrote them on the chalkboard in alphabetical order, in groups of mainly four for us to copy.

"Once you memorize the first eight, move on to the next four or eight until you've memorized all of them. Recite them on the school bus, at home, on the weekend. Sing them to your favorite song, substituting the prepositions for the song's words. Practice, practice, practice," she advised.

I tried, but sometimes I got confused. My parents helped me because English wasn't my strong subject. When I had the first eight done, I moved on, but then I forgot the first ones. Slowly, eventually,

I succeeded. Grammar became easier once I could spot and write prepositional phrases, just as Sister Joan had promised. While challenging us, she made grammar fun. She truly cared about us.

In addition to singing the prepositions, she shared other useful language nuggets. I still remember her catchy phrase: "Good better best, never let it rest, until your good is better, and your better is best."

After high school and a stint in the Army, I enrolled in college on the G.I. Bill, majoring in — my parents couldn't believe it — English!

In creative writing class in my junior year, I recited the prepositions for my professor and classmates. I explained how my eighth grade teacher, Sister Joan, had often said that a strategically placed prepositional phrase could add depth and variety to sentences. Impressed, my professor asked for a copy of Sister Joan's list and other tricks of the trade that I remembered.

After graduating from college, I landed a job teaching eighth grade English in a New Jersey public school. I bent over backwards to make grammar easy and fun the way Sister Joan had. I started with a unit on the eight parts of speech, with prepositions coming first. Memorization was the cornerstone.

Before long, the students were singing the prepositions to their favorite tunes. One year, since it was near Christmas, we all sang the prepositions to "Jingle Bells." As I recall, it was quite boisterous. The principal stuck his head in my classroom door. "George, is everything okay?"

"Of course," I assured him.

I also required students to recite the prepositions in ten seconds or less. If you thought that was impossible, then you don't know eighth graders. They welcomed the challenge, and with no homework as a motivator, they got right down to business. I pulled out a stopwatch and timed the students daily to gauge their progress: 21, 16, 12, then bingo, 10 seconds!

I taught eighth grade English for thirty-eight years. Looking back, teaching English was a tough but worthwhile job, and I loved every day. One of my former students, Sharon, followed in my footsteps and became a middle-school English teacher. She pushes her students to gallop through the prepositions, too, with excellent results. "How low can you go?" she roars, with stopwatch in hand. I laugh at the sight and see elements of myself and Sister Joan in her.

Now when I meet former students in town or at the mall, they rarely say, "Hi, Mr. Flynn. How are you?" Instead, they smile and belt out the following: about, above, across, after; against, along, amid, among; around, at, before, behind; below, beneath, beside, besides; between, beyond, by, down; except, for, from, in; into, of, off, on; over, through, throughout; till, to, toward, under, until, unto, up, upon; with, within, without.

~George M. Flynn

28

The Tools

When you catch a glimpse of your potential,
that's when passion is born.
~Zig Ziglar

I walked into your classroom frustrated. I felt as though no good could come from this situation. I was nine years old and had just been diagnosed with a visual-spatial learning disability, one that required me to leave my previous school and enter yours.

I was mad at my parents for taking me away from my friends, at myself for not understanding, and at you for placing me in a class of only five students. Your room was full of beanbags, computers and games, and yet I longed for the normalcy of crowded spaces and rows of desks.

When I came to you, I was in third grade and couldn't read or write. I was unmotivated and in a constant state of distress when it came to schooling. I had come from a private school that could not teach me in a way that worked for me. I was transferred to your public school, one known for its special-education programs.

I hated being different and feeling like I was stupid and less worthy than other students. I was embarrassed when you would take me from my regular classroom and bring me to yours for the day, indicating my "special status." You could tell I was upset and you took me under your wing. You started where I was and provided me the tools to move on.

It took two months to respect you, a year to understand you, two years to learn my own ability, and three years to move past your safe space. You broke those years into moments and got me excited about learning. You not only taught me what I needed to move past my disability, but you supported me in all that I did outside of it. You attended my theater performances, built a relationship with my parents, and helped me advocate for myself.

A girl who once had to be bribed to read, forced to write, and was unsure in her abilities was transformed. You showed me that we each learn differently, and that success would arrive with hard work.

I have not seen you since my youth, but I still think about you. I ponder what my life would have been like if I had never met you. I think of how unhappy and jumbled I was before I entered your classroom. I would love to cross paths with you now and show you all I have accomplished because of you.

Now, I intern in an elementary school filled with children who face the same kinds of uncertainty that I faced all those years ago. I work one-on-one with these children as you worked one-on-one with me. When I see a child who is struggling, I think back to the tools that you gave me. When I see a child in need of support, I advocate for her like you taught me. I hope I am touching the lives of these children the way you touched mine.

Before you entered my life, I was not fully me. So, thank you, thank you for giving me dreams and aspirations, and most of all, thank you for giving me the tools to give back to others what you gave to me.

~Ariela Solomon

29

The Power of a Promise

Music is the shorthand of emotion.
~Leo Tolstoy

hen I was in fourth grade, my classmates and I took a test to see how well we listened and discriminated between various pitches and chords. Apparently, I passed the test because my parents received a letter saying that I had qualified to play in the school band. My mom went to a parent information meeting and brought home a clarinet, an instrument I had never heard of before. I started attending lessons and band practice with a nice man who told us to call him "Mr. Ed."

I enjoyed playing my clarinet. I never had to be reminded to practice because I loved new challenges, and I liked being able to play new tunes each time I went to my lessons. When I was in sixth grade, Mr. Ed encouraged me to enter a solo and ensemble festival with seventh and eighth graders. What an eye opener! I learned even more about what I could do if I worked hard enough.

About halfway through my second year of band, Mr. Ed told us he was leaving. He had received a Fulbright Scholarship and would be going to London for a year. I was devastated. But Mr. Ed gave us his address and told us to let him know how we were doing. "If you write to me, I'll write back," he promised.

I continued to play clarinet and wrote to tell Mr. Ed about it. As promised, he wrote back and told me about the marvelous places he'd been and the things he'd seen. London sounded like a place I wanted to see for myself. If he was able to do it playing his tuba, then maybe I could travel the world playing my instrument.

We were so happy when Mr. Ed came back, and when I graduated to junior high, Mr. Ed was still my band director. He convinced me to switch from clarinet to oboe and I loved this new adventure. Now we played even more challenging music, and we earned high ratings at district and state festivals. But just after our triumph at the state festival, he informed us he'd be leaving again. This time, he was going to Illinois. And this time, the move was permanent. He'd been named the tuba instructor at Illinois State University. But again, he told us, "I want to hear from you. Write to me, and I'll write back."

So once again, I wrote. I told him about my new teachers, about studying and practicing my new instrument, about going to music camp and learning lots of things and playing wonderful music. I even auditioned and won a spot in the American Youth Symphony and traveled to Europe, where I saw some of the sights he'd written about. And he wrote back, encouraging me and telling me about the university and the wonderful people there in central Illinois. I told him I wanted to study music and be a band director like him, and he encouraged me to attend Illinois State University and audition for a scholarship. On one of his visits back to Michigan, he took the time to visit my parents and assure them that he would personally look out for me if I went to ISU. Although I auditioned at several colleges, ISU offered the best scholarship so I packed my bags and traveled south.

My time at Illinois State was magical. I made many new friends and became certified to teach music, but I missed my home and family. At the end of four years, I made the wrenching decision to return, knowing I'd miss my friends and the support I had at ISU. But once again, Mr. Ed reassured me by saying, "Write to me, and I'll write back."

For thirty years, we exchanged Christmas cards and other communications. I became a music teacher, then a regular elementary classroom teacher, and then a college professor. I raised a family and watched them marry and have kids of their own. I did a lot of traveling, too, and managed to see more of the places Mr. Ed had written about so long ago. Mr. Ed also married, and we exchanged photos and shared stories about our families.

Three years ago, Mr. Ed passed away. I made the seven-hour trip back to Normal, Illinois, for the memorial service and sat with dear friends from my time at ISU. We listened as others shared their stories of what this great man had done for them. I thought about his legacy as I drove home. Would my years of teaching ever measure up to the influence he'd had?

I realize it's silly to compare my teaching career to someone else's. But what I *can* do is reflect on what he taught me and try to emulate it. From Mr. Ed, I learned the joy of making music. I learned how to share that joy with others. And I learned the power of a promise kept.

~Patricia Gordon

A Life Once Touched

What we have done for ourselves alone dies with us;
what we have done for others and the world
remains and is immortal.
~Albert Pike

I recently retired from twenty-three fulfilling years as a classroom teacher. One of the treasures from my classroom is a little wooden apple painted with the saying "To teach is to touch a life forever." Throughout my career, I thought a great deal about the idea of touching lives, of making a difference. I always measured my success in hugs, mementos, and smiles from my students, not by data and test scores. I always prayed that I would have a positive influence on each of the young lives I touched.

I know how powerfully one teacher can impact the life of a person who does not believe in herself, because I was a high school dropout. No matter where we lived, we were always the poorest family in town, that low-class bunch from the wrong side of the tracks. I was the oldest of nine kids, raised on welfare with an unemployable father and a mentally ill mother. I didn't stand a chance. I quit high school to get married at sixteen, and a few years later found myself a divorced, single mother with no education, no skills, and no future. Factory jobs, waitress work, and night shifts barely kept a roof over our heads.

The one thing I had going for me was my stubbornness; I did not want my children to be raised on welfare, so I worked. Then I had an accident and couldn't work for several months. The world as

I knew it ended.

I sank into a deep despair. While my physical injuries healed, my remaining confidence disappeared into a hopeless depression. Still, with growing boys to feed, I did not have the luxury of giving up. Searching the classified ads, I found a notice that our local community college offered training for those who qualified under a government program. It included a stipend for the hours as well as the training. One requirement was a high-school diploma or GED certificate. Years earlier, I had taken the GED test and received my certificate, but with such low scores that I was ashamed to show it to anyone. I felt stupid, certain that I had little to offer other than a willingness to try. I dug through my papers until I found the envelope with my GED scores and went to the school to meet the advisor who would assess me. Her name was Ruby Martin.

I sat nervously waiting while Mrs. Martin looked over my score sheet, her expression changing to a deep frown. My heart fell. I was prepared to hear her berate me for my failure, my low scores, and wasting her valuable time. She looked at me for a long moment before she spoke.

"Why did you apply for this training program?" she asked. "Why aren't you applying to college?"

With my mouth dry, my eyes filling and my face burning with shame, I could only whisper, "Because I am stupid, poor, and desperate. I thought maybe…"

She laid her glasses down and looked sternly at me. "Why do you think you are stupid?"

"You have my test scores. You can see for yourself."

"Didn't anyone ever explain these scores to you?" she asked. I just shook my head as I stared at my clenched fists in my lap. For the next hour, she explained how the GED scores are not based on percentages the way most tests are, and that my numbers were very high indeed. She assured me that I was not only *not* stupid, but that I would make an excellent candidate for the job-training program. I was speechless.

The twelve-week training course occupied my days with academics, technical training, and a seminar on how to interview and dress professionally. Throughout those weeks, Ruby Martin came in every few days and walked around the room, stopping to speak to several of us, including me. She was positive, encouraging, and supportive. The basic skills we learned in that program made it possible for me to get a job as a retail clerk and bookkeeper, but the words of Ruby Martin echoed in my mind: "Why are you not applying for college?" I caught myself daydreaming at times of a real education, hoping for a future that I had been certain was out of reach for me.

One day, armed with little more than a tiny spark of hope and a million questions, I dropped by her office without an appointment. Ruby Martin took the time to guide me toward the financial-aid office and assure me that I could qualify for help. She encouraged me to apply for college admission. I was listed as a "non-traditional student," a thirty-eight-year-old, high school dropout.

College proved challenging and exhausting, yet incredibly rewarding. At graduation, I scanned the faculty in their regalia, and there she was, smiling back at me. I knew she always participated in graduation, but at that moment, I felt she was there just for me.

I transferred my credits and associate's degree to the university, earned a bachelor's degree in English for Education, and set out on my own career as a teacher. Still hungry for more learning, though, I applied for graduate school and kept going while teaching middle-school reading and English.

At times, it felt like a hopeless task — teaching young teenagers who had already given up on themselves. Still, I hoped to fulfill that "touching a life" cliché. So I struggled to be both teacher and student, often neglecting my own younger child, then a senior in high school. Though I often felt I was in over my head, ready to quit, I prayed for strength to finish what I had started. As the time drew near for graduation with my master's degree, I was compelled to tell Ruby Martin how much I appreciated her encouragement back when I felt at my lowest.

I dropped by her office, again without an appointment. As I watched her assist another student, I was overcome with gratitude and the realization that she had truly given me a new life. The student turned to leave, and I stepped forward. "You probably don't remember me," I said, "but I went to school here about five years ago. I just want to thank you for your help."

"Of course, I remember you," she spoke softly. "You'll have to tell me your name, but I remember your face and your story. How have you been doing?"

I told her I had graduated *magna cum laude* and was earning my master's degree in Education, that I had been teaching for two years, and that I owed all of my success to her. "If you had not taken the time to make me feel as if I had some potential, if you had not believed in me and encouraged me, I would never have gone to college. Nobody ever believed in me before." The tears came — my tears, her tears, and those of the two people who had come into the room unnoticed while I was talking.

Years later, after a long teaching career, I was standing in the checkout line of a local grocery store when I heard a hesitant voice behind me. "Excuse me, miss, but I think you were my seventh grade teacher." I turned and had to look up at the speaker, a young man well over six feet tall. He told me his name, and I instantly remembered which class he had been in, where he had sat in my room, and even how he had hated reading. We chatted briefly, and I asked what he was doing these days. "I am going to college," he answered. "I want to be a reading teacher."

"Wait a minute," I said. "The Eddie I remember *couldn't* read, *wouldn't* read, and *refused* to read."

"Yes, ma'am. That was me. I figured if you could reach somebody as stubborn as I was, maybe I could help somebody, too. Because of how you never gave up on me, I now believe I can make a difference."

I saw Ruby Martin's obituary in the local newspaper a few years ago and felt tremendous sadness at her passing. But I also experienced great joy in knowing I had taken the time to show my appreciation. Teachers often become just background in the everyday lives of students. We may never know how much influence we have had on them, but when a former student reaches out and says, "Thank you," we feel a warmth that sustains and strengthens us for the next round. Ruby Martin touched my life forever. I hope she understood that she continued touching the lives of my students as well. A life once touched is forever changed.

~Virginia Reeder

31

When Steven Came Back to School

A teacher affects eternity; he can never
tell where his influence stops.
~Henry Adams

I've been in the teaching profession more than thirty years, and one of the best teachers I've even known was Mr. Rowe. I was lucky enough to co-teach fourth grade with him in an open classroom many years ago. We had fun teaching together, and our kids had fun learning.

Mr. Rowe had infinite patience and understanding, and I learned so much from watching him. He could perform miracles, like the one he performed with Steven, one of the unhappiest kids I ever saw. Steven couldn't stand school. He didn't like being picked last for kickball, he didn't like the kids who raised their hands and knew all the answers, and most importantly, he didn't like himself.

The first day he walked into Mr. Rowe's classroom, he ignored the other students, scowled, and slid into his chair, knocking a couple of textbooks onto the floor.

Mr. Rowe walked over to him and touched Steven's shoulder, but Steven pulled away. Nevertheless, Mr. Rowe welcomed him: "Hi, Steven. I'm happy you're in my class. We're gonna have a great year." Steven looked around the room as if Mr. Rowe must be mistaken. No teacher in his right mind would want Steven to be a part of his classroom.

So, while Mr. Rowe seemed cheerful and relaxed that very first day of school, it seemed like Steven was angry and confused. He stood up, knocking his chair over, and kept looking around the room. "Are you talking to *me*?" he shouted, a little too loud. "You *can't* be happy that *I'm* in your class. No one is *ever* happy when I'm in the room."

Most kids nodded in agreement. A very brave kid laughed out loud. Steven's eyes narrowed, and his hands knotted into fists.

But Mr. Rowe gave him a wide, genuine smile. "Believe what you want, but this is a new day and a new beginning. This year, you can become the Steven *you* want to be."

"Yeah, right," Steven grumbled, but he seemed to smile a little to himself as he sat down.

That day, Mr. Rowe chose Steven to pitch the kickball at recess. "Hey, Steven," Mr. Rowe commented, "you're pretty good at pitching. Let me show you my secret trick." Mr. Rowe taught Steven a one-of-a-kind pitch that rolled straight just until a kid's foot was about to make contact. Then that ball would curve quickly to the right.

Not a single kid could score with that trick ball. Steven tried the pitch; it wasn't perfect, but it was good enough. His team cheered him on, and a kid or two even patted him on the back. "Way to go!"

After recess, Steven sat as close to Mr. Rowe as he could. When a question was asked, Steven lit up; he knew the answer. He raised his hand timidly, barely in the air at all. And he looked down, eyes focused on his feet.

Mr. Rowe called on him. When he answered, his voice shook. A few kids laughed, and Steven scowled. And then he got the answer right.

So that was pretty much how Steven's first day at school went. And later, when his former third grade teacher asked him, "How's fourth grade?" he shrugged and said, "It stunk." But I had a sneaking suspicion it was the best first day of school Steven ever had.

That is not to say that every day went smoothly. Sometimes, Steven would act out. But Mr. Rowe always pointed out the good things that Steven did, and calmly and quietly helped Steven regain control.

It was evident that Steven grew to love Mr. Rowe more and more with each passing day.

Time passed quickly that year, and before we all knew it, it was the very last day of school, and kids were boarding the buses to go home.

Our school has a very special tradition on the last day. The teachers fill the sidewalk, waving goodbye to the kids as the buses pull out with their horns honking. It's a parade of yellow school buses filled with happy kids going off for summer vacation.

But on that particular day, Steven walked slowly to the bus, his head down, tears in his eyes. He boarded the bus reluctantly, hesitated, and then ran back off of the bus to hug Mr. Rowe one last time. Steven sobbed, "I don't want to leave you! I don't want to go."

Mr. Rowe had a tear in his eye, too, and he whispered, "I know, Buddy. I'm gonna miss you, too."

Many years later, Mr. Rowe and I were surprised when a handsome young man walked into our classroom. He stood tall and proud in a Marine Corps uniform.

He hugged Mr. Rowe, and then Steven said quietly, "I came back to school today to say thanks."

I hope that every child has a teacher as life changing as Mr. Rowe. It is my hope, as well, that every teacher gets to have the experience of a former student coming back to say a very simple "Thanks." That is the true measure of a teacher's success.

~Katherine Mabb

Chapter
4

Inspiration for Teachers

Making a Difference

*Ideal teachers are those who use themselves as
bridges over which they invite their students
to cross, then having facilitated their crossing,
joyfully collapse, encouraging them to
create bridges of their own.*
~Nikos Kazantzakis

32

Unforgettable

How wonderful it is that nobody need wait a single
moment before starting to improve the world.
~Anne Frank

I was teaching a unit on the Holocaust to my freshman class and we were starting with *The Diary of Anne Frank*. I hadn't taught this subject before, so I was looking for some ideas. Someone told me about *Paper Clips*, a 2004 documentary about a school in Whitwell, Tennessee that taught about the Holocaust in a way that was meaningful and relevant for the students. They tried to realistically represent the numbers of those killed in the Holocaust by collecting paper clips for each person. That project really spoke to me as an educator. I wanted to try something similar within my own classroom to see if I could help my students connect to the Holocaust in a meaningful way.

At the time, I was very interested in scrapbooking, and so it dawned on me that we could make scrapbook pages to pay tribute to some of the victims and learn the stories of their lives before they were killed. I called it "The I Remember Project." The students chose from a list of victims and created "Remembrance Pages" for each person, with as much information as they could glean about the victims' lives.

When they were completed, the Remembrance Pages were hung on the walls outside my classroom creating the Wall of Remembrance. Later, we took them down and put them in scrapbooks that we kept in the classroom. Each year, we made new Remembrance Pages, learning about and honoring as many victims as we could each year.

That first year of the project made a huge impact and one of my students, Jessie King, did something extraordinary. She wanted to reach Irene, a Holocaust survivor she had learned about through her Remembrance Page. She sent an e-mail to the United States Holocaust Memorial Museum, which we had used as a major source for the project, and they passed her message along to Irene, who lived in Toronto, Canada. Irene's daughter Judy responded, and when Judy learned that we had never had a Holocaust speaker at our school, she said she would drive her mother the 350 miles to our school in Albion, Pennsylvania to speak to us. Our little, middle-of-nowhere school was being given an incredible opportunity. The kids were beyond excited, and they made T-shirts and banners in preparation.

The lives of our students and staff would never be the same after seeing Irene and hearing her story in person. It was a story that far too many people could tell, and from which a lesson could be learned that is sadly still applicable to today's world. And all this happened because one young woman whose heart was touched reached out to share those feelings. Because of her actions, my whole world changed, as a teacher and as a human being.

But the story doesn't end there. Incredibly, a fire was lit, and other students came on board. This was a time of major budget cuts, and our school would never be able to pay for speakers like this, so we took matters into our own hands. We created the "I Remember Committee" to fundraise in order to bring individuals to our school who could expose our students to real-life stories of discrimination, prejudice, and inhumanity. Fortunately, Irene's daughter Judy had been working to promote diversity and improve race relations within her own country of Canada. She became our "Angel from the North," setting up interesting speakers for the next several years, including another Holocaust survivor, Max Eisen; Marina Nemat, a published author and survivor of an Iranian prison; Tanya Khan, a devout Muslim woman whose personal mission was to debunk the stereotypes surrounding her faith; and human-rights activists Danny Richmond and Toni Silberman.

When Jessie King walked into my classroom, I had no idea how she would touch my life and afford me the opportunities to meet such incredible people. She became my inspiration. And as she has graduated and moved on to pursue other dreams, she has become my friend. Over the years, she has tirelessly given of herself for a cause in which she believes: to make the world a better, more knowledgeable place in which to live.

~Patricia Wood

33

Bonus Pay

*Don't live down to expectations. Go out there
and do something remarkable.*
~Wendy Wasserstein

ost of my students with special needs had neurological problems that affected their language processing and communication skills. Danny did not, but he was having such behavioral issues that my supervisor asked me to give him a chance in my classroom.

When I reviewed Danny's records, I understood why he might act out. There was no way he could keep up with the sixth grade curriculum. He could barely read or write. He was still printing his name, refused to even try to write a sentence, and recognized only a few words. His first response when asked to try something was belligerence.

Once he understood that I would quietly persist, with the gentlest of encouragement and a firm belief that he could do the task, he stopped the belligerence. Instead, his shame and embarrassment surfaced. I decided to leave the textbooks behind and focus on real-world examples, like street signs and fast-food restaurant vocabulary. Danny was quietly pleased that he could finally understand menu-board words and not have to order by picture, by what someone else was having, or by using words from television commercials.

I remember the day I informed him he could read more than 100 words. He did not believe it until he sat down and counted out the 4x6 homemade word cards himself. He allowed me to share this victory with his classmates, and their joy and pride in him chipped away at his defensive shell. That was the day he became a true member of our class.

It was evident he had a kind heart. Some of his classmates had balance difficulties, and he always seemed to be right there to catch them as they tipped. I noticed that he watched them carefully and could assist them so discreetly that an outside observer might not even notice the bobble. Danny knew what it was like to be singled out and teased, so he helped other kids avoid the same fate.

I assigned him to help our youngest students, always positioning him as an expert. He'd sit with students who were reading along with a book on tape. He was there to set up the recorder, matching the title on the tape and books to the assignment card I gave him. He never realized that as he helped the younger kids read along, he was reading, too. It gladdened my heart to see him slip into that center during free time and listen to one of the books himself.

The boy who wanted nothing to do with books suddenly liked a few. I arranged for him to practice one, *The Berenstain Bears and the Spooky Old Tree*, until he could read it perfectly and with great drama. Then I had him read it to a group of preschool students. When he returned to our classroom with a thank-you certificate in his hands, he had a swagger in his walk and a huge smile on his face. He radiated confidence. He asked me to laminate that certificate, and he kept it taped to his desktop.

I only had to show him once how to set up the learning center for math activities, and he took over the job. He loved having the markers sorted and in cups, the paper stacked, and the manipulatives set up before I could even ask. Danny was better with numbers; he could do basic addition and subtraction, but refused to even attempt multiplication. Nothing budged him until I told him it was a fast way of adding. "I already can add, but I'd like to be fast!" was his response, and we were off and running.

At the end of the first grading period, when I called his mother and identified myself as Danny's teacher, her response was a surly "Now what?" I explained I wanted to share that he was doing well, and I was delighted he was in my class. There was a long pause, and with a catch in her voice, she said, "No one from school has ever called me to tell me something good." With a catch in my voice, too, I told her she could expect more calls like this. The next day, Danny greeted me with a wide grin. "You called my mama, and she was happy!"

Danny continued to blossom, becoming in many ways my teacher's aide. One day each week, my class and I went into the community. Once, while riding the Regional Transit Authority bus on a field trip, he reached over and took off my glasses. I am extremely nearsighted, and without my glasses the world is a blur. "These are dirty," he said. He proceeded to spit on each lens and wipe them clean with his shirt. When he tenderly placed them back on my face, my vision remained blurred for a bit — maybe from residual spit, or maybe from my unshed tears.

On the last day of school, we had a party and awards ceremony for the students moving on to junior high. Danny had made so much progress in his one year with us, and I was looking forward to honoring and celebrating him. I was heartbroken when he didn't get off the school bus that morning. We wouldn't even get to say goodbye.

Then around 10:30, I heard all the kids gasp. There was Danny, smiling ear-to-ear, and with him was his mother carrying a sheet cake. They used public transportation to go to the grocery store and buy a cake, and then come to school. This would have involved transferring buses several times, a complicated and time-consuming journey. The class rose as one, enveloping Danny and his mother in a circle of joy and hugs. We all cried: me, Danny, Danny's classmates, and Danny's mother. And we all stuffed ourselves full of cake and laughter and thankfulness for one another.

Teaching may not pay me the big bucks, but where else do you get a bonus like that?

~Jude Walsh

34

Be Someone's Grapefruit

*Common sense and a sense of humor are the same
thing, moving at different speeds. A sense of
humor is just common sense, dancing.*
~William James

Do you remember bringing your eighteen-month-old daughter to preschool with knotted hair, a milk mustache, in a princess costume, while her older brother trailed behind in his superhero pajamas? No? I do. And I remember what a blessing it was to be around people who laughed along with the joke, people who knew that fighting over Cinderella and Superman outfits just isn't worth it sometimes.

The year my middle son was three and his sister was eighteen months old was chaotic, to say the least. Their older brother, who was four, went to school a bit farther away, and my husband dropped him off, leaving me to get the two younger kids ready for school and pack their lunches.

Packing lunches wasn't, honestly, my thing. It requires buying the food, then making the food, and then cramming the sandwiches into the teensy rectangles in the Pottery Barn squares made for monogrammed lunch boxes. This never works out in real life the way it does in the catalogs.

Trying to make nut-free sandwiches in the shape of a star and a flower while my daughter danced the tango naked with baby wipes trailing from her bottom wasn't working. If Cinderella wasn't waltzing in the nude, chances are she was swinging from my hip begging for "chocwat," while I tried to patch together some sort of acceptable meal. I figured if self-parenting was good enough for the children of the 1980s it was good enough for my kids, too. And that is how my three-year-old ended up on lunch duty.

Ultimately, I did what any good delegator would do: I put my handy three-year-old son in charge of lunches. There were rarely problems because he is the middle child and wanted to please his mama by packing acceptable lunches while I chased his sister who was riding the dog.

It turned out he wasn't making great lunches but the teachers — loving and nonjudgmental — never mentioned the quality of food going into those lunch sacks — until the day when one of my daughter's teachers told me, very sweetly, not to pack medicine for lunch.

"Huh?" I said. I needed to decide if I was going to play along as if I was the one actually packing the lunches and take responsibility for whatever "drugs" were in the lunchbox, or throw myself under the pre-school bus and admit that I had the three-year-old running the show.

It turned out it was just a Pedialyte bottle my son had mistaken for a Gatorade. I wasn't in too much trouble, but I did feel like I needed to tell my son's teacher what had been going on just in case he had been peddling Pedialyte and peanut butter in class.

I walked to my son's classroom. Miss Brenda wrapped me in a big Louisiana hug and smiled so wide it lit up the dim hallways. I wasn't worried about telling Miss Brenda about my error. I knew she would chuckle and make me feel better. Liam, my son, loved Miss Brenda, and it was easy to see why. She was one of those rare birds who sprinkle sunshine in their wake all the time. She may have had bad days, but you never knew it.

Every morning, I walked my son to his classroom and stood in the hall to watch his little face as his morning routine unfolded. Liam would stand shyly in the doorway, his chin tucked down, looking up through his thick eyelashes. The moment Miss Brenda saw him, she would smile and kneel down with her arms wide open. "There's my Liam," she would say, and he would run into her arms. His joy was my joy. Leaving my baby with someone who clearly loved him so much was manna from heaven. It allowed me a few precious hours to shower, and to feed and walk our dogs. Not enough time to get lunch food, but that's okay.

I approached Miss Brenda about the lunch/drug situation, and she smiled as I walked toward her, a twinkle in her eye.

"Miss Brenda, I need to talk to you about lunch."

"Uh-huh?" She laughed, a big, tooth-eating grin spreading across her face. She wasn't one to reprimand, but she might draw this out for the fun of it.

"Well, obviously, I haven't been making the lunches, and I probably shouldn't have put such a large responsibility in a toddler's hands. I am sorry if his bringing Pedialyte to school caused any problems or lawsuits or anything."

She just hugged me and laughed. She was a mom; she got it. Miss Brenda didn't judge you; she rolled with you. She was always on the inside of any joke because that's where the joy lives.

"Helen, I knew he made the lunches. He brings ten cookies, a fruit punch and a piece of bread every day. But you know what's funny? He loves grapefruit."

I looked at her. "You sure we are talking about the same kid? Grapefruit? It's sour."

"Nope," she said, "he loves it. Every day, I bring a grapefruit for lunch, and he eats half. It's his favorite part of the day."

I looked at her, and my heart swelled, the way it does when you discover someone is taking care of you but not saying anything. They are just silently loving you from the sidelines.

"Miss Brenda, you are giving him half of your lunch every day? I wish you had told me. It's one thing to starve my own children, but I feel awful that I have been starving you."

Miss Brenda looked at me. "I love sharing my grapefruit with him; I just wanted you to know so you could buy some for him to have at home." Just like that. Grace.

I bought grapefruits for my little boy, and I still do. Miss Brenda made my life better in so many small ways. Her smile, her wit, her *joie de vivre*. Half the time when you walked into the classroom, she was dancing with all of the kids. She loved New Orleans, and at the end of the year I gave her the fleur-de-lis belt she had seen me wear. She loved it.

Miss Brenda passed away last week. She was too young to go, and she was loved by everyone who was lucky enough to know her. We hadn't stayed in touch, and I learned about her passing on Facebook. But I was deeply saddened. She was one of the good ones. She was the light that makes the bad days more bearable.

Every time I buy a grapefruit, I think of Miss Brenda. Every time I cut a grapefruit for my kids, I say, "Remember Miss Brenda?" When I heard about her passing, I thought about how many lives she touched. I know that everybody who loved Miss Brenda has their own grapefruit story. Sometimes we strive for fame, glory, money, status or power in the hope that these things will render us immortal. But it's being someone's grapefruit that truly allows us to live forever. I realized that, more than anything, I want to be someone's grapefruit. And I will feel Miss Brenda's love for the rest of my life, every time I buy a grapefruit.

~Helen Boulos

35

Everyone Deserves a Second Chance

I always prefer to believe the best of everybody,
it saves so much trouble.
~Rudyard Kipling

I've been a substitute teacher for nearly a decade. I'm in a classroom one day and out the next. The closest I've ever come to being a "real" teacher were some long-term assignments that lasted anywhere from one month to an entire school year.

I rarely get to have an effect on the life of a student, and I don't have the benefit of finding out later, as I have already moved on. But I'm pretty sure that I made an impact the time I landed a long-term assignment at a juvenile detention center.

There were only twenty-four students in the entire school, and all of them except one seemed to be cooperating. The one holdout would come into my reading class, sit at his desk, and do nothing for ninety minutes. If he failed his classes, he would either be sent to the normal prison or have to repeat his sentence at this school, and he was already repeating once. I needed to reach this student so he wouldn't be sent to the normal prison.

One day, I asked him what he wanted to do when he got out of the program. He told me he really wanted to work on cars in a shop.

This got me thinking. My brother had been in an automotive

program when he was in high school many years before, and I recalled there were textbooks he had studied. Later that day, I went to the head of the program and told him about the student not wanting to do any work. I explained that I was worried he would repeat the program again, or worse, and that I wanted to try reaching him with an automotive textbook. I got permission to try, with the stipulation that I would have to pay for any books myself.

I ended up buying a used automotive textbook online for $18. The next day, I told the student that I had purchased this book for him to use in reading class. He asked, "How much was it?" I told him. Then his eyes almost filled with tears as he replied, "You spent $18 for me?"

In that moment, I realized it wasn't about the book. He was surprised that someone would worry about his education, about his possibly being moved to the normal prison. He didn't know that anyone cared enough about his future to spend their own money for him.

When the book came in a few days later, he devoured it. I assigned sections of it for reading comprehension, and once he answered the questions, he kept reading. He kept a dictionary nearby. When he came across a word he couldn't find in the dictionary, he would ask me.

He didn't repeat another year. I never did find out if he ended up working in a repair shop, but I'd be willing to bet that he did.

~Bradley Hall

36

The Sponge

Be thou the rainbow in the storms of life. The evening
beam that smiles the clouds away, and tints
tomorrow with prophetic ray.
~Lord Byron

I taught children for thirty years and retired last year. At one point in my career, I worked in a juvenile prison for teenage girls. Many of these young women had endured physical, sexual and emotional abuse, draining them of self-worth and robbing them of innocence. Many had turned to alcohol and drugs to soothe the pain. Others acted out in violent and inappropriate ways.

Earning their trust was not an easy chore.

One particularly difficult girl, Ashley, had to be removed from the classroom numerous times due to belligerence. When the class was asked to write autobiographies, she wrote three words and signed her name. This was while the other girls were writing long, detailed descriptions of their lives.

"My life stinks," wrote Ashley.

When we had meetings with her to discuss her progress, or lack thereof, she sat there like a statue, lifeless and silent.

One day, I found her drawing on the desk. Ordinarily, this would have resulted in a reprimand and a "consequence" for violating the rules. But to this point, no type of discipline had seemed to faze her; she had already endured numerous room restrictions, and loss of movie and commissary privileges. They did nothing to alter her behavior. More punishment would be futile.

I ignored the violation. I looked at the drawing she created and was impressed. It was a sketch of a mother swinging her young daughter in the park. It was done with great clarity and detail, and I stood there a long time studying it.

"That's very good," I said. "You're talented and should redraw this on a piece of paper." I left it at that and returned to my seat.

After the weekend, I returned to work. Ashley was absent. I was told she received a disciplinary ticket on Saturday for cursing at staff and intimidating other youth, and she wouldn't return until Thursday.

I asked Hope, a friend and classmate, for some insight into what Ashley enjoyed reading. She informed me that Ashley enjoyed reading *Harry Potter* books, and also loved the music of the sixties and stories about The Beatles. After lunch, I found *Harry Potter* books and stories about The Beatles in the library.

I returned to my office and gathered math and English texts, crossword puzzles and word searches, and a sketchpad and pencils I had purchased over the weekend.

I wasn't allowed to visit Ashley, so I wrote a note expressing my hope that she was feeling better. The security officer assured me she would receive it.

Ashley returned to the classroom Thursday morning. I asked if she had completed any assignments I had given her. She shook her head no. I reached for the sketchpad, but she grabbed it and pulled it to her.

"That's okay," I said. "It belongs to you."

I smiled, returned to the front of the room, and began teaching the lesson. Several times during the period, I felt her staring at me.

When the bell rang, the class exited — except for Ashley, who stood in front of my desk.

"Thanks for getting me stuff when I was in confinement, especially the sketchpad and pencils. They helped me get through some tough days," she said.

"You're welcome," I responded.

She turned to leave, but I stopped her.

"Wait a second, Ashley. I'm leaving on vacation, and there are some books I want to lend you."

I placed a box of books on my desk.

"What's this?" she asked.

"These are some poetry books and novels I thought you might enjoy."

I pulled one of my favorites from the box. It was a book by Shel Silverstein called *A Light in the Attic.* I held up the book for her to see.

"Sometimes, when I'm feeling low and the world seems to crowd me, I thumb through the pages and laugh," I said. "I always feel better afterwards."

I returned to work after vacation, and the only recognizable face in class was Ashley. She'd been denied parole and ordered to spend three more months at the facility.

I walked to her desk, and said, "Didn't go well at the parole board, huh?"

She looked at me and shook her head.

"Hang in there," I said. "Look for the rainbow beyond the clouds. This is your life right now, but it doesn't have to be forever." I left a peppermint twist on her desk.

I often had students work for me when class was not in session. One day, I called Ashley, and she accepted. She swept and mopped the room and graded papers. I offered her a Pepsi and homemade oatmeal cookies I had baked the previous evening.

She sat at the desk and began talking.

"I haven't been a good person. I have hurt myself, my family, and my friends," she said.

She talked for ten minutes without stopping, and then looked at me.

"They will forgive you," I said. "They love you. You're not to blame; you're a victim. And the power to change lies within you."

It was a mild summer day, and I suggested a walk around the grounds. She agreed. When I returned her to the dormitory fifteen minutes later, she broke into a wide smile and said, "Thank you."

Ashley turned her life around. She completed daily assignments, raised her grades and made the honor roll. She was pleasant and engaging, and worked diligently to become a better person. She volunteered to tutor struggling students, and earned a job working in the administration building delivering mail.

The day her parole was granted, she stopped by my classroom. She was excited about reuniting with her family and friends, and moving on with life. We talked, and she showed me drawings and poems she had created.

I looked at them and said, "I'm very proud of you."

She blushed and turned away. I handed her a tissue. After a deep hug, she departed, and I leaned back in my chair and inhaled.

I noticed a manila envelope on my desk and opened it. She had left several poems and drawings, and a photo of herself.

On the back of the picture, she'd written, "Thank you, Mr. E., for believing in me."

The human spirit is a sponge. It absorbs what it is given.

~Jerome Elmore

Puppy Therapy

There is no psychiatrist in the world
like a puppy licking your face.
~Bernard Williams

I loved teaching fourth grade and I loved acting like a kid with the students. I used humor to reach them. Our class mascot was a rubber chicken in pajamas that went everywhere with us. Our days ended out on the playground doing the chicken dance together. Learning was accomplished through participation and teamwork, emphasizing much-needed social skills along the way. The kids loved our unique classroom style, and it worked — they were motivated and enthusiastic.

Then, one year, I was assigned a particularly unreachable student. Jeremy had been born with fetal alcohol syndrome, which probably accounted for his severe learning disabilities. He was impulsive and had no attention span. He also had few social skills and always seemed ready for a fight.

Jeremy didn't smile and he clearly didn't want to be in the classroom. Getting him to lighten up became my goal that year. Oh, sure, I wanted him to read, write and know his math facts. But more than that, I wanted him to experience happiness and excitement about learning.

I modified all his fourth grade work to make it easier for him. I let him take many of the tests orally. He needed encouragement or he would stop trying. I needed to boost his self-confidence.

I tried so many of my usual methods but I wasn't reaching him.

So I set up a conference with his mother. When I told Jeremy, he just shrugged. Then, without making eye contact, he said, "My mom won't come. She never comes to conferences."

"Yes, she will," I said, more confidently than I felt.

"No, she won't," said Jeremy. "Wait and see."

Now this woman *had* to come, if only to show Jeremy that people could change. I added a little note to my conference request. "If you are unable to come, I will be glad to drive over to your house to meet with you there. Just let me know what day and time is good for you."

Lo and behold, I got my conference! In the first five minutes, I understood a lot about Jeremy. His mother turned her back on him while we were talking. She never once looked at him. She did not speak any words of encouragement. She expected the worst.

At other conferences, teachers had told her everything that was wrong with Jeremy. Instead, I told her about the effort he was making and that he was trying. His mother had never had a good conference before. She did not believe in her son.

I realized that Jeremy was on his own as far as his education. He had no homework help. No one checked his planner. So Jeremy's homework became morning work. Each morning, he rode his bike to school early and worked in my class before school.

Yes, he still got in trouble in the cafeteria and in the halls. But while he was in my class, he knew the rules and followed them.

I continued to work with Jeremy on his academics. He had a long road ahead of him and always would. But I had more pressing matters: I still needed to make him smile.

How I tried! I walked beside him in line and told him funny stories, acted pretty silly for a teacher, and even put him in charge of R.C., our rubber chicken. No smile. A permanent scowl wrinkled his brow.

My husband heard about Jeremy every night. We discussed how to get him to lighten up. He needed so much more than I could provide. And I only had until June.

After the winter holiday break, my husband brought our brand-new miniature Dachshund puppy, Maggie, to school to show my students. I talked about her all the time, and the kids were looking forward to meeting her. At the end of the day, George, my husband, was waiting outside our classroom door with Maggie in his arms. The kids could pet her, but not hold her, just in case she wiggled her way out of their arms.

George and Maggie were immediately engulfed in a sea of fourth grade students all wanting to pet her. Maggie was a kisser, so each child was repaid with very wet doggy love. Jeremy stood near the back of the group watching. I took a chance.

I offered to let him hold my beloved puppy. He agreed. I had him sit down, and we placed Maggie in his lap. Of course, within three seconds, she was all over his face and licking it from forehead to chin with her own brand of puppy love.

Jeremy exploded with giggles. The whole class stood and watched, knowing that something out of the ordinary had just happened. Jeremy lay back on the ground and allowed her to lick him all over his face until we took pity on him and pulled her off. No one else asked to hold her; everyone knew it was Jeremy's time. My husband and I were both in tears watching Jeremy get his puppy-love therapy.

Jeremy would be about thirty years old now. I hope he remembers that day as vividly as I do. I don't recall his reading score or his math progress from that year, but I remember the sound of his laughter. I still see the crooked little grin that appeared more frequently with each passing day after Maggie the puppy's visit.

I don't know if I affected Jeremy, but he most definitely affected me. The memories I have of Jeremy embody what teaching is truly about. Teaching is not about test scores and mastery of tons of information. Teaching is all about heart.

~Jeanne Kraus

38

I Believe in You

*To be a champ you have to believe in
yourself when no one else will.*
~Sugar Ray Robinson

Our class was preparing for the sixth grade Olympics, a campus-wide event at our large middle school, with close to twenty classes participating. Leading up to the Olympics, the students needed to choose their track and field events.

I could have just posted a sign-up sheet and saved myself time and effort, but instead I took the time to sit down with the students individually and ask which events they would like to try. Most students were beaming with excitement and told me right away.

But this was not the case with Eric, a child with special needs who was mainstreamed into our class and often bullied around campus. When I met with Eric, he looked down and mumbled that the only thing he could do was throw a Frisbee a little. "The Frisbee it is," I told him with a smile, trying to meet his eyes. "I believe in you, Eric — I know you can do it!"

On the first day of the event, my students were scattered all over the ball fields as they participated in their individual events. I quickly sought out Eric and stood alongside him for support as he waited for his turn. Eric stepped up, took a deep breath, and threw the Frisbee just far enough to tie for eighth place and earn a half point for our team. I gathered a few students, and we celebrated his success together.

At the end of the second day of events, the physical education teachers totaled up all the points and assembled the classes for the awards ceremony. Coach Kenny, the P.E. teacher who led the event, shook his head with a smile, and said to all the sixth graders and teachers: "In the history of our school, we've never had an Olympics that has ended this close." Then he announced that our class had won... by an astonishing half a point!

The class went absolutely bananas as we ran to the stage in celebration. I truly felt like I had witnessed a miracle.

When we got back to our classroom, I told my students that I would like to reveal the MVP of our class's team, without whose efforts we would not have won the entire event. Everyone's heads turned toward our pentathlete, Parker, who had finished first in his events and earned many points for our team.

Instead, I called Eric to the front of the classroom. I explained that without Eric's perseverance and his half point, we would not have earned first place. The entire class gave Eric a standing ovation—clearly the first in his life.

A few days later, Eric's mom pulled me aside and said, "I don't know what you said to my son, but for the past two weeks he has practiced every day throwing a Frisbee against the fence in the back yard." She thanked me for giving him something to strive for.

I have based the core of my teaching philosophy on these four words: "I believe in you." When children know their teacher believes in them, they are free to take chances, to open up to learning, and to begin to believe in themselves. I only have to think of Eric to know how important this is.

~Martin Reisert

39

Beyond the Classroom

We were born to unite with our fellow men, and to
join in community with the human race.
~Cicero

Mark was a great kid from a bad neighborhood. A scholarship fund provided his tuition to Catholic High, where he contributed — and not in a small way — to the sports program. On the football field he showed considerable talent, running the ball past the opposition and even jumping a mound of fellow players to make the touchdown. But it was a mound of a different sort that showcased Mark's greatest talent — he was a pitcher. In his junior year, scouts from pro teams lined the bleachers right alongside the college coaches. His 85–95 mile-an-hour pitches and excellent strikeout stats made him a much sought-after recruit.

But Mark struggled in the classroom. He was plenty bright, just behind, perhaps due to a difficult home environment. Mark's mom died from a drug overdose while he was in high school. I remember the funeral and watching Mark cry as he hung his head over the casket. He moved in with an elderly grandmother.

The area where Mark's grandmother lived was dangerous, and he was soon the victim of a drive-by shooting. The school community jumped to his aid, working behind the scenes almost immediately. While the ambulance sped away, a student's dad who was a surgeon accepted Mark as his patient. He met the ambulance at the hospital and whisked Mark away to surgery, removing the bullet and making arrangements for physical therapy. Another family — whose son Kevin also attended Catholic High and played sports — fixed up a bedroom for Mark. Kevin and Mark became best friends, and Kevin's dad took a personal interest in Mark, even attending his parent/teacher conferences.

I met Mark in my resource room. At first, his teachers sent practice sets and homework for me to help him complete. When I had a better idea of his needs, I began remedial tutoring so that we could address the gaps in his education. Despite the attention from pro scouts, Mark wanted to attend college. The interest from several universities was high, but Mark's scores on his college entrance exams were low. He needed to improve his ACT score.

Several teachers discussed Mark's needs. We agreed that he required help far beyond what we could offer him within the time constraints of our class periods. After-school tutoring wasn't possible because of football and baseball practice. Some felt Mark should give up sports and concentrate on schooling. But his opportunity to attend college was linked to sports, so to miss practice would have been counterproductive. One of my fellow teachers, Mrs. Banks, offered to tutor Mark in math at her home. I scheduled Mark to come to my house for all the other areas of the ACT. No one paid us. Mrs. Banks summed it up this way: "Payday doesn't always come on Monday."

When we were not working with Mark to improve his skills for the ACT, the coach and Kevin's dad took him to various colleges to talk with both baseball and football program coaches. He settled on the college that offered him scholarships to play both sports. As you might expect, we were all elated, but a little concerned. If Mark did not score the minimum required by that university, he could not attend, no matter how talented he was. The day came for Mark to take the ACT. I picked him up and took him for breakfast, and then delivered Mark to the testing center along with pencils, candy bars, and apples supplied by his other teachers.

It takes weeks to receive the results. But then, one afternoon after school, I heard quite a commotion in the hallway. Mark burst through my door, lifted me out of my chair, spun me around, and jubilantly shouted, "I'm going to college! I'm going to college! I'm going to college!"

"I guess you got your score?" I asked, once he set me down.

"Well, YEAH!" he laughed. "And guess what? It is one point more than I need to be accepted. One point extra! Thank you, thank you, thank you! Now, where's Mrs. Banks? I've got to tell her, too!" And he was off and running again.

Until that moment, I had never quite understood the meaning of "Payday doesn't always come on Monday." But the meaning became clear the instant Mark ran into the room to announce his news. No amount of money could ever replace my spin in the air at the hands of a boy who finally had a chance at a better life.

~Eloise Elaine Ernst Schneider

Today, I Was

There is nothing impossible to him who will try.
~Alexander the Great

Today, I was an ad designer, creating posters for our upcoming event.

Today, I was a nurse, cleaning and bandaging a small wound.

Today, I was an actress, playing a role no one has ever played before.

Today, I was the plumber, for "the toilet wouldn't flush."

Today, I was a writer, being creative with the hope that others would be creative, too.

Today, I was a computer operator, showing others how things run.

Today, I was an environmentalist, setting up recycling stations and enforcing the rules.

Today, I was a storyteller, giving life to the characters in a book.

Today, I was the pitcher, for I was the biggest in the kickball game.

Today, I was a singer, leading the group in song.

Today, I was a friend, giving a hug or a smile when someone needed it.

Today, I was a choreographer, trying to get them all to move along.

Today, I was a forest ranger, leading a group through the woods.

Today, I was an interior decorator, creating magic with paper and little more.

Today, I was a secretary, answering calls and typing away.

Today, I was a detective, gathering all the "facts" and figuring out which ones were true.

Today, I was a repairman, because "it just broke in my hand."

Today, I was a clown, doing ridiculous things to capture my audience's attention.

Today, I was an artist, drawing pictures on the wall.

Today, I was a transportation coordinator, ensuring everyone got where they belonged.

Today, I was a supervisor, delegating jobs to those who were here to help.

Today, I was a reporter, writing notes on the day's events.

Today, I did ALL these things and more, because...

Today, I was a TEACHER.

~Pamela Berardino

Yes, the Little Things Count

A complete stranger has the capacity to alter the life of another irrevocably. This domino effect has the capacity to change the course of an entire world.
~J.D. Stroube

I had been teaching at the Southfield Christian School in suburban Detroit for three years when I had a particularly talented class assigned to me. The students included a little girl named Mary Kay who spent only one year at our school, the year that I had her in my third grade class.

Her father was Billy Kim, a famous evangelist, the South Korean version of Billy Graham. He had brought his family to the United States for a year of speaking, fundraising and ministry.

Mary Kay spoke beautiful English, and had a radiant smile and gracious demeanor. She had tremendous respect for authority and learning.

One day, the class was being irritating the way that eight-year-olds can be. That day, I was wishing I had twenty more students just like Mary Kay.

I had gotten the students quiet and together for their next segment of study. As we turned toward Social Studies, I asked Mary Kay to read a section of our book out loud. I was surprised when, despite the beautiful, flowing English she spoke, she read haltingly, stumbling over certain words and mispronouncing others completely. I hadn't meant to put her in that position. Her spoken English was so wonderful that I didn't realize her ability to read it was not equally good.

Immediately, the kids in the class began to laugh at her. One, who I'll call Johnny, said, "What a dummy. She can't even read from a third grade book." Well, that was not okay. My heart went out to that little girl.

I said to Mary Kay, "Why don't you go and write some words in Korean on the board for everyone?" I also had Johnny, her critic, come to the board to experience Mary Kay's language himself and perhaps learn a lesson.

Mary Kay's eyes suddenly brightened, her tears drying as she walked with a smile to the board, brimming with newfound confidence and security.

The other children watched as she wrote word after word along with her name in the very distinctive symbols of the Korean alphabet. The teasers quit teasing and watched with a bit of awe, not pity. Then one of the students said, "Write my name, Mary Kay." And she did. Then another. And another… and another… and another. Soon, the whole class had their names on the board, and Mary Kay was a hero, not the little foreign girl who couldn't read. Mary Kay could do something the others could not. She went from feeling inadequate to feeling special.

That happened back in the 1970s, back when I was a new teacher. Fast-forward to several years ago, when I was visiting my sister in suburban Detroit, not far from the school where I taught Mary Kay. Coincidentally, her father was going to be speaking one evening at the church connected to that same school.

I was planning to have dinner with a friend in the area, so I asked her if she would join me for this special meeting with Reverend Kim, and she agreed to go. After he spoke, I joined the press of people trying to talk to him. I wanted to let him know that his daughter's third grade teacher was still alive and well!

Of course, Reverend Kim had many people to see and was accompanied by some of his associates and assistants to help him manage the crowd and attention. However, I was soon able to get close enough to touch his arm and say, "Reverend Kim, I just wanted to take a moment and re-introduce myself. I'm Jackie Sinclair, formerly Miss Sanders, and I was Mary Kay's third grade teacher when your family was living in the area."

All of a sudden, his eyes got big, and he said to me, "My daughter has been looking for you for forty years!" He pulled out his phone and said to me, "Just a minute. I need to call her." He quickly dialed the number, but she didn't answer so he left a message.

He looked at me kindly and commented, "Miss Sanders, she *will* call you! She so wants to speak with you."

I left the auditorium and returned to my sister's home. Not long afterward, the phone rang. It was Mary Kay Park, now a grown woman and a professor at Biola University in Southern California. What a wonderful treat to be speaking with little Mary Kay, all grown up.

She told me about a YouTube video she had made describing how her life as a little Korean girl had been changed because of her time in my class. The video had been commissioned by the Asian/American Pacific Islander Initiative 2011, a White House story project, and thousands had seen it. The majority of her story was about that day in my class! Mary Kay had gone on to Harvard, earned a Ph.D., taught at the university, and continued to impact lives for decades to follow. She became an advocate for others who might face what she faced. And she wanted me to know.

Scores of influential people, myriad experiences and lots of hard work contributed to Mary Kay's success. But I was reminded of this: One action matters. It's like a domino that starts a chain reaction. The rest of the pieces will fall as long as someone knocks over the first one. And teachers are so often those who start those reactions. I'm glad I had that moment and actually heard about the outcome. Knock a domino over, and you just might get your moment, too.

~Jackie Sanders Sinclair

The Power of the Basics

The beginning is the most important part of the work.
~Plato

His name was Eduardo. He was a student in my eighth grade math class. Other kids teased him constantly, mocking his inability to do simple things like add and subtract or tie his shoes. For as long as he or his mother could remember, he always failed every subject.

One day in class, I heard a student tell Eduardo, "You are so dumb, you don't even know how to tell time!" Laughter bounced off the concrete walls.

As Eduardo shrank in his seat, I walked over to him and quietly asked if that was true. He shrugged. It was a heartbreaking, defeated kind of shrug, loaded with meaning. I then asked him the most simple, yet profound, question a teacher can ask: "Why?"

"I don't know," he said, with another shrug as he sank lower behind his desk.

I pressed him for an answer.

Finally, he exclaimed, "Nobody ever taught me!"

"What about your parents?" I asked.

"Nope." Shrug.

I turned and got the class started on an assignment. Then, I took the clock off the wall, sat down next to Eduardo, and quietly explained how it worked. Within ten minutes, Eduardo knew how to tell time.

Nobody had ever taken the ten minutes to show him how a clock worked. Many had simply dismissed him as "unable to learn." He *could* learn. After that day, his confidence began to increase. He even became interested in learning, because he knew he *could*. He began doing some of his homework and started performing better on tests.

Throughout my teaching career, I've taught math to kids of all kinds. I've taught the quadratic formula to highly advanced sixth graders, and I've taught high school students who were struggling to pass the high school exit exam.

And throughout it all, I've come to know that the most successful students have one thing in common: they've mastered the basics.

Sometimes, we place so much emphasis on collaboration that we overlook teaching students to look someone in the eye while shaking their hand. Sometimes, we place so much emphasis on critical thinking that we forget to make sure students can actually read. I often think of legendary basketball coach John Wooden who, upon meeting his newest class of college recruits each year, would first spend considerable time teaching them how to properly lace up their sneakers. Improperly laced sneakers lead to blisters, and blisters can lead to a missed shot when the game is on the line. The basics.

For years, I watched kids struggle in my Algebra class, having never mastered the basics. In Algebra, the missed basic usually means the times tables. The past several years, I've traveled the country speaking, writing and coaching educators, and I always ask the teachers their biggest challenge in teaching math. "So many students don't know their times tables," they've told me.

I've thought about this a lot. Beneath all the complexities of education and learning, curriculum and policy lies one thing — the importance of the basics. Just as reading is the basic, critical foundation to succeed in writing and language arts, knowing the times tables is the basic, critical foundation to succeeding in math beyond elementary school. I tossed and turned at night for many months thinking about how amazing it would be if all kids could learn their times tables. If I could help them do this, in an engaging way. It became my new mission, and one I embarked on with a passion.

I created an interactive, online program to help *every* kid master his or her times tables, without the stress. I combined my own teaching (on video), my own music (times-table raps, to be exact), cutting-edge technology, and a few bad jokes, to create a program that is actually accomplishing this simple, yet profound, mission. Now, kids all over the world are using the program to master this basic skill, so they can grow more confident in math, and in life.

And to think it all started with an eighth grader named Eduardo, a shoulder shrug, and a clock.

~Alex Kajitani

Chapter
5

Inspiration for Teachers

That First Year

*The true aim of every one who aspires to be a
teacher should be, not to impart his own
opinions, but to kindle minds.*
~F.W. Robertson

The Colors of Us

Everyone is kneaded out of the same dough
but not baked in the same oven.
~Yiddish Proverb

Nevaeh angrily proclaimed. "I'm not black! I'm white!" She was one of the many beautiful mixed-race children in my preschool class. It was October, and I was only a couple of months in as a first-year teacher. Fresh out of college, I was both excited and terrified by what this year had in store for me. We had already established our daily routine, and I was picking up on what made each of my students tick. This proclamation, however, was a curveball. It needed to be addressed, but how?

"I'm white, and Maya's black!" she said again, referring to her lighter-skinned younger sister.

"Better than being orange like Dylan!" chimed in another boy.

Something needed to be done.

Fortunately, one of my last college classes was children's literature, and I had read a wonderful book entitled *The Colors of Us* by Karen Katz. In it, a little girl wants to paint a picture of herself with brown paint, but it's not quite right. As she walks through her neighborhood, she sees her friends and family and realizes that each is brown, but a different shade of brown, like honey, cinnamon, dark chocolate, or the sandy beach.

I had the book and pitched an idea to my director. Race and skin tone had become a negative topic in the classroom. I wanted to read the book with the class and see how they identified with each of the delicious (positive) descriptions. Then I wanted the children to mix paint to create their own skin tones. We would use the paint to stamp their handprints on a large banner with the words, "The Colors of Us." The purpose was to tear down the black/white fence and help them to see that we are all different shades of brown, created from the same base. It's not one or the other, but a spectrum. She agreed, but we needed to let the parents know what was happening. We included it in our weekly newsletter and invited parents with any reservations or concerns to address them with us. The letters were sent home, and my co-teacher and I began preparing, both the materials and ourselves.

The following Monday was the big day. We began with our "Good Morning" song and Circle Time activities. At last, it was time.

"Okay, class. We have a very special book to read today. Someone wrote a book about *us*!" I said. "It's about a group of friends, just like all of you, and they had to paint themselves. What colors do you think they used?" Most of the answers were the expected black, white, and brown, but a few were different.

"Umm, I don't really know what color I would use 'cuz I'm kinda both." And another, "Yeah, I don't think they make this color." It was the perfect segue. "That's a very interesting observation, Michael, because the friends in this story had that challenge, too. Let's see how they solved it."

So, we read. The pages were filled with colorful pictures of the little girl describing her friends and family using tasty descriptions like "cinnamon sticks" and "hazelnut." With each description came a comment from the kids. "Hey, that's like me! I'm like cocoa!" Or, "That's like my momma. She's like peanut butter and Daddy's like milk chocolate!" It was beautiful. The children were excited to identify with the characters and to have a positive association with all the different shades. Now came the tricky part. "How would you guys like to make handprints with your own skin color?"

There were lots of excited "Yeahs!"

We set black, white, and brown paints on the tables. When I asked Nevaeh what color she needed, she looked at the white paint and then down at her arm. "I'm not white, am I, Miss Deborah?"

I held my very Caucasian arm next to the white paint. "Hmm… I must not be white either."

She giggled and said, "Of course, you are! You even have white hair. Well, kinda yellow. But that paint is not your color."

Then I brought out some of the various flesh-toned paints, and none of them were a perfect match either. I asked, "What do you think we can do to make your color?" We had mixed colors before. Blue and yellow. Red and blue. The week before, we had used white and black to make colors like pink, lavender, and maroon. The stage had been set, and Nevaeh performed right on cue.

"This color," she said, "is kinda close, but not dark enough."

"What can you do to make it darker?" She dipped her brush into the black paint, swirling it with the tan paint to create a beautiful mocha. Smiling, she swiped some on the back of her hand and held it high in the air.

"I did it!" Nevaeh proclaimed, "I found me!" And indeed she had.

~Deborah Elaine

Ask First

All truths are easy to understand once they are
discovered; the point is to discover them.
~Galileo Galilei

fter twenty years in advertising, which thrives on relationship building and persuasion, I went back to school,
earned a master's degree in education, and became a
teacher — a profession that also thrives on relationship
building and persuasion. I somehow ended up teaching high school
English even though my original mission was to embrace the awkward weirdness of middle school. My first semester as an educator
quickly turned into another semester as the kids taught me about
high school and life, and what was important to them. It had been
twenty-five years since I graduated from high school, so I had a lot to
learn. I listened. I took notes. I asked a lot of questions.

My students endured more hardship than I had been familiar with
at their ages. Many came from fatherless homes; some had parents
in prison; most qualified for free lunches and their families survived
on government assistance; and some of them were already parents
themselves. Comprehending their circumstances proved impossible,
but loving them came easily.

When my second semester began, my classroom welcomed a host
of new students, including one young man who lit up the space every
time he passed through the door. David stood tall at six feet, four inches,
and from the back his broad shoulders and muscular build gave him

the appearance of a grown man. His wide smile and sparkling eyes charmed every person in the room. He was smart, too. David knew the answers to seemingly everything. For weeks, he controlled the atmosphere of my class. He led group discussions, encouraged others to participate, and earned the highest grades.

I was so impressed by him and his abilities that I didn't ask a lot of questions. I didn't really take time to get to know him as I had with my first-semester crew.

A few weeks passed, and we entered the month of February. David strode quietly into class, sat firmly in his seat, and refused to remove his headphones. David's engaging smile disappeared. He looked sullen and sad. I asked if he was okay, but he didn't respond. I encouraged him to participate, but he angrily refused. I reminded him of the class rules, and he threw a tantrum as big as his size 14 Jordans. So I sent David to a buddy room. Three days in a row…

Finally, I called another student down to my room. He was a young man with whom I had developed a strong relationship. I had noticed him walking in the hallways with David on a regular basis.

"What in the world has happened to David?" I asked.

"Oh, ma'am, this week is his mom's birthday, and she just died three months ago."

I was shocked. I excused the student, and I cried. I had failed David during a very difficult time.

The next day, I let David keep his headphones on. As soon as the bell rang and the other students scattered, I stopped him at my desk.

"I'm sorry," I said, placing my hand on his left shoulder. "I should have asked questions. I should have found out what was going on, and I shouldn't have had to ask your friend to figure it out. What do you need from me? What can I do to help you through the next couple of weeks?"

David shrugged. I suggested that we come up with a plan that would allow him to keep up with his work, and he agreed. David also agreed to let me know when he was having a rough day so I could put our plan into motion.

"Are you sure there is nothing I can do for you?" I pleaded.

"I don't know what I need," he cried. "I just miss my mom."

"Can I give you a hug?"

David leaned down and hugged me for a very long time. We both cried.

The next year, David was a senior. I moved to another building in the high school to teach freshmen, but David made his way to my classroom at least once a week to get his hug. That May, when David graduated, I stood at the end of the stage so I could be there to hug him after he received his diploma.

Sometimes teachers are the students. There is so much our kids have to share with us if we are willing to listen. I learned a valuable lesson about not coming to conclusions without first getting to know my students, even the ones who start halfway through the year.

~Michele L. Rausch

45

Chicken Soup for the Soul

The Awakening

*When you're teaching a hard concept and the students
all have puzzled looks on their faces and then suddenly
you can see that "aha" moment, that they got it,
that's just an incredible thing.*
~Anant Agarwal

I was a new teacher filled with enthusiasm and energy. I had known, from the time I was ten years old, that I wanted to be a teacher, and now here I was with my own classroom... my own students. I was teaching second grade. It was a dream come true. It was *my* dream come true... except for the math part of the equation. Math is not my strongest subject, although I can get along most of the time as long as I'm not asked to solve one of those word problems. You know the ones I'm talking about. The ones where the train leaves the station on Tuesday at 9:00 a.m. going ninety miles an hour... Thank goodness I was teaching second grade; I could do that math. Easily. Yes, I could *do* the math, but could I *teach* the math?

My biggest math challenge was Annabelle. She had long brown hair and blue eyes — the most expressive eyes ever. All of her emotions and feelings — happy and sad, scared and delighted — were expressed through her eyes. And her smile. She was that one student whom every teacher wishes to have in her classroom. She was good and never caused any problems; she was helpful and always wanted to go that extra mile; she was smart, a fabulous reader who was reading way above grade level; but she struggled with math. Maybe that's why I felt such a connection to her. I tried not to show it, but she was the teacher's pet. My pet.

The math unit we were working on was subtraction. We had already covered single-digit subtraction, and everyone, including Annabelle, seemed to grasp the concept pretty well. But now we were at the point in the unit when we were moving on to a more complex subtraction concept: borrowing or regrouping. The taking away of something from the whole. I explained the concept of place values — the ones column, the tens column, and the hundreds column. I explained that you couldn't take a bigger number away from a smaller number unless you borrowed or regrouped the number. I made charts to show that the number 13 is made up of one ten and three ones. If you want to take 5 away from 13, you have to regroup the one ten into ten ones and move it to the ones column. Then you can take five ones away from thirteen ones. Confusing at best!

Most of the students got the concept. Most... but not Annabelle. She had the blankest, most confused expression on her face. I tried every which way to explain the concept to her. No progress. I brought in ice cream sticks and rubber bands and had her count the sticks into groups of ten and rubber-band them. I showed her that the number 13 was really one group of ten sticks with a rubber band and three loose sticks. And how she couldn't take five sticks away from three, but if she borrowed ten sticks from the tens column and added them to the three ones in the ones column, she could.

I used beans. I used little sparkly stones. I used pretzels. I used marbles and rings to demonstrate to her what the concept of borrowing was all about. Well, call it borrowing, call it regrouping, call it anything you want, she just couldn't get the concept. I was frustrated. Annabelle was beyond frustrated. She was really trying, but she just couldn't grasp it.

Until... one afternoon. She and I were working after school on regrouping. I tried once more to show her the sparkly stones and how the columns of ones and tens worked. Nothing. I tried again. Still nothing. I switched to the ice cream sticks and the rubber bands and tried… again. And then she got very quiet. She stopped squirming. She took a deep breath. She sat very still and looked up at me with her big blue eyes.

And in that instant I knew that she understood. She got it! A light went on. No words were needed. It showed in her eyes. It showed on her face. For the first time in a long time, she smiled. She understood. And I, as her teacher, had that amazing WOW moment! That moment when I knew that all of the time and the effort I had put into explaining a concept had just paid off. All of the gadgets and ice-cream sticks and rubber bands had finally gotten through. The concept was hers! She now explained it to me correctly. We clapped. We yelled and cheered. We hugged. We ate the pretzels!

But did she really understand? I needed to know that this was not a fluke. I challenged her using different numbers, and she got them all! Every one. She understood. It was like in *My Fair Lady* when Professor Henry Higgins is trying to teach Eliza Doolittle to speak with a proper English accent. After trying and trying, she finally got it. Annabelle finally got the math concept of borrowing that had eluded her for so long.

I had Annabelle in my classroom years ago, but I have never forgotten her. Nor will I ever forget her. She made my efforts as a teacher so very rewarding. Her "getting it" was the first ever WOW moment I had in my career. I have had others over the years, but that exact moment when the breakthrough occurred, when her eyes lit up, she smiled and she understood, will always be the one I remember most. The one I cherish. As a teacher, I made a difference to one little girl. As teachers, we have the privilege of guiding and enlightening students. And as teachers, we have the pleasure of being rewarded when those students "get it." WOW!

~Barbara LoMonaco

46

A Change in Strategy

Compliments are like verbal sunshine.
~Steve Curtin

On the first day of school, Belinda stuck a pencil in Rory's eye and called him a very bad word. That earned her a place in "time-out."

"Time-out is like jail, Mistuh Buhsell," she said, and she would know, as she had spent the majority of her time there that day. "You should call this jail."

Belinda was right. From that time forward, when students misbehaved and ignored their first two warnings, they went to an isolated desk known as "jail."

My first year of teaching was probably not too different from anyone else's. I drew praise for my enthusiasm and hard work while secretly realizing I hadn't a clue what I was doing. Belinda knew.

"Mistuh Buhsell, you too young to be a teacher," she said on day two.

Belinda, like many of my students, had grown up "street smart," with very little use for schools and books. She was easily the smallest person in my class, and many teachers had fallen into the trap of believing she was "too small and precious" to hurt anyone. They might as well have thought the same about a bumblebee.

"Jail" was not working, so I kept Belinda in at recess. I made her wash all the desks and pick up all the garbage lying around. *That'll teach her,* I thought. Belinda, though, was smarter than me.

"I like cleanin', Mistuh Buhsell," she said. "Can I do this every day?"

On the third day, I caught Belinda fighting with José. I walked over to their table and asked what the problem was.

"She keeps calling me a bad word," José said. Being the smart, idealistic new teacher, I asked José to whisper the bad word into my ear.

"She said I'm 'stupid.'"

I was relieved to hear that at least Belinda had toned down her language. *Baby steps toward improvement,* I told myself. Belinda wrote standards after school while I gave her another lecture on behavior.

"Belinda, tomorrow is a new day," I said. "Keep your head up and try your hardest and you're bound to improve."

The next day, I caught her fighting with José again. Exasperated, I shouted across the room to ask why they were fighting. Again, José accused Belinda of calling him a bad word.

"Stop calling José 'stupid,'" I bellowed.

"I didn't call him stupid, Mistuh Buhsell," she yelled back. "I called him a (bleep)!"

That was it. Belinda had finally earned a call home. But Belinda informed me that her mama didn't have a phone. She even smiled when she said it. Determined to win this battle, I told Belinda that I would walk her home after school and talk to her mother in person.

And for the first time all week, Belinda became silent.

The rest of the day, she sat still in her chair. Eerily still. At any moment, I anticipated she'd smack somebody or throw something across the room, but she just slouched in a trance, even with kids teasing her.

"It's not going to work, young lady," I told her. "You already earned a walk home, and behaving now isn't going to change that."

For the first time since I set eyes on her, Belinda was just a cute little girl sitting subdued in her seat. I sympathized, but "experts" advised that to survive as a teacher I had to stand firmly by my decisions.

When the final bell sounded, Belinda dashed for the door, but I reminded her of our appointment. Her shoulders slumped in defeat. I took her by the hand, and we began the two-block walk to her house. Along the way, I nervously pondered what to say to her mother. Here it was only four days into the school year, and I had lost control of a three-and-a-half-foot-tall seven-year-old.

Belinda took me through the gate to her yard, heavily littered with debris. I heard a big dog barking inside the house. Belinda went inside to get her mother while I waited on the porch like a struggling insurance salesman.

"Where you been, girl?" a nasty voice screamed. Babies cried loudly inside.

"My teachuh's here," Belinda said softly, and I still couldn't see inside through the heavily barred front door.

"Hello," a deep voice barked. I could barely make out the outline of a shadow behind the door.

"Uh, I'm Mr. Brassell, Belinda's teacher."

"What'd she do this time?"

I suddenly decided to try a different approach. "Well, I didn't come to tell you what Belinda is doing wrong. I came to tell you what she is doing right."

There was no response, so I continued.

"Belinda really likes to participate in class," I said, searching for whatever true, positive comments I could find.

Still no response.

"Belinda is also always at school on time, and I wanted to thank you for that," I said. "I really appreciate your support."

The door opened, and a rather skinny, short woman smiled. She was in her thirties, but looked much older, with scars all over her arms and face. I finally caught a glimpse inside the cramped little house: there were empty 40-ounce malt liquor bottles, crumpled newspapers, and fresh "doggie deposits."

"I'm Ms. Johnson," she said, offering me her hand to shake. She practically blushed as she fidgeted with the curlers in her hair.

I smiled and described every positive thing that Belinda had done over the past week, from sitting quietly as she did her independent work to cleaning the room. I failed to mention that Belinda only sat quietly when I put her alone in "jail" or that she cleaned the room during recess as a punishment for bad behavior. It seemed that Ms. Johnson had heard those stories about her daughter too many times in the past.

"Well," I concluded, "it was really nice to meet you, Ms. Johnson, and I hope you feel free to visit our classroom anytime."

Now it was Ms. Johnson who was standing uncomfortably in the doorway.

"My Belinda's helpin' other students in her class," I overheard Ms. Johnson yell to neighbors as I departed. "Her teacher says she's really improving."

The next day at school, Belinda gave my knees a big hug.

"My mama bought me a new backpack," she said with a smile bigger than her tiny face could hold. "And she said she'd get me a new dolly if I get good grades in your class."

"Are you going to try harder to get along with other people in here?" I asked.

"Yes, sir," Belinda said. "You the best teacher."

That made me smile. I had completed my first week of teaching, and despite all of the questions I had in my head, one positive comment from a little seven-year-old made all the difference in the world to me.

~Danny Brassell

47

The Twenty-Minute Lesson

To share your weakness is to make yourself vulnerable;
to make yourself vulnerable is to show your strength.
~Criss Jami

I woke with a racing heart and fluttering stomach. Today would be my first parent-teacher conference. Like everything else that first year of teaching, I expected I'd learn a lot. What I didn't expect was that a twenty-minute conference would change me forever.

Akif was a happy, good-natured boy. His thick, black glasses only magnified his smiling eyes. He was a bit immature — as middle-school boys often are — but he was kind to his classmates and he didn't misbehave. His homework, however, was chronically late. He struggled to keep pace with the class, even when he assured me he understood the assignments. I gave him effort grades when I could, but the problem was getting worse. By November, despite messages left on the home answering machine, it was time to meet the parents.

At my middle school, we collaborate for conferences. Akif's work was incomplete in most subjects, so other teachers joined the meeting. I was grateful I wouldn't be alone. My colleagues could show me how they resolved issues with parents. I needed to learn, and I really wanted Akif to succeed.

Akif's father entered the classroom uncertainly. His blue acrylic sweater, oversized and misshapen, hung on his thin frame. The old Mobil gas station logo — with the flying red horse — covered his left chest. I realized he carried no coat on this cold November morning. Yet despite his disheveled clothes, his graying beard was neatly groomed and his hair was covered with a white crocheted cloth. Its intricate weave looked handmade. He walked in nervously, quickly sitting in one of the empty desks we'd circled for the conference.

We welcomed him and began introductions when his thin hand went into the air to stop us. In a shaky voice, he asked to speak first. I was surprised, but could sense his anguish.

He poured out his story. Akif was his youngest child. They'd moved from India, and he worked two full-time jobs to support his family. As he spoke, I noticed he wouldn't make eye contact with us. Then he shook his head ruefully and explained his wife and children also worked. Everyone pitched in however they could. In India, he said, he devoted time to his children. But here, with all of the demands, he hardly saw them. He couldn't guide and help them anymore. The more he spoke, the more I understood what he was trying to say: He blamed himself for Akif's struggles.

"All of God's creations need attention," he stated. "Whether it is a tree or a deer or a child, they all need the same thing. Nurturing. I have not been able to give Akif what I gave my older children. I can't give him the attention he deserves. I keep telling him he must ask his teachers for help with his schoolwork. Surely, they will understand. That is their job."

Then he stopped. His head hung as he covered his face with his hands. He began to weep.

No one in the room moved. I felt suspended in time. I was overcome by his humility and desperation. I knew in that moment, I was in the presence of something far greater than myself. He embodied selfless, unconditional love. His burden overwhelmed him, and he begged for mercy and help from complete strangers.

"I would be forever grateful if you could give Akif help," he said as tears rolled down his cheeks.

We sat in shocked silence. I forgot all about being a first-year teacher. I prayed for the right words and spoke from my heart, reassuring Akif's father that we would help his son succeed however we could. For the first time, the man looked directly at me, and I saw his face relax with relief. Then he bowed his head and thanked me deeply.

I know we created an action plan for Akif. I remember lunch periods and before-school sessions. As a teaching team, I am sure we focused on study skills and homework strategies. But I honestly don't remember details. Akif moved on to high school, and I lost track of him. Yet that parent-teacher meeting changed me in powerful ways — as a teacher, but also as a person and eventually a parent.

Those twenty minutes taught me about selflessness, honesty, and love. I witnessed the powerful sacrifice of a parent, and the burden created when our best isn't enough. I learned people can surprise me, and not to assume things before I hear someone's story. And I was taught the beauty of vulnerability and the importance of asking for help.

It was one of the important lessons of my life... all in twenty minutes.

~Katie O'Connell

48

The Girl Who Didn't Get It

*With but few exceptions, it is always the underdog
who wins through sheer willpower.*
~Johnny Weissmuller

As a first-year, sixth grade math teacher, I thought there were three kinds of students: those who immediately got it, those who eventually got it, and those who never got it.

When I gave up a successful career in journalism to try teaching, my hopes were high. Perhaps a tad too high. I envisioned myself as Michelle Pfeiffer in *Dangerous Minds*, saving inner-city kids one school day at a time until peace and harmony prevailed in the land of public education.

But after two months I was drowning in lesson plans, parent-teacher conferences and grading rubrics. *I will never be able to help the kids who don't get it*, I thought. By Thanksgiving, I was ready to quit.

The kids who did get it were easy. Two of my students, Steven and Derek, seemed to grasp mathematical concepts almost by instinct, their brilliant minds able to understand new skills before I even finished explaining them. I often felt like I was wasting their time by continuing with the lesson.

One day in class, I decided to separate the kids into three teams and have them compete to solve math problems, relay-style. By luck of the draw, Steven was up for Team 1, Derek for Team 2, and a girl named Alyssa for Team 3.

My heart sank. Alyssa was the opposite of Steven and Derek. She was the one who didn't get it. She had no mind for math and took forever to pick up new concepts, if she ever learned them at all. She also happened to be one of the sweetest girls in class, one who always wore a shy smile and never said a bad word about anybody.

Part of me felt guilty for pitting her against the two future NASA engineers. *Should I put an end to the game in favor of a more traditional lesson?* I wondered. Steven and Derek were already at the board, chalk poised, eager to go. Teams 1 and 2 exchanged smug looks, knowing this was a two-man battle. The students on Team 3 rolled their eyes and sank in their chairs dejectedly.

My heart broke for Alyssa, but really, wouldn't any kid in the class lose to Derek and Steven? I gave Alyssa a smile and forged ahead.

"Express the fraction 13 over 80 as a percentage," I instructed. "Go!"

The boys were off like racehorses, setting up the problem correctly and whizzing through the execution. Alyssa stared up into the atmosphere, waiting for the answer to appear in a cloud above her head. By the time she started writing, Teams 1 and 2 were screaming wildly. Steven and Derek were already done.

"Steven was first, Mrs. Zimmers!" Team 1 yelled. (They insisted on calling me "Mrs." even though I wasn't married.)

I moved toward Steven to check his work. Unbelievably, he had the wrong answer. He had successfully divided 80 into 13 to get 0.1625, but he had only moved the decimal to the right one place instead of two, making his final answer 1.63% when it should have been 16.25%.

"I'm sorry, that's incorrect," I said.

Team 2 burst into cheers, believing the victory was theirs. I moved over to check Derek's work, assuming this would be the end of the round. Poor Alyssa was still dividing away in her slow, methodical manner, but I was pleased to see she had at least set up the problem correctly.

As I looked over Derek's answer, I couldn't believe what I was seeing. He, too, had the decimal in the wrong spot. He had made the same mistake as Steven. I was incredulous; they so rarely made errors.

"I'm sorry, Derek. That's also incorrect."

"This is a stupid contest!" Steven grumbled.

The boys turned back to the chalkboard, trying to figure out where they went wrong. As I watched them futilely rework their division, I also watched Alyssa, who was inching closer and closer to her own answer. My heart started beating a little faster. *Go, Alyssa, go! Kick those boys' butts!*

"I just checked it, Mrs. Zimmers," Derek insisted. "The answer is right."

His division was right. But his final answer wasn't.

"I'm sorry," I said firmly. "It isn't."

They were two boys who were used to getting high-fives and pats on the head for every answer they gave. And now nothing. They were flustered. And both their teams were screaming at them, adding to the pressure. They were a No. 1 seed in the NCAA basketball tournament, with a lowly 16 threatening an upset.

Through it all, Alyssa kept working. Team 3 suddenly came alive, as they realized Alyssa might actually score them a point.

"Come on, Alyssa! You're beating them!"

I am embarrassed to admit this, but I joined them. I began screaming my head off, jumping up and down, and clapping my hands like a crazed seal for Alyssa.

"You can do it, Alyssa! You can beat them! Just keep going!"

Steven and Derek turned to me in surprise and anger.

"No fair, Mrs. Zimmers! You're not supposed to take sides!"

I definitely wasn't supposed to take sides. I knew that rooting for one student meant I was effectively rooting against another, and good teachers don't do that. But the idea that this girl — the one at the bottom of the class, always in danger of failing the next test, never being the kid who got it — could triumph over these two was overwhelming. Derek and Steven had experienced a lifetime of academic triumphs. This was possibly Alyssa's only shot.

I never stopped screaming. Right or wrong, I couldn't help myself.

Alyssa finally finished, taking a full minute, it seemed, to make the chalk stroke on the last digit of her solution. The room became quiet as everyone waited for my nod of approval. Did she have the right answer?

She did. 16.25%.

"Point goes to Team 3!" I yelled with more enthusiasm than was appropriate for a teacher. I hugged Alyssa as the rest of Team 3 leapt out of their seats and cheered.

The profession of teaching ate me alive. The high hopes I had had when I started were quickly obliterated, and I gained a newfound respect for those who lasted in the job. I managed only a year before I went scurrying back to journalism like a frightened mouse. But when I think about that year, the bright moments outshine the tedium of the job and my own failures. I see brilliantly bright, blinding moments like Alyssa remembering what she learned about decimals at the perfect time.

I no longer think students — or any of us — fit into three categories. We're all just human. At times, we make mistakes; at others, we achieve the impossible.

~Jenine Zimmers

49

Meant to Be

*As long as we are persistent in our pursuit of our
deepest destiny, we will continue to grow. We
cannot choose the day or time when we will
fully bloom. It happens in its own time.*
~Denis Waitley

I had graduated from college and was looking for employment when my oldest sister brought home an application for an alternative teaching program. Those accepted would earn a Master's of Art in Teaching while working full-time in the classroom. When I was a little girl, I had a list of careers that I wanted to pursue and teaching was one of them. So, I decided to apply to the program.

They were looking for a hundred teacher candidates. I made it through the first round and was invited for an interview. I made it through the first interview, but not the second. I received a wonderful rejection letter in the mail extolling my virtues as an excellent candidate for urban teaching. The letter contained a list of urban education programs, but none were offering a free master's degree.

I had gotten really excited about the program, and I was disappointed when I wasn't accepted. I was sitting in the back yard talking with my sister about it when she pointed out that people are not always able to keep their commitments. "You never wish anyone any harm, but things happen," she said. "What God intends for you, no one can take from you." Her words soothed me.

Because I had a bachelor's degree, I was able to become a substitute teacher. I was subbing when I received a call from the director of the program a few months later. They had a vacancy at a school, and I was on the list in case any of the one hundred candidates selected didn't work out for some reason or another. He told me to report to the school the following morning. I heard my sister's voice in my head and smiled. "What God intends for you, no one can take from you."

The next morning, I traveled by two buses and a train to get to the school. I saw a bald guy with a big smile on his face. I asked him for directions to the office. He pointed toward the stairs and said, "Second floor on your right." When I got there, a dead ringer for Al Bundy and a heavily made-up woman were sitting in a back office talking. The woman ushered me in. He was the principal, and she was the teacher mentor for the program.

I could feel the butterflies fluttering. Even though I was a full grown woman, all of my fears of being in the principal's office came flooding back to me as I looked at this blank-faced man who did away with all formalities and asked, "What took you so long?" The mentor introduced herself and explained what was expected of me: sit in the class and observe.

The mentor took me up another flight of stairs to Room 301 and instructed me to sit in the back. There was a young Clark Kentish-looking guy looking clueless. He didn't appear to know anything more about teaching than I did. The classroom reminded me of my seventh grade classroom — chaos and confusion. He was talking, but nobody was paying attention. Little did I know he was teacher number three, and it was only October.

I stayed in the classroom watching him "teach" until lunchtime, and then the mentor returned and took me to the three-in-one — lunchroom, auditorium and gym — for more observation. At the end of the day, I found myself once again in the principal's office, and the butterflies had returned and brought a few friends. I sat quietly while the principal and the mentor discussed — debated really — my fate. I had been called to fill a vacancy, but the program director had sent two of us — me and Clark Kent. Clark had arrived an hour before me and was immediately placed in a classroom.

The principal suggested that Clark Kent and I both remain for the rest of the week, alternating teaching, and whichever one of us was still standing by the end of the week would get the job. But the mentor did not agree. She thought that since Clark Kent had arrived at the school first, he should fill the position. She argued that grad-school classes had started, and that waiting another week would put the teacher even further behind.

My fate was decided. I had to leave; Clark Kent stayed. I went home confused and disheartened. I had come so close that I could feel the chalk dust on my fingertips, but it was all for nothing. The next day, I returned to subbing with the words of my sister still playing in my head: "What God intends for you, no one can take from you."

The following week, the principal called me back. Clark Kent had quit. The next day, I reported to work without a clue as to what to do. I didn't even want to be a middle-school teacher! I didn't want any grade higher than fourth grade because my middle-school years had been so awful. I didn't want to return to that even as a teacher. But once again, my sister's words came to me and calmed me. "What God intends for you, no one can take from you."

It was a trying experience that first year. I was the fourth teacher in four weeks, and the revolving door of teachers had become a game to some of the students. They told me they were waiting to see how long I would last. Some of them tried to help me find the door, but I refused to leave. Others confided in me that they were tired of new teachers. They needed stability, and I didn't want to let them down.

I thought back on my junior-high days, and I vowed to give my students a different experience from the one I had—a better one! There were many days when I didn't know what I was doing, when I asked myself, *Why am I here?* But I knew that I was exactly where I was supposed to be. I was at my first school for ten years and this year marks my twenty-third year of teaching. My sister was right. What God intended for me, nobody could take from me.

~Stephanie J. Gates

50

The Learning Curve of a Sub

*You never really know a man until you understand
things from his point of view, until you climb
into his skin and walk around in it.*
~Harper Lee, To Kill a Mockingbird

I just finished my first year of substitute teaching, working in the same three buildings. The most common question the staff asked me all year was, "Who are you today?"

They meant *who was I subbing for*, but the question always made me smile, because being a substitute does have that schizophrenic feel.

After all, I've been in classrooms ranging from kindergarten to high school. I've covered subjects ranging from honors English to remedial study skills. I've been a librarian, a gym teacher, an art teacher and, once, a band teacher.

School is about learning, and I learned a lot.

I learned the immense value of the school office. They have the keys, the codes, the copy machine and the chair where the challenging children sit.

I learned every classroom includes a version of the same three kids.

There is the kid who wants to be the teacher. This one is very vocal about how things are usually done, how things should be done, and how to handle the uncooperative students. This kid is never far from my elbow.

Then there is the kid who wants to get away with murder. This one never stops misdirecting, slyly suggesting the class do things their real teacher never lets them do. This kid is never far from my other elbow.

Unfortunately, there is also the kid who is lost. Sometimes quiet, always heartbreaking—this one needs individual help. Rarely do I have enough control of the classroom to give that help. This kid *should* be at my elbow.

I feel bad about this.

I've learned that all kids, regardless of age, use the bathroom for independent wandering. That said, I always let them go. I'd rather be duped than clean up... stuff.

I learned flicking the lights is the best way to garner attention.

I learned fifteen minutes until the bell can feel like fifteen hours.

Substituting in a grade school taught me that one's place in line is a sacred, sacred thing, not to be messed with or dismissed.

Substituting in a junior high taught me that nothing has changed for kids who are becoming teenagers. It is still a minefield of whispers, judgment, and alienation.

Substituting in a high school taught me to collect assignments at the end of the hour. It creates a sense of urgency for at least twenty minutes.

"Who are you today?"

That question was never as important as what I was supposed to be doing that day—teaching.

And I struggled. Mightily.

I walked in a lot of teachers' shoes, and every walk confirmed how amazing teachers are. They come to school with a plan and are flexible enough to execute that plan in a variety of ways amid a variety of challenges.

And if that plan fails, they come up with another one.

I learned to appreciate this tenacity. Every sub assignment contained a low moment when I realized how outnumbered I was, how off track we were, and how much I wanted to quit.

My guess is real teachers have those moments, too. After all, these kids are not their kids. They are somebody else's kids. Perhaps that is the most amazing part about teachers. The good ones feel parental responsibility toward somebody else's kids.

If you don't think that's impressive, try taking over someone's classroom, just for an hour. You'll learn.

~Nicole L.V. Mullis

51

A Mother's Day Gift

The manner of giving is worth more than the gift.
~Pierre Corneille

As a first year middle-school teacher, I often felt like the old woman who lived in a shoe. Remember her? She was the one who had so many children that she didn't know what to do.

My first year of teaching was an emotionally exhausting job with few rewards. I was young, inexperienced, and had class after class of twenty kids just waiting for me to make a mistake.

After a particularly long night of going to graduate school, grading papers and thinking about how many weeks I had left until I could breathe, I had one of those mornings when I began to question my job choice. I had become a teacher to help kids. Instead, I felt like I couldn't even help myself anymore, and I was so tired. It had just been Mother's Day, and as I sat at my desk surrounded by lesson plans, I wondered how I would ever have enough energy to have children of my own, much less continue teaching.

That was when I heard a knock at my door. One of my students came in — the too-cool-for-school, basketball-playing country boy who had accidentally broken my favorite snow globe and become one reason why I couldn't display nice things in my classroom. He shyly handed me a large flower that probably came from his family's farm. He had stuck a bird feather in it.

"I got you a Mother's Day gift," he said. Most middle school and high school teachers don't receive presents. Christmas and Teacher Appreciation Day had already come and gone without any gifts. I was so shocked that I just stared.

Flustered by my silence, he said, "You know… since you are like a mother to us and all that, I thought you should get a present, too."

I smiled and told him he was the sweetest person in the entire world, and I just loved it. Based on his smile, I knew that I had done an adequate job of making him feel quite proud of himself. What possessed that twelve-year-old to bring me a homemade present, I'll never know. Once he left the room, I locked the door. And I cried. That moment took me through the rest of the school year and several more.

~Jessica McIntosh-Brockinton

52

First Impressions

Poetry is a language in which man
explores his own amazement.
~Christopher Fry

I stood in the middle of a classroom full of third graders. "Okay, everyone, take out your writing journals," I said. It was the third week of school during my first year of teaching, and I was pleased that my students were already getting the hang of our classroom procedures. They had just finished putting away their books and were waiting quietly for instructions, with their hands folded on their desks. Things were going pretty well. I had been holding morning meetings with my students and making sure that they all got to know each other through community-building activities.

I had harmony among my students, and I was proud that I had accomplished that. And I felt lucky because I had been assigned such a wonderful group of kids. But on that day, after my students had started enthusiastically writing in their notebooks, a short boy with chubby cheeks, curly brown hair, and an unkempt appearance walked into my classroom looking quite confused.

"Which classroom are you supposed to be in?" I asked.

"This one."

"What's your name?" I asked.

"Carlos," he responded.

I looked at my roster. "You're not on my list," I said. He shrugged his shoulders. "Who brought you up here?" He shrugged. "How did you get here?" He looked past me and shrugged again. I looked in the hall in case someone was waiting for him, but there was no one there.

No one seemed to know where he had come from, but he was mine now.

That evening, I went home exhausted, wondering if things would ever be the same. As the days went by, things only seemed to get worse. Carlos was uncooperative, never did his homework, and came to school unprepared. It usually took twenty minutes just to get him to write his name on a piece of paper, and there always seemed to be a mess under his desk — scattered crayons, pencil shavings, and crumpled paper.

After one week with Carlos in my classroom, I was completely drained. I cried in my car on my drive home, asking God why he had allowed the peace in my classroom to be broken by this little boy. I felt like everything about Carlos was a disaster. He was a mini-tornado going through my classroom every day. The other students also had a difficult time taking to Carlos because he seemed indifferent to the opinions and expectations of others.

Learning to work with Carlos took time. But I developed my skills as a teacher and learned about the types of interventions he needed, as well as the steps I needed to take in order to refer him for additional services. And I got to know him better. It turned out that he was witty and had a natural knack for comedy and entertaining the class. His sense of humor and street smarts were advanced for a boy his age. As much as I tried to keep a straight face when he cracked a joke or made a funny comment, I couldn't help but chuckle or smile.

By spring, I had learned to decipher his writing. His inability to spell or use punctuation, coupled with his terrible penmanship, were definitely a challenge, but I mastered the art of reading his short responses. I learned to be more patient with Carlos, to give him more time to complete his assignments, and to give him extra direction and to work one-on-one with him. Still, he seemed unfocused and disengaged.

One spring day, I announced that we would be learning to write poetry. I started by showing the students short examples of poetry, and then I went over the rules for writing a haiku — a three-line poem using five syllables in the first line, seven in the second line, and five in the third line. After practicing a few times, I had the students share their poems. Some stood in front of the class nervously rocking back and forth or holding their papers up to their faces as they read, but not Carlos. He walked up, proud of his work, and read his poem to the class. It was about spring, and it was beautiful. He bowed comically and said "thank you, thank you" when he was done. The students clapped in approval.

We moved on to different types of poetry within the next week. I had never seen Carlos so excited before. Every day during writing he would look over at me with a big smile and say, "Teacher, are we going to do poetry today?"

I introduced their final poetry project — an "I Am" poem about themselves that would go through a peer-editing process and would then be typed and submitted to a citywide competition. A month after submitting the top five poems in the classroom to the competition, we heard back. Carlos had won first place for the third grade poetry contest. He couldn't believe it. "I have never won anything before, Teacher," he said in disbelief. His classmates were a little jealous, but in the end they cheered for him, knowing he seemed like the most unlikely to win something like this.

On the last day of school, Carlos came up to me and gave me a big hug. "I'm going to miss you, Teacher," he said.

"I'm going to miss you, too," I responded.

There were many things I didn't understand about Carlos when I first met him, like why he was always disheveled, cranky, and unfocused. With time, I learned. There were occasions when I would let him take home apples or snacks that were left over, because his family didn't have enough food to eat. He always lost his books because his family seemed to move from home to home. He had been the victim of abuse, one of his parents had been incarcerated, and he had also been institutionalized for some time before appearing in my classroom. This little boy had been carrying the weight of the world on his shoulders, but it didn't break his spirit. His sense of humor was intact, and his ability to write poetry was astounding. I never knew he would hold such a special place in my heart. Even today, years later, I think about him and send prayers his way, hoping life is being kind to him.

When Carlos walked into my classroom on that fateful day in the third week of school, I felt he had so much to learn. In the end, I discovered that the real lesson had been for me.

~Daisy Franco

Chapter 6

Inspiration for Teachers

My Teacher Changed My Life

One looks back with appreciation to the brilliant teachers, but with gratitude to those who touched our human feelings. The curriculum is so much necessary raw material, but warmth is the vital element for the growing plant and for the soul of the child.
~Carl Jung

What If I'd Dropped That Class?

Education is not the filling of a pail,
but the lighting of a fire.
~William Butler Yeats

On the first day of my sophomore year, I wandered the hall searching for my third-period classroom. My schedule said Latin. I knew that must be an error, but I needed to be somewhere before the tardy bell rang. I found the room, rushed in, and took a seat in the front row.

The teacher, a tall, lanky woman with short, tight curls, spoke in a strong voice. "Welcome to Latin. My name is Miss Hofer, and I tolerate no loafers. If you're one who interrupts or does not complete homework, leave now." She turned to write her name on the chalkboard. When a snicker floated from the back row, she wheeled around and aimed a penetrating stare at the perpetrator.

During lunch, I shared the experience with my friend, Alice. She frowned at me. "Latin? You're not going to college, are you?"

"No. My schedule must be a mistake, but I hate changing classes. Anyway, Latin might be fun."

She shook her head. "Not with Hofer. Latin! You'll probably fail."

That irritated me. At that moment, I decided I wouldn't drop Latin, and I'd pass.

Although difficult, I loved the challenge of the subject. Also, I enjoyed Miss Hofer's keen sense of humor, as well as her sincere interest in her students. In a quiet way, she demanded order and respect, unlike my Algebra I teacher, who threw erasers at talkers.

Often, she asked a student to remain after the dismissal bell. Then one day, it was my turn. My stomach churned as I shuffled toward her desk, expecting a reprimand for something, but I didn't know what.

"I discovered you're enrolled in typing," Miss Hofer said. "Do you know how to use these?" She removed some stencils and a bottle of correction fluid from her desk drawer. When I shook my head, she explained how to correct the stencils, and then handed me a copy of the prior year's Latin Club banquet program and a schedule for the upcoming one. I regretted I had raised my hand at a Latin Club meeting to volunteer my help with the annual spring banquet.

At first, I made numerous errors, but soon I managed to slow down enough to not need the messy correction fluid. After a week of hard work, I placed a box of assembled programs on Miss Hofer's desk. She smiled and nodded at me.

The next week, I added Latin II to my schedule for my junior year. Not only was I passing, but I had earned an excellent grade in Latin I. I knew I could do the same in Latin II in spite of my friend Alice's new set of warnings.

There were only two years of Latin available, but Miss Hofer also taught a Word Study class, recommended for college-bound seniors. I included it in my schedule for senior year.

Alice again questioned my choice. "You're working at that drive-in place and playing in the band and orchestra. Your senior year is supposed to be fun. Why suffer with Hofer again?"

I didn't bother to explain that I liked this teacher.

One day, just as the bell rang, Miss Hofer said, "Nancy, I need to see you." No longer afraid of her chats, I waited for her request.

"What are your plans after graduation?" she asked.

"I'll get a full-time waitress job. Maybe I'll go to secretarial school someday."

"I looked at your transcript," she continued. "You can be admitted to the state college."

"I can't afford college," I replied.

She handed me a business card. "Call my friend, Mrs. Johnson. She's a language teacher. If you can get a work-study job, I'll help you apply for a tuition scholarship. It won't cost much if you live at home."

"My family expects me to get a job."

Miss Hofer sighed. "Think about it."

When she called my name a few days later, whispers drifted from all parts of the room.

"Silence," she bellowed. "She's not in trouble, but you're going to be."

I traced the grooves in the desk with my finger until the other students left.

"Did you contact Mrs. Johnson?" she asked.

After a long pause, I replied, "No, I didn't know what to say."

She handed me a piece of paper. "Write it down."

I found a nearby desk and wrote: "My name is Nancy Lewis. I'm a senior at Central High School. My Latin teacher suggested I call you about a possible work-study job. May I schedule an interview with you?" I handed it to Miss Hofer.

"Take out the word 'possible' and change 'Latin teacher' to 'Nellie Hofer.' Mrs. Johnson and I are good friends."

I considered calling, but my family needed the extra money I could earn as a full-time waitress. No one in my family had gone to college, and I knew it would be difficult. This was not an option for me. However, my self-talk changed as the week progressed. A few days later, I took the paper from my notebook, deciding it wouldn't hurt to call. Within two weeks, I had the promise of a full tuition scholarship and a work-study job. I wanted to try this, but what would I tell my parents?

One evening, as I helped Mom prepare supper, I took the plunge. "I can start college this summer. It won't cost anything, but I can't work full-time like Dad wants."

Mom didn't say anything.

I continued, "I'd like to live here and go to Southwest Missouri State. They'll give me a part-time job and a scholarship. I can still do waitress work on the weekends. I'd like to major in education, to be a teacher. I can do it."

"I'm sure you can," she said. "It's just a surprise. You've never mentioned college before. Of course, you should go. I'll talk to your father."

The next day, Dad's conversations with his buddies changed from inquiries about my future job possibilities to bragging about my college opportunity. That weekend, Mom, who never spent money calling long distance, phoned my grandmother in Illinois with my college news. I smiled to myself, realizing how proud they were of me.

The next week, it was my choice to stay for a talk. I told Miss Hofer, "I received an acceptance letter for the scholarship to SMS. Mrs. Johnson wants me to start this summer. I'll be typing Latin worksheets and grading papers. Thanks for your help."

She smiled. "I understand you're going to be an elementary teacher. You'll be a wonderful one. Don't forget to come back to visit me."

Three years later, my parents beamed as I walked across the auditorium stage to accept my college diploma with a major in elementary education. My father even purchased a suit for the occasion. Ten years later, I received a master's degree in reading.

Today, at seventy-five years of age, I sometimes glance at the two framed documents above my computer and wonder how my life would have turned out if I had chosen to drop Latin I. Many people and events have affected my life's journey, but Miss Nellie Hofer may have been the greatest influence of all.

~Nancy Lewis

54

When the Going Gets Tough

If you are always trying to be normal, you will
never know how amazing you can be.
~Maya Angelou

It was the first day of my senior year and we were choosing our classes. There were two choices for English: Mrs. McCabe, a lovely lady approaching retirement whose curriculum consisted mostly of showing films based on literary classics; and Mrs. McDougal, who was known to be a no-nonsense, students-are-here-to-learn taskmistress who assumed all her students were going on to college. Mrs. McDougal had been known to fail students who didn't apply themselves, too.

I was going to college, so I swallowed hard and chose Mrs. McDougal's class.

The following day, classes began. My English class with Mrs. McDougal was the last period of the day. Shortly after all the students were seated, Murrel McDougal moved slowly into place behind her desk as if she were a praying mantis stalking her next meal. She turned and smiled wickedly at us.

"So, you're the lucky ones who chose to be challenged this year." Surprise, surprise. Mrs. McDougal had a delightfully dry sense of humor.

Her curriculum was challenging, as she wanted us to be prepared for college. She had structured the year into several blocks: basic grammar and parts of speech, spelling and vocabulary, writing styles, and literature. We didn't see one film. But we each read at least four novels from her College Prep Reading List and gave a ten-minute book report on one of our reading assignments. But it was in the writing assignments that I discovered a part of me that I truly enjoyed. The assignments were Essays, Critiques, Reports and Creative Writing. And Mrs. McDougal proved true to her reputation. We worked for our grades.

One day, while we were all quietly reading, Mrs. McDougal came to my desk, winked at me, and motioned for me to follow her into the hall. I had very mixed emotions, not knowing if I had committed some unpardonable breach of English usage or was about to be asked to drop her class. When I walked into the hall, she was leaning against the staircase smiling. She motioned for me to join her. I really wasn't prepared for what she shared. She told me I was more than just a good writer; I was a promising author, and she strongly encouraged me to write on my own — and submit my work for publication. She told me she had already sent one of my essays to a textbook publishing company, and they were going to use it. I was flabbergasted and teared up, thanking her profusely. I floated for the rest of the term. The terrifying Mrs. McDougal thought I was a fine writer!

I did finish college and go on to get a Master of Fine Arts degree in creative writing. I spent time in the Army, and the years flew by. I did some screenwriting and sold several scripts, produced several of my plays and published five novels.

At my senior class's 50th Reunion, I was delighted to share old stories with my classmates in Mrs. McDougal's demanding college-prep English class. As we talked, we discovered something none of us had realized at the time, so long ago.

The dear lady had taken each of us aside privately and encouraged us to follow a talent in which we seemed to have shown proficiency. Some became teachers or professors; others became professionals in various disciplines who wrote reports, texts and surveys. And, although our professions were different, we were all nurtured by Mrs. McDougal, whose "toughness" helped each of us overcome any doubts or fears

| My Teacher Changed My Life

about whether we could or couldn't. Her approach led to quite a few very productive lives. If she knew how positively her approach and encouragement enriched the lives of her students, Mrs. McDougal would be very happy.

~Lonnie D. Groendes

55

Chicken Soup
for the Soul

A Lesson in Kindness

In life, there are no mistakes, only lessons.
~Vic Johnson

"Did you bring it?" I nodded and returned my gaze to the front of the classroom where Mrs. Hudson stood. The "it" was my new orange skip ball. I couldn't wait until after school when my friends and I would get to jump for an hour until our parents picked us up. I was only eight years old, but I was as tall as a fifth grader and could jump over the rope really well.

There was a loud creak as the door opened. Miss Swann, the guidance counselor, walked into the room. A girl, as tall as I was but with shorter blond hair, limped in behind her. She kept her eyes focused on the floor.

Miss Swann spoke. "This is Margaret Cooper. She just moved here to Sebring from up in north Florida. Be sure to welcome her to our school."

I couldn't take my eyes off what should have been the girl's left leg. It wasn't really a leg, just waxy, bumpy skin — a mass of scars with a shoe. The leg-thing was not only scarred but shriveled up, gross and much smaller than the other leg. Girls were not allowed to wear pants to school, but I thought Margaret should be given special permission so she could cover up her leg.

Mrs. Hudson, our motherly gray-haired teacher, placed her arm gently around Margaret's shoulders and guided her to a seat toward the front, then bent over and whispered something in her ear.

Mrs. Hudson was always so nice to everyone. I adored her. She finished explaining the math problem on the board and announced, "Milk-break time. See you in ten minutes."

Connie, Rose, and I were the first to race out the door and line up to accept the little red-and-white cartons of milk and paper straws provided by the school. My friends and I huddled on the far corner of the concrete breezeway, near the sweet-smelling jasmine bushes at the edge of the patio. Sarah-Jane spoke up first. "I think Miss Swann said her name was Margaret Cooper Pooper, didn't she?"

Everybody got the giggles. Cooper Pooper. I looked around to make sure we were alone, leaned in and nodded my head. "Yup, she *is* Margaret Pooper. Or is that Maggot Pooper?" My friends laughed even louder at my brilliance, so I continued. "Today, let's meet at the far end of the sidewalk. And make sure she doesn't follow you!"

I left my friends and skipped back to the classroom before recess ended. I wanted to say hello to my beloved Mrs. Hudson and find out if she liked my latest book report. With her usual big smile, she took my paper from the top of the stack on her desk and handed it to me. But this time she didn't release her grip on my paper with its big A+ on top until I looked up, directly into her eyes.

She began, "Wendy, you are a good student and a nice person. In fact, I've noticed that you're kind of a leader in the class."

I basked in her warm approval and smiled. Shifting my weight from one foot to the other, I was a little embarrassed that Mrs. Hudson liked me so much. But I loved how she seemed to know me so well. It was like having a third parent, but better. In her class, I wasn't the middle child like I was at home. The way she smiled when she called on me in class and her comments let me know how much she appreciated having me around. One time my friends tried calling me the "teacher's pet," but I took it as a compliment.

My cherished teacher continued in her quiet voice. "That's why I am sure you, of all the students in the whole class, will help Margaret Cooper get used to being here and being one of us. I just know you will invite her to play with you and your friends after school today.

Thank you for being the quality person you are, honey."

Her confident words were clear as ice, frozen daggers aimed at my heart, which was now pounding in fear. Guilt erased my smile and made it hard for me to breathe. Did she guess, could she possibly suspect what we had been saying about the new girl? Could she know how awful I was?

I managed a weak smile and nodded. My swirling thoughts and fears made me want to throw up.

I managed to include Margaret in our group although it wasn't easy, since skip ball required skillful jumping. I know without a doubt that we became friends that day.

While many school memories have faded over the years, the lesson Mrs. Hudson taught me has stayed with me. Margaret Cooper and her family moved away at the end of the school year, but my life was changed forever.

Mrs. Hudson gently guided me, challenging me to think for myself and do the right thing. She believed in me, and because she did, I rose to the level of her expectations, both for Margaret long ago and even in my choice of career.

With the goal of helping others always the guiding force in my life, I have counseled hundreds of potential dropouts, disruptive students, and many dysfunctional families in my lifetime.

I think Mrs. Hudson would be proud.

~Wendy Keppley

56

A Mother When I Needed One

You cannot save people. You can only love them.
~Anaïs Nin

It was November 7, 2014, my eighth grade year. My teacher had asked me to come in after school. I didn't know why. I certainly didn't think she knew about my suicide plans.

I had been planning to kill myself on November 11th for months. I remember looking at the calendar and choosing the date. It was shortly after my mother's birthday, but before the holidays. It was when it would all stop — all of the pain, all of life.

Normally, teachers called me in after school to ask if they could keep my papers, but not about this. Most teachers just saw my good grades, and I suppose to most of them that meant I must be okay.

However, that day, I stayed after school with my teacher for four hours, revealing everything that had led up to this point in my life: the divorce, the abuse, and the escape.

I watched my strong, brave teacher cry as she tried so hard to crack my tough shell. She wouldn't leave me until I was safe, and because of that, I owe her my life.

Throughout the rest of the school year, we met once a week. During a rocky period in my life, she was there for me when no one else was, and that's all I needed: someone who would listen, someone who would care, someone who would love me.

She was the best counselor anyone could ever ask for, the best friend I never had, and the best mother when I didn't have one.

The end of the year came, and I constructed a quote with my newly gained wisdom from her. With graphite handy, I sketched the words into unbreakable tree branches amongst blooming flower buds.

Every now and again, I still go to visit her, and there, high on her wall, it hangs in a black photo frame: "Beautiful is the one who's constant in making others' lives beautiful."

And she is beautiful.

~Brie Dalliant, age 16

57

The Code Reader

*One of the basic needs of every human being
is the need to be loved, to have our wishes
and feelings taken seriously, to be
validated as people who matter.*
~Rabbi Harold S. Kushner

I was twelve when life overwhelmed my mother and she signed herself into a psychiatric facility. We lived in rural Northern California where my dad worked as a logger. He left the house before dawn and returned after dark. The oldest of five children, I did my best to help my elderly grandmother care for my three younger brothers and sister. Money was tight, but we always ate well, had clean clothes and a warm bed to sleep in.

In those days, my mother's condition was called a "nervous breakdown." I was just old enough to know she was in trouble, but not old enough to know where I fit into what "drove her crazy" or what might make her better. I wrote cheerful letters, hoping to boost her spirits and remind her how much she was missed. We loved her and hoped she would be home soon. Of course, we all promised to behave and not upset her.

No matter how much I tried to concentrate at school, my mind wandered and my grades slipped. My heart ached with confusion and uncertainty. Years later, I would learn the "problems at home" that I thought were invisible to a certain teacher were actually obvious to her.

Gladys Hue, the local high-school public-speaking teacher, also worked in the elementary schools as a speech therapist. She was tall, about fifty, with a blond pageboy and dancing blue eyes. The day she walked into my sixth grade classroom to screen children for her special program, Mrs. Hue, dressed in a pastel blue dress, reminded me of the golden-haired angel we always placed atop our Christmas tree.

She explained she was there to listen to each of us and, just like a hearing test, see who might need a little extra help with their words. In the company of a few colorful puppets, she commenced a student-by-student series of private interviews. By the time she got to me, I had perfected a heretofore nonexistent stutter.

When I sat down at the small table in the back of the room with Mrs. Hue, I became the center of her attention and sputtered out my name: "Ja-Ja-Jackie." Her smile never faded as she asked several questions and listened intently to my now faltering pattern of speech. Not once did I sense judgment or suspicion. To the contrary, I felt important — like I used to feel with my mother. But most of all, deception aside, I felt like I was being heard.

For all the things I was about to learn from Mrs. Hue, the most profound remains the realization that a child's inability to express her feelings is not a reflection of how deeply she feels. Fledgling humans that they are, children often communicate, for lack of a better term, in code. Gladys Hue was a code reader, and on that day she saw a freckle-faced girl with curly hair reaching for what we all long for — to feel valued and understood.

For a brief few weeks, Mrs. Hue's speech-therapy class filled the void left by my mother. There were about ten students. Some had lisps; some substituted the letter "w" or "y" for the "r" sound; and others, like me, stuttered. We practiced enunciation with puppets, performed dramatic narrative sentences with dress-up hats, and sang with the accompaniment of tambourines and triangles. Miraculously, my stutter vanished within a few days!

Years later, I confessed to Mrs. Hue that I really hadn't had a stutter. The ever-present twinkle in her eye brightened as she revealed she had known the truth all along. To my surprise, she added, "You know, you needed me as much as I needed you." She went on to explain she didn't have the heart to deny me something I so clearly wanted and secretly used me as a "diction model" for the other students.

Mom was home by the end of summer, and our family set about the business of trying to regain our stride. Unfortunately, turmoil in one form or another persisted. Headstrong and prone to help the most helpless, Mom took on a new role as a mental-health advocate, and our home became a local group-therapy hub. By the time I started high school, my parents were on their way to a divorce, and I again sought refuge in a class taught by Gladys Hue.

Popular opinion holds that most people are more afraid of public speaking than death. Perhaps if more people had a teacher like Mrs. Hue, that ratio would shift significantly. "Tell them what you're going to tell them," she taught us. "Then tell them, and then tell them what you told them." This was her hallmark message to those of us who dragged our feet to stand behind the podium in her classroom, grateful the structure hid trembling knees and provided a handhold for sweating palms.

Religiously, she counted how many times speakers said "uh" to help us better string together words and thoughts. Her critique on organization and content balanced the positive and negative. "Jackie, this is a wonderful idea," she once said to me about a speech on world peace, "but reading it is like trying to swim through a muddy pond." Because her praise mattered so much to me, I did what any aspiring young public speaker would do: I broke into tears and ran to the library.

Eventually, through trial and error, I earned my way onto Mrs. Hue's competitive forensic-speech team. The challenge was fraught with fear and doubt, but her unwavering faith in me, her magical ability to see potential where I saw none, kept me striving. I even achieved the highest honor of any of her students as a California state finalist in the 1968 Annual Lion's Club Student Speaker Contest.

Shortly before I delivered my speech, Mrs. Hue, known for her stylish elegance, removed the sparkling earrings she wore. "Now that you're a young lady," she said, handing them to me, "we're going to doll you up."

I placed second that day, but had so far exceeded my own expectations that I came to realize the greater prize was having been one of Gladys Hue's students. More than teaching, she embraced and inspired, nudging some, prodding others, tirelessly challenging each of us to wrangle our fears and fully engage our imaginations.

I last visited Mrs. Hue shortly before she passed away in 2010 at the age of ninety-five. I recall marveling at how little the years had diminished the graceful flick of her hand as she spoke or the all-knowing light in her eyes. I told her, "I owe so much to you." She shrugged, alluding to a philosophy she shared with many teachers — she had simply opened doors for her students. It was up to us to walk through them. Her attempt at humility soon melted into a twinkling of delight and pride, and once again, decades later, student and teacher needed each other. I needed her to know as much as she needed to hear how deeply valued she was as a code-reading educator who changed my life.

~Jackie Boor

History in Our Hands

If you want to understand today,
you have to search yesterday.
~Pearl S. Buck

The bullet hole seemed too small, as though it went about the lethal business of warfare without much of a fuss. Despite its size, it had pierced the helmet I held in my hand and killed the boy who wore it. I knew his name and what he looked like. I knew that he was only eighteen years old when he died because I held in my other hand the photo ID badge that was taken from this German soldier as a souvenir, along with the helmet.

At fourteen, I couldn't reconcile the fact that someone would make a choice to take these things and dehumanize a young man who became an unidentified body to whoever found him. I couldn't imagine the injustice to his mother never being certain of her son's fate for the sake of a souvenir, or that a young girl, half a world away and many decades later, would learn what his mother never had.

I knew of certain horrors of war, but I had never heard of taking mementos from the men you killed. This was a common practice by both sides during the world wars, and my History teacher's uncle was no different from any other soldier. He took these things from the war, and they made history come alive for my ninth grade History class.

These were not relics locked behind museum glass, where they would make war seem somehow mythical, like it didn't really happen to flesh and blood soldiers. Holding these things in our hands proved the war happened, that teenagers were killed, that they wouldn't live the lives that we looked forward to. Holding these things helped us to think about history as a means to save us from ourselves rather than just regurgitating a rote list of facts.

Before ninth grade, we viewed History class as something to endure. We had so little available to us that mattered historically in our south Texas town. The old courthouse, a once cherished piece of architecture visited by presidents and state leaders, stood rotting on the bay front. Why would students value history if we saw no evidence of it in our lives? Our teacher understood this and began our year by showing us historical photos of our town as well as current photos he took in the exact same locations. He spent days perfecting these shots to provide us with something beyond our required curriculum. He wanted us to understand that history belonged to us, that we could touch it, see it, and evolve with it.

Our teacher also brought things for us from each period we studied, all things from his own family, making post–Civil War American history meaningful to us. Chapters became more than facts and numbers. They became stories populated by humans and, as the year wore on, we realized that history was also populated by those we knew and loved.

The Vietnam War touched most of our homes. We were born as the war ended, but our fathers had served, and we knew their stories — at least those they were willing to tell. Our teacher brought his draft card and explained the system to us. We were fourteen years old, and in just four short years, this could be our story, too. He passed around his high school yearbook, and we enjoyed seeing a teenage version of our teacher in a yearbook for our same high school. He had walked our halls as a kid, had friends and girlfriends here. He was just like us. As we continued looking at the yearbook, however, we noticed that some boys were circled. These were the boys in his class who had died in Vietnam.

"Did you know all of them?" we asked.

"Yes. Like you, I had gone to school with them since I was a kid. Look around the room and imagine that some of your pictures will be circled in four or five years."

We couldn't look at each other. We lived in a military town, and the weight of that statement left us silent. I thought about the young German soldier whose helmet I had held in my hands earlier in the year. I wondered if these circled boys came home with all their belongings or if their things were taken as souvenirs by unknown soldiers in Vietnam. The bell rang a moment later, marking the end of another day of real learning.

Our teacher never indicated any political point of view. He simply humanized history, made us care about it, and inspired us to ask questions or research history on our own. We were squirmy freshmen in every other class, but he never once had to ask us to be quiet or pay attention in his. He didn't have to. We didn't want to miss a thing.

~Tanya Estes

English Escape

Reading is not just an escape. It is
access to a better way of life.
~Karin Slaughter

I stood in front of a panel of expectant faces, hoping the speech I wrote would be good enough to read at graduation. The board sat before me, an assortment of high-school teachers I didn't recognize, except for one, Mr. Timmons. He had been my sophomore English teacher.

Mr. Timmons had a warm smile and genuinely cared for his students. From the first day of my sophomore year, I knew I'd enjoy his class. It didn't take him long to discover my love of literature. I had begun to read *The Iliad*, and he was impressed that I chose to read that in my free time. As I progressed and we discussed what I was learning from Homer's epic storytelling, Mr. Timmons realized my appreciation of different perspectives and began suggesting other books he thought I would like. He could not have known that I immersed myself in other worlds to escape my rocky home life. It probably never occurred to him that school was my reprieve.

From as far back as I could remember, my father struggled with his past and binge drank on some weekends. He could be a mean drunk. I grew up feeling it was my job to protect my mom and sister from him, so he would occasionally take his anger out on me. My mom finally gained the courage to leave him, but my sister went off to college and my grandpa died, leaving my mom struggling to take care of her mom while working long hours on the night shift at the Chrysler plant.

I had always been independent, so she left me to my own devices, parenting me the best she could when she felt it important. It seemed to work, but inside I was crumbling. There were days when I wouldn't see my mom at all, and I refused to speak to my father after we left him. I just couldn't do it anymore.

Mr. Timmons became the only constant father figure in my life. He listened to me, and he encouraged my love of all things written.

I clung to the stories he suggested and read them like crazy. Despite his efforts, things got really rough in the second semester. I started dating a guy who was very much like my father. He grew controlling, and our relationship moved quickly, leaving me with bruises all over my body by the time it ended.

My friends didn't understand. My mom was busy. I hadn't spoken to my father in six months. Life began to feel hopeless. English class became my only true escape.

I felt that everything was my fault. I had allowed everything to fall apart. Everyone was upset with me. I couldn't take it anymore. I went to a party, got drunk and found a bottle of pills that I swallowed, hoping to end it all.

After that, everything was chaos. There was the hospital, in-patient, and the release. My mother told me she couldn't handle me anymore and sent me to live with my father, a fate I feared more than anything. By the time I walked back into Mr. Timmons' classroom, my life had completely shifted. The simple act of sitting at my desk offered a sense of normalcy that felt like coming home.

Mr. Timmons talked to me like he always did. So many teachers, family members, and friends had begun treating me like I was a little kid, handling me with very careful words. Some even avoided me, but not him.

He decided to give the class a treat and show the movie *Dead Poets Society*. I loved it instantly, but about halfway through Mr. Timmons asked me to step out into the hall with him.

The empty corridors seemed so lifeless compared to the shuffling crowds that usually filled them. I wasn't sure what he had to say, but I knew it involved what I had been through. "Are you enjoying the movie?" He watched me as he closed the door behind us.

"Yeah, I love it."

"Jessie, I'm going to tell you the ending because of what you've been through. The main character kills himself."

I appreciated his straightforward approach, but I couldn't say anything. I just stared at the floor.

Mr. Timmons brightened his voice. "I'm sorry for what you've been through. But I'm here for you, and I don't want you to ever do anything like that again."

It felt so good just to hear that. It seemed so simple. "I won't," I promised.

Reading my graduation speech in front of him a couple of years later, I had never been so grateful. My sister and I were sharing our own apartment, and my life had finally started to feel like my own. At first, I had written the usual cookie-cutter speech about *carpe diem* and all the possibilities the future can hold, but it didn't say anything about me.

What I held in my hands instead was a different kind of speech, one that spoke of the sanctuary school had become. How it had helped me to escape the pain that plagued my life. Starting from scratch helped me to reflect on my learning experience and the teacher who had helped me through my sophomore year. It was a speech that had little chance of being read at a celebration for hundreds of students, and I knew it.

Somehow, I got through reading it without stuttering or crying. My body shook with anxiety, but I took some deep breaths and felt satisfied by the end.

Afterward, Mr. Timmons came to speak with me. He praised my writing and beamed at me like a teacher whose student had won a Pulitzer. The essay was not selected, but that didn't matter. I know he voted for it. I had said what I needed to say to the teacher who made the biggest impact on my life.

~Jessica Marie Baumgartner

My Teachers' Gifts

Teaching kids to count is fine, but teaching them what counts is best.
~Bob Talbert

I once had a teacher who taught me to read
and how to spell words that I someday would need.
How could she have known where that someday would lead
when she shared her gift with me?

I once had a teacher who taught me to sing.
A song in your heart is such a wonderful thing.
I wonder if she knew the joy that would bring
when she shared her gift with me?

I once had a teacher who taught me to draw.
She opened my eyes to the beauty I saw.
She taught me to see the beauty in us all
when she shared her gift with me.

I once had a teacher who taught me to play
as part of a team — not always just my way.
He taught me a lesson on sharing that day
when he shared his gift with me.

All of these teachers shared lessons that were free.
What I do with these treasures is up to me.
If I share them with others, thankful they'll be
that they shared their gifts with me.

~Tom Krause

Chapter 7

Inspiration for Teachers

Lessons from Non-Traditional Classrooms

Tell me and I forget. Teach me and I remember. Involve me and I learn.
~Benjamin Franklin

Michael and the Tokens

Hold yourself responsible for a higher standard than anybody expects of you. Never excuse yourself.
~Henry Ward Beecher

I glanced up at the seating chart on the bulletin board to see which students I would be teaching that hour. I recognized two names. The third one, Michael, was new.

At two minutes to the hour, the director opened the door to the afterschool learning center, and the students came in. My regulars quickly seated themselves, and I handed them their first assignments. A heavyset boy of about nine lagged behind. The director walked him over to my desk. "Michael, this is Harriet, your instructor."

I smiled and stretched out my hand in welcome. Michael offered me a limp handshake and plunked into his seat.

His shirt was crumpled, stained and tucked in halfway. Brown hair fell over his eyes, and a ring of purple, probably grape juice, stained his mouth. As I leaned over to talk to him, the smell of unwashed boy wafted toward me.

Breathing shallowly, I forced myself to smile. He did not smile back. His glance slid past me and darted around the room.

"Michael," I said, keeping my voice bright and friendly, "let's get started."

He continued to ignore me.

"Michael," I repeated, "please look at me when I'm talking to you."

He turned to me and sighed. His sigh said it all. He did not want to be here.

A quick glance at the other students told me they were working well, so I had about five minutes to devote to Michael. "You're going to be working on three to five reading and vocabulary exercises each time you come," I said. "I'll check your work after each exercise before moving on to the next. And at the end of each session, you'll get special tokens to buy toys in our store at the back of the room."

At the mention of toys, Michael's eyes lit up. "I get toys?" He swiveled around in his chair to stare at the store display.

I gave him a moment before tapping on the table to regain his attention. When he turned to face me, I continued, "Yes, you get toys, but you earn them by working hard. You save the tokens, and when you have enough, you can buy something. So let's start earning those tokens."

I handed him the first exercise and described what he needed to do. We worked on the first example together. When I was sure he understood the assignment, I turned to one of the other students.

Within a minute, Michael piped up, "I'm done. How many tokens do I get?"

A quick check of his work showed mostly errors. "Michael, I think you can do better. I want you to read this again slowly."

"But what about the tokens?" His voice had taken on a whiny tone.

"You get the tokens for working hard, not for working quickly or carelessly."

He shrugged and went back to work.

The next two months were a repeat of the first session. Michael would barrel through his work with little care for the right answer. When forced to do it again, slowly, he'd get most of the questions right. He was smarter than his original test scores indicated, but he was sloppy and didn't seem to care how well he did.

The only thing that motivated him was tokens.

Since his regular school didn't give out tokens, I knew I had to figure out some way to improve his self-discipline and motivation that went beyond our one-hour sessions. I tried praise. That didn't work. I tried pointing out how hard other students were working. That didn't work either.

After another three weeks passed with little improvement, I talked to the director. "Michael and I are both getting frustrated. Maybe he'd do better with another instructor."

She agreed. We tried him with three other instructors. He did worse. The day I walked into the center and saw his name back at my table, I was ready to quit.

Just before the students entered the classroom area, the director came over to me. "Michael's mother spoke to me in the waiting room. When she checked the board and saw that Michael was back with you, she was pleased. You're his favorite teacher."

Favorite teacher? But before I could process that, the students filed in. Michael took his usual seat with me and raced through his first assignment, as usual. But this time, I didn't react as usual. Instead, I turned to him. "Michael, you know how I decide how many tokens you get each time?"

He nodded.

I smiled. "Let's try something different. From now on, you'll decide."

"Me?" he said, looking right at me.

"Yup, you. I think you're a good judge of how hard you're working."

At the end of the session, I handed the other two students eight tokens for a job well done. Then I turned to Michael. "How many tokens do you think you earned?"

He paused for a moment, his face scrunched up in thought. "Two?" he said. "I made a lot of mistakes."

"Okay," I said, "we'll go with two today. But remember, the tokens aren't only for correct answers. They're also for working hard."

Over the next two months, Michael worked himself up from two tokens to five or six. He still sometimes slipped into his old ways and rushed through the work, but that happened less and less. By the end of the third month, he was routinely giving himself seven or eight tokens, and he deserved them.

He had conquered his reading and comprehension problems.

More importantly, he had taken responsibility for his learning. On the day he "graduated," I'm not sure who was prouder — Michael or me.

~Harriet Cooper

62

Wisdom from My Elders

*Education is the best provision
for the journey to old age.*
~Aristotle

I was accustomed to teaching college undergrads, so this summer gig was a bit outside my comfort zone. The university's Senior Scholars program wasn't for college upper-classmen, but for *senior citizens* — people much older than my twenty-seven-year-old, graduate-student self.

Still, I'd signed on to teach Broadcast Media History to Senior Scholars in order to put a few dollars in my threadbare pockets. I compiled all my notes and slides, planning to start with some historical theory, then go over major radio and television events that shaped U.S. popular culture. (Sounds fun, right?)

I found my classroom in the basement of the senior community center and was greeted by a bright group of fifteen students already seated — women and men with silver hair, wrinkled skin, and lively spirits. They were chatty and clearly eager to learn.

"Ahem," I said, clearing my throat and standing tall at the front of the classroom. "Thank you for coming. I'll be teaching you about Broadcast Media History." I noticed some sly smiles and sideways glances.

I proceeded to teach for the full forty-five minutes. And, by that, I mean lecture, with perhaps a few directed questions sprinkled in.

Class ended, and I waved goodbye with a professional smile as they ambled out of the room talking in hushed tones.

The next day, as I walked through the senior center lobby, I noticed a few of my students sitting in the lounge area chatting. I gave them a small wave and a slightly confused look. Arriving in the basement classroom, I found the lights out and every seat empty.

I looked at my watch and double-checked my class info sheet. The time was correct, as was the day and the classroom. But nobody was there.

Classes were optional in the Senior Scholars program — no grades or anything — but fifteen students had signed up for mine. And not one of them had come back for the second day.

My stomach lurched, my cheeks reddened, and my breath grew shallow as the realization hit me: *They didn't like me. I was awful yesterday.*

I plopped down on a plastic chair and dropped my head into my hands on a desk. Tears pooled at the corners of my eyes.

What was I going to do?

I was being paid to teach Broadcast Media History to fifteen students. And every last one of them had jumped ship after "the young professor" had bored them to rebellion.

Taking deep breaths in an attempt to quell my panic, I thought about how to get myself out of this mess. How could I redeem myself to these students, lure them back to this basement classroom, and fill it again with light and oxygen?

Finally, I had an idea. It was slightly mortifying, but it might work. I stood up from the plastic chair, squared my shoulders and then relaxed them. With my gut quivering, I marched out of the classroom with a new approach, hoping I wouldn't be facing a firing squad.

Ascending the basement stairs cautiously, I walked into the lounge. The seniors were waiting there with raised eyebrows to see how this young whippersnapper would handle their walkout. I inhaled and exhaled deeply. "Hi, everybody," I said. Some of the men crossed their legs and sat back in their cushioned chairs, grinning like they were about to watch a boxing match.

"So, I realize... I blew it yesterday," I said. "I apologize. I was trying to teach like I thought a university course should be. It was boring. And… obnoxious."

They giggled quietly like a group of schoolchildren as I lowered my chin and grinned sheepishly, my eyes scanning them.

"I am asking you to please give me another chance."

The room was silent as they looked at one another, communicating silently.

"I commit to you that, this time, I will make it more interesting," I continued. "I won't lecture… In fact, what I was thinking is that I could ask *you* to tell me your *own* experiences of the events of Broadcast Media History. After all, you were alive for most of these, right? What do you remember about them? What did you think about them?"

It felt as though all the tension whooshed out the windows then, like air releasing from a balloon. They started to laugh and chatter and talk over one another.

"Remember Ed Sullivan?"

"Oh, I actually met Walter Cronkite!"

"We closed our shop early once a week for *I Love Lucy*!"

They had so much to share, so much they wanted to talk about.

"Yes, yes!" I said, raising my voice above the din. "We'll talk about all of that. Starting today with the *War of the Worlds* radio broadcast. How many of you remember that, with Orson Welles?"

The room erupted with affirmations and stories.

"Okay, great. Yes!" I said, nodding and raising my hands, trying to bring their attention back to me. "So… would you all be willing to come back to our classroom and talk about it there?"

With heads held high they picked up their purses, notebooks and coffee cups and filed down the basement stairs. They had made their point. Thankfully, I had heard them.

We had a wonderful summer discussing the events of Broadcast Media History, the events of their lives. I learned as much about these events from their stories as I'd learned in all my graduate courses. I even threw in some historical tidbits here and there that they didn't know. (I told them that CBS had a minister, a priest and a rabbi screen every *I Love Lucy* episode for "offensiveness" when Lucy was pregnant, a TV first. They told me that Lucille Ball was a natural brunette.)

From my worst moment of shame in my teaching career came one of my greatest lessons. Nobody wants to be lectured at. No matter their age, people want to be heard and seen. I've approached every single class I've taught differently after that summer — and I have the mutinous, wise Senior Scholars to thank for that.

~Megan Pincus Kajitani

63

Teaching Future Heroes

The art of teaching is the art of assisting discovery.
~Mark Van Doren

I drove cautiously down the lane toward the small country school, acutely aware that the students were on recess break and could dart onto the narrow roadway in the flash of an eye. They scampered happily in the large grassy area at the center courtyard that I was slowly passing, frolicking under the watchful eye of the playground supervisor.

My car rolled to a stop outside the main entrance of the traditional red-brick school, where the teacher I had come to interview was waiting for me.

"Perfect timing!" he exclaimed. "They're just outside for recess. Come and see them from the upstairs window!"

Without another word of greeting, he turned on his heels and nearly skipped through the door, a big smile lighting up his face. No wonder he had won so many teaching awards and citations, I thought. I followed him into the building and up the narrow staircase to the second floor.

He was already at the window looking proudly down to the courtyard below. I came to stand quietly at his side, realizing I hadn't actually said a single word to him yet. I looked from him to the activity in the courtyard and back again. He was pointing out individuals and describing the distinct differences that were already apparent in his young students.

It was fascinating to watch this renowned teacher discuss his young charges with so much affection. I knew from his long history of success that he was known for his discipline and high expectations. It was comforting to know that was tempered by such gentleness, given that his were the youngest students in the system.

He continued his spirited assessment of the students, pointing to their current interaction as proof of their character, heartiness, innate goodness, and innocent desire to please. And their potential to save lives.

"Oh, sorry," he said, suddenly embarrassed as he finally glanced in my direction. "You probably want to know how we make heroes out of all these adorable puppies. I just get really distracted — I love watching them play!"

We were both laughing as we shook one another's hands in a delayed introduction. He began leading the way back down the stairs toward his office.

"They are just so cute to watch at this stage," he continued, talking over his shoulder as he moved from the kennel area to the corporate offices of the police dog training center. We passed the Wall of Fame, where photos of the canine partners were mounted alongside plaques and awards and photos of thankful political dignitaries. For decades, this facility has graduated German Shepherds that have gone on to become distinguished members of police forces all over the world. These highly skilled and loyal canines are the stuff of legends, and the latest act of heroism by a canine officer was the reason for my interview on this day. I was assigned to write about the multi-step, complex process of selection before a police officer–dog team graduates from the intensive program. But I arrived to find the real story on this day was a level of compassion and devotion that was totally unexpected.

"This place is the same as any other school," he explained to me once we were seated in his office. "Schools everywhere are bursting with students who are full of potential and teachers who are devoted to helping them reach that potential. School communities everywhere work together to shoulder the challenges that present themselves as students advance through the years. All teachers are identifying skills and streamlining pathways that will lead to the most success for each student."

"But most students," I told him, "aren't being trained to save lives or sniff out a bomb or stop a terrorist attack. Teachers don't expect *all* their students to become heroes one day."

"Well," he replied, "maybe they should."

~Sandy Kelly Bexon

64

On Being Bad

Sandwich every bit of criticism
between two layers of praise.
~Mary Kay Ash

I'm an English teacher because I love to read, write, and analyze the heck out of things. I'm confident that I can tackle tough works and come to some level of understanding. I'm confident that I can say something intelligent about the literature, or at least ask the right question so that one of my brilliant students can.

In this arena — English — I can become smug. I can get cranky over people being unable to distinguish "then" from "than." I can forget that the students in the hard, plastic seats in front of me are trying, or at least they'll try unless I overdo the red pen and squelch their enthusiasm.

All public schools require teachers to do hours of continuing education to maintain their credentials. Sometimes, what is allowed seems odd to people. I teach English, and my time volunteering as a violinist in the American River College Orchestra counts for continuing education.

And here's why it *should* count: because I'm really bad at it.

I can't count. I have no ear. I don't really understand key signatures. But I'm trying. I'm trying because my fellow musicians are kind. They always patiently answer questions I have about notation. Even if I've asked before. They don't judge. They are just happy that I'm giving it my best effort.

This can happen in the classroom, too. Students can love and support one another, and they usually do if the environment allows it. The environment is my responsibility. The most important thing to me is respect, and somehow I have to grow that respect in the classroom. The only way I have figured how to do that is to model it myself. That is easy when the students are brilliant, and many of them are. But when they are in need of remediation, it can be hard.

In the orchestra, the culture is controlled by conductors. They can be prima donnas, flapping around like some bird of paradise and squawking at the musicians. Or not. They can be patient, kind, and generous. They can let the love of the music hold the ensemble together. When you go into their office, crying because your pride is broken and the music is hard and your fingers are old and you're not getting any younger and you don't really get how all the B's can be flat, they accept you for who you are. You learn something about teaching from that.

I learn that my students, too, are trying. That the love of words can be sustaining. That we all know they meant "then," and the communication hasn't been lost. I learn that it has always been about love, and that the greatest gift I can give them is patience.

Maybe I have just come from a rehearsal where we're playing Brahms Symphony No. 1. Maybe of the 28 million notes, I can hit 139. That is a lot of awkward faking going on. There are times when I just feel exposed in my inability.

I often remind myself that this is what it feels like to suck at English. There are reminders everywhere that you aren't getting it, and you can see everyone around you happily discussing the underlying metaphors in Camus's *The Stranger*. You know if you open your mouth, you'll be discovered, like when I pull my bow across the string and the guy in front of me realizes that I don't know I'm flat.

Pulling the bow takes courage. Asking questions in class takes courage. Offering an opinion takes courage. I learn to honor the grit of the "bad" student.

And I learn how to be a better teacher.

~Kate Wells

65

Nature's Classroom

Heaven is under our feet as well as over our heads.
~Henry David Thoreau

I t was one of those crisp, cool November days, when the leaves are all colors, and it is glorious to be outdoors. It was 3:00 p.m., and we were on a yellow school bus about to pick up a class of fifth grade "at-risk" students for an overnight camping experience at the Outdoor Environmental Education campsite.

When we arrived, the students were all waiting outside their school with their duffle bags of bedding and a change of clothes. Some had their things in trash bags, and some had very little in the way of bedding. It was obvious that these kids had no one to help them prepare for the overnight, even though we had given them an hour-by-hour itinerary and recommendations for what to bring.

As I stepped off the bus, the principal of the school greeted me. He took me aside and asked if he could have a private discussion. When we reached his office, he informed me that he had kept eight boys after school for misbehavior, and they were no longer to be included on the field trip.

I reminded him that our whole program had been designed for just the kind of students he had forbidden to go on this adventure. Those eight boys needed to see a part of our world totally different from the one they had come from that morning. I begged him to reconsider his decision and let them go. He listened, and then said, "Well, I guess

I can delay their punishment until next week." Then he called those eight boys in and told them he had changed their punishment. They could go, after all.

The boys were excited, but they had no extra clothing or bedding for sleeping. We always had extra clothes and bedding in case of emergencies at the site, so this was not a problem.

I had talked the principal into letting these troublemakers go, so I told the rest of the staff that I had my group of eight, and they could divide the rest of the class between the three of them.

Most of the students from these "at-risk" schools had never been out in the woods, sampled the rippling waters of a stream, or heard the calls of the whippoorwills or coyotes yapping at night. They had never fallen in the meadow grasses and pretended to be deer or rabbits, and hadn't hiked a trail lit by moonlight.

And the wonders, with these eight boys, were just beginning. The first job upon arrival at camp was to set up tents and fetch water from the pump. Then I led them into the deepest part of the oak-hickory forest, far enough so they were completely worn down and dependent on me to show them the way back to camp. We were discovering wildlife tracks, fungi, and other things of interest as we hiked. Now I had the upper hand. They needed me to show them the way back with a compass and map.

These boys found many things to explore. They lifted the side of an old watering tank and discovered ten or twelve tiny garter snakes. They asked if they might pick them up, and I said yes; they were not poisonous. One of the boys wanted to take one home to scare his sister, and I explained the special job these creatures have in nature. Then I asked him why he wanted to scare his sister with a tiny snake, and he said, "Because she's big and mean and makes me do stuff I don't want to do." We put the snakes back where we found them and moved on.

At the stream, so clear that the rocks lining the bottom were visible, the boys asked if they could remove their shoes and socks, and wade in the water. It was still warm enough, so I said yes. They found tadpoles, crawdads, minnows, and insect larvae, which begin their short lives attached to rocks in the water. These boys were full of wonder and asked many questions about the things they were observing.

The boys dried off their feet on their trouser legs, and put their socks and shoes back on. We continued our hike, stopping each time one of them found something of interest. And the "wonders" they found. Travis (the apparent ringleader of this group) found some owl pellets beneath an oak tree. "What's this?" he asked. In all my twenty years of field studies, I had never found an owl pellet. Not only had Travis found one, but he found one containing a complete skull of a field mouse. "Can I take it home to show my mom?"

I said, "Let's take it back to camp and share it with the group. We do not take things like this home because it isn't sanitary, and your mom wouldn't want you handling it." We put it in a plastic bag for safekeeping. On the way back to camp, Jessie (the quiet one) pulled on my shirt and pointed. He had found a rare, wild, fringed orchid growing there for us to see, but hidden away from the rest of the world.

In the evening, we had a good time roasting hot dogs and making s'mores by the campfire. We sang all the silly songs we knew, and ended with a beautiful one called "Moon on the Meadow." They liked it so much that we sang it several times until they knew all the words by heart. Just before retiring, we took a short hike down to the lakeshore in the moonlight.

Next morning, we woke everyone to scrambled eggs, French toast and cocoa. Then we hiked again to the shoreline to look for arrow points and bits of old Native American pottery. The boys found tiny arrow points called "bird heads" and "friendship rocks" (rocks with a hole through the middle). We let them keep the friendship rocks, but re-buried the arrow points where they were found. The kids were talkative and excited about their "finds" as we returned to camp.

After lunch, we hiked one last time before leaving. The boys found a hollowed-out sycamore tree, big enough for all eight of them to fit into. Then they discovered the tree was still alive, as it had tall branches with green leaves. It was a chance to talk about how a tree grows, the parts of a tree, and the function of each. As we were talking, Jessie said quietly, "What's that?" He was pointing at an evergreen about five feet tall... a red cedar. Nestled among the branches was a small bird, quietly looking at us. I dug out my bird book and identified it as a full-grown screech owl, even though it was tiny.

Wonders never cease. Up to that point, Jessie was the one holdout in the group who didn't seem to be enjoying himself like the others. Now he was talking a mile a minute about finding things none of the rest of us knew anything about… and he was ecstatic! He was going to have some things to tell his family when he got home.

Most of the group slept all the way back to school. It had been a beautiful overnight experience for all of us. The principal met us as we arrived and invited me into his office to tell him how things went. He was extremely anxious about the eight boys he had reluctantly allowed to go on the trip. As it was, he had more to tell me than I told him. When I asked permission for Travis to take his owl pellet home (which we had carefully placed in a glass specimen bottle with a tight cap), he said the boy could keep his treasure to show his mom, but confided his mom was a prostitute. His dad was in and out of jail. He spent most of his time with his older big sister. Yes, that big sister! Two of the other boys had one parent in jail, and Jessie was in his fourth foster home.

I had tears in my eyes as the principal thanked me for insisting that these boys be allowed to go with us. As he observed the happy looks on their faces, he said, "It was just what they needed!"

The boys made discoveries that day they will remember for a lifetime — not just discoveries in nature, but discoveries about themselves. They had used compasses and topographic maps to find their way back to camp (with a little help). They had assembled a tent, slept on the ground with only a blanket, cooked and cleaned, pumped and carried water, gathered wood to make a campfire, and shared all of this with school friends. I have thought about those eight boys through the years, and I've wondered how much that weekend might have changed their perspective and improved their futures.

~Yvonne Evie Green

66

Transformative Teaching

*If you take advantage of everything America has to
offer, there's nothing you can't accomplish.*
~Geraldine Ferraro

When a local community center put out a plea for experienced volunteer teachers, I abandoned an unreward-
ing early retirement to accept the challenge. I hoped to
regain a sense of purpose with a familiar and comfortable experience — teaching.

But on that first day, as I stood in front of the classroom and
surveyed my twenty gray-haired and wrinkled students, I realized
that this teaching experience would be a totally new adventure. These
eager students were aged refugees, permanent residents in America
for less than five years, and this class was their next step to American
citizenship.

As the first session progressed, I was impressed with their strong
reading and writing skills. Speaking was their weakness. Each could
manage the minimal oral communication required for placement in
the citizenship class, but they lacked the crucial conversational English
skills needed to pass the Immigration and Naturalization Service (INS)
oral test and interview.

To encourage good, old-fashioned practice, I decided to empha-
size oral interaction rather than lectures and student-written reports.

Additionally, I would begin each three-hour class with a short period of casual conversation to ease their self-consciousness and encourage English usage. By the end of that first day, I had quickly regained my "teacher legs," determined the best course design for my students' success, and recaptured my long-lost enthusiasm.

My sixty- to eighty-year-old pupils demonstrated exceptional determination. They worked hard to master their adopted language. I found their dedication awe-inspiring. They came early and stayed late. So did I. By week three, we were assembling an hour before class just to chat in English. They especially wanted to talk with me, so I often found myself in the center of three or four ongoing conversations at once. It was exhilarating.

Toward the end of the ten-week course, the students began to receive notices for their INS interviews and tests. I was confident they would pass, but they were all nervous anyway. On the day prior to each student's interview, he or she stayed after class to privately talk with me and receive encouragement and a hug.

As they passed the dreaded INS ordeal, each student returned in triumph. Amazingly, even though they no longer needed the preparatory class, they continued to attend, acting as mentors to those who awaited final interviews. We became a team: a teacher and her naturalized-citizen helpers.

On the last day of the semester, all twenty students took their usual seats. The room fell silent. One of my newly minted American citizens stood and spoke in halting but understandable English. As class spokesperson, he thanked me for helping them earn their U.S. citizenship. When he sat down, twenty pairs of hands reached into brown paper bags and emerged with special gifts — homemade ethnic foods carefully wrapped in aluminum foil, hand-picked garden flowers, candy bars, even a plastic key ring from San Francisco. The elderly refugees, dependent on meager government assistance, passed these generous offerings forward to make a small pile on my desk.

I thanked them for their eloquent words of gratitude and their thoughtful gifts. Then I added a sincere "thank you" for their greatest gift to me — helping me find a new sense of worth, contentment with retired life, and a renewed vigor for public service. There were many tears all around, with lots of tissues and hugs before we said our final farewells. In the empty classroom, I stared at the gifts, awash in contradictory end-of-school-term feelings — proud my students were able to move on, yet not wanting to let them go.

~Lynne Daroff Foosaner

67

Still Teaching

Few things are harder to put up with than the
annoyance of a good example.
~Mark Twain

any athletes look for new, competitive outlets after their high school "glory days" have ended. When my friends and I finished high school four decades ago, we turned to softball. Fast-pitch, slow-pitch, it didn't matter. We just couldn't hang up our spikes at age eighteen.

The summer of 1981 was very successful for our slow-pitch team. One local tournament was especially appealing to us because of the nominal entry fee and the prize money being offered. The local Elks' Lodge sponsored an annual tournament that, for a mere $100 entry fee, awarded $300 to the champions and $150 to the runners-up.

We liked our chances of winning the tourney because this particular slow-pitch event attracted many "veteran teams." We were young and cocky and could certainly out-run, out-hit and out-play guys in their thirties!

As the tourney progressed, it was obvious that there were two dominant teams destined to meet in the championship game — ours and one other. The other team breezed through its bracket, relying on the homerun ball and good pitching. We enjoyed an equally easy path through the twenty-four-team field to the finals.

What was interesting about this opposing team was that it was comprised of teachers — most of them our former high-school teachers.

Their pitcher was our senior class advisor; the jazz-band director played first base; even the school custodian roamed the outfield.

So when we squared off in the title game, it was more than just recreational softball. There were several sub-plots and plenty of bench jockeying. One of my teammates hoped he could pay back one of our opponents for a detention he had received many years before as a high-school sophomore. One of the educators heckled us from the outfield: "Hey, don't you guys still owe me some homework?"

In a high-scoring game, we prevailed 16–14 and headed to the Elks' banquet hall where they were hosting the tournament awards presentation. We were celebrating our victory, already running up a hefty bar tab — knowing that our prize money for winning the tournament would probably cover our drinks well past midnight.

The tournament director took the microphone and began the awards presentation. He thanked all the participants and reminded the two hundred people present that the tournament had raised a significant sum of money for the Elks' cerebral palsy charity. He then called the second-place team to the front of the hall to present them the runner-up trophy and a check for $150. The team of teachers accepted the trophy, graciously thanking the tournament committee. Before the team captain, our former senior English teacher, put down the microphone, he said, "And by the way, we'd like to donate our second-place prize money back to the Elks to help fight cerebral palsy."

In the midst of our own revelry in the back of the hall, we just barely heard those words: "donate" and "prize money." Uh-oh. Instantly, our team had the proverbial devil hovering over one shoulder and angel over the other. Of course, we had only a minute to decide. The devil was advocating for us to "Keep the money. Party on. You won it fair and square." While the angel encouraged us to "Do the right thing; people are watching; you have to donate the money back, too!"

Interrupting this moral dilemma was the tournament director, back on the microphone. "And will our champions now come forward."

We strutted through the crowd, high-fiving each other all the way to the podium. We enthusiastically accepted the trophy, and somewhat reluctantly donated our $300 prize money back to the Elks' cerebral palsy campaign.

We learned a valuable lesson from our former teachers that night, and it wasn't in the Chemistry, History, or Geometry classroom. It was a lesson about doing what was right — a lesson that I remember all these years later.

~Mike McCrobie

68

Teaching from a Wheelchair

The only disability in life is a bad attitude.
~Scott Hamilton

Following her graduation from medical school, Caroline completed her residency program in Obstetrics and Gynecology, got married, and opened her practice. But then her bright future changed when a car accident paralyzed her from the neck down. I received the sad news from my daughter, Lori, who had attended medical school with Caroline.

The tragedy made it difficult for me to teach my third grade class. When I shared the news of the accident, the students wanted to become involved, and they sent letters and colorful pictures to cheer "Dr. Caroline." They became her pen pals, and some asked questions about her disabilities. "What do you do all day? How do you brush your teeth? Do you ever feel sad?"

Dr. Caroline sent the class a videotape that began with the title, "Howdy, Hillbillies" (our class name the children derived from my name, Mrs. Hill). Then a beaming, articulate Dr. Caroline appeared on the screen with greetings to the students and appreciation for their letters. She was seated in her wheelchair.

For an hour, Dr. Caroline educated her new friends about her disability. She demonstrated the gears on her motorized wheelchair as she spun out of control in "crazy gear number two." She ventured outside to her handicapped parking space and taught them about the Americans with Disabilities Act that reserved spaces for the disabled. She demonstrated her red van that was equipped to raise and lower her wheelchair and commented, "I think my van looks like a big, red Coke can, don't you?"

Inside her apartment, she strapped a metal device on her hand that enabled her to pick up a fork and eat. She showed her special computer with equipment modified for her disability so she could send us e-mails, banners, puzzles, and letters. Our class picture was propped against her monitor.

Dr. Caroline continued to be my team teacher for several years. She created a website and asked people around the world to send our class interesting information. Within two months, we had received over 10,000 responses, including one from the governor of Colorado.

All of my classes wished they could see Dr. Caroline in person, so one year she and her husband put their Coke-can van on a train and traveled from Washington D.C. to our school in Clearwater, Florida. The pen pals in my current class, and those from past classes, filled the decorated auditorium to meet their special friend.

Afterward, a teary Dr. Caroline summarized her relationships with the students over the years.

"It seemed that whenever I was having a dreary, gray day, or I was frustrated, something would come from the kids. In their own way, they said exactly what I needed to hear. These kids have given me the reassurance that I belong and am worthwhile, whether it's for a group of third graders or in an academic medical center. They made me feel like I am a valuable person."

Dr. Caroline's life was changed after that tragic car accident, but she has a new career in health care… and a special place in the hearts of her pen pals.

~Miriam Hill

Chapter
8

Inspiration for Teachers

Breaking Through

*The dream begins, most of the time, with a
teacher who believes in you, who tugs and pushes
and leads you on to the next plateau, sometimes
poking you with a sharp stick called truth.*
~Dan Rather

69

Tough School

From a little spark may burst a flame.
~Dante Alighieri

lthough I'd taught many years, this was my first year at this particular school—a South Florida high school located in a town so poverty-stricken it didn't even have a grocery store. During orientation, I found myself sitting beside another teacher new to this school. We shook hands and he introduced himself. "I'm Jim, a college professor from Indiana. I'm teaching English. I asked for the toughest school. I want to make a difference in these kids' lives."

"I'm teaching intensive reading to juniors and seniors who can't pass the state test," I answered. Unlike Jim, I hadn't asked for this school. I had simply been assigned, and it was a challenge in many ways. I commuted fifty miles each way, leaving home at 5:30 to get there by seven, driving past endless fields of tall, green sugarcane.

Tough school? That was an understatement. My students threw things, ignored directions, cursed, even threatened physical harm. One day, they stole my grade book off my desk while I helped a student in the back of the room. They kept asking, "Miss, you coming back tomorrow?" hoping the answer would be "no." But I kept saying "yes."

I'm one of those people who love a challenge. Tell me I can't do something, then get out of my way because I'll try twice as hard.

I asked other teachers for advice.

"They're going to test you," they said. "Don't show them you're afraid. But don't turn your back on them, either."

I gamely followed my lesson plans, ignored the kids who abruptly jumped up and ran out of the room screaming curses, and drove home exhausted each afternoon. I wondered how in the world anyone could ever learn anything in this environment. I racked my brain for some way to reach them.

One day, I ran into Jim again. He was carrying a carton of books out to his car. "This is the most dysfunctional, disorganized school I've ever seen," he declared. "And these kids! Their only goal is getting teachers to quit. Well, they win. I've had it. I'm going home." He'd lasted less than two weeks. That wasn't unusual; one teacher didn't make it through her first day!

Despite all the challenges, or maybe because of them, I came to love those kids. They were coarse, rough and untamed, but just as smart and funny as kids anywhere. What they lacked was civility, background knowledge, and context. They had abysmal vocabularies, asking, "What that mean?" about common words. My heart bled for their lost opportunities.

Drug abuse was rampant; gangs roamed the hallways; many girls became pregnant; violence was a daily occurrence. One of my students — a sweet sixteen-year-old boy who struggled in class but shined on the football field — was shot dead one Saturday night by another teen, simply because he had been in the wrong place at the wrong time. I spoke at his funeral, held in the gym, the following weekend.

I struggled to find some way to make reading enjoyable for the kids. One tried-and-true exercise, which never failed at other schools, involved Readers Theater. Kids worked in groups, practiced a short script, and then read it aloud to the class. For two months, I handed out scripts each Thursday, hoping to see a spark of joy. They grumbled and mumbled and stalled and complained about yet another dumb thing this teacher was making them do.

One Thursday, I gave them the scripts as usual, wondering why I even bothered. But that day, a group of three students got a script about some catty girls. When they presented the skit, they invested the characters with humor and emotion, acting out the comments, striking poses, and shaking fingers in faces.

The class roared its approval — stomping, applauding, and whistling. That's when they realized Readers Theater wasn't about what I liked; it was about what they could do with those scripts to shine in front of their peers. The next group couldn't wait to present theirs, to see if they could do it better than the girls, and so it went.

"Miss, we do that play thing again?" they asked. And, yes, we did that "play thing" again every Thursday.

Readers Theater improved their pronunciation and pacing. They had to read at a certain speed to make it sound like ordinary conversation. They discovered that *how* they said something influenced its meaning. They paid attention to punctuation — pausing for a comma and coming to a full stop for a period — something many had never grasped before. They learned to be comfortable speaking in front of people. Most of all, perhaps for the first time, reading was fun.

The best day came when I had to attend an in-service training program, spending the day in the school auditorium rather than in my classroom. I met the substitute who would run my classes. One of the students wandered into the room and spotted the worksheets I'd prepared.

"Naw, Miss, it be Thursday," he pointed out. "We do that play thing today."

"It's too complicated to explain to a sub," I said, but he smiled and shook his head.

"We teach her how," he said. So I gathered up the worksheets and left the scripts instead, giving the sub a list of "helpers" she could call on each period. That day, my students ran the classes themselves, practicing and presenting their scripts. The sub left me a note: "I never had an easier or more enjoyable day covering classes, especially at this school."

By the end of that year, most of my students had passed the state test. They were relieved, but I hoped they took something more important with them: the memory of being captivated and entertained by written words, and seeing, perhaps for the first time, that reading and fun weren't mutually exclusive.

That summer, I rested, recuperated, and got ready to return to my dysfunctional school. The first day, a crowd of hulking seniors shuffled in and found seats. One boy picked up a textbook and hefted it, clearly about to launch it at me. Another boy leaned over and grabbed his arm.

"Naw, man, she cool," he said, then turned to me. "Miss, I heard 'bout you. We do a play thing?"

~Ellen Rosenberg

70

Preconceived Notions

I have a dream that my four little children will one
day live in a nation where they will not be
judged by the color of their skin, but by
the content of their character.
~Martin Luther King, Jr.

As I walked into the school, I was worried. I was definitely out of my element on this one. What had possessed me to move to a small town where the nearest movie theatre was an hour away? What in the world had I been thinking to take a job in a town where I was the only visible minority?

I guess being desperate for a job will do that to you.

My home city was Toronto, and it was not easy finding work there. I had heard of teachers working for years on the supply list because there was nothing else available. Landing a teaching contract as a first-year teacher, I should have been grateful, right? Well, I certainly didn't feel that way when I walked through the halls of this high school about two hours from Toronto. I stuck out like a sore thumb. Everywhere I walked, eyes turned toward me. As the principal gave me a tour of the school, I heard students whisper as I walked past: "Is that a new teacher? No, she can't possibly be. She isn't from around here."

Standing before my first class, I saw a sea of faces of one colour—a completely different colour from my own. I reminded myself that I was there to help students not only learn the curriculum, but to effect change in a new generation. I was there to inspire, not allow myself to be limited by racial divides. Summoning up my courage, my rollercoaster of a year began.

I sat through moments in science class when I gave lectures on how vast and black space is, and students responded with "Miss! That's racist!" and "How can she be racist, idiot, when it's her own race? Duh!" I sat through moments in chemistry class when we discussed drugs and narcotics, and I had students ask me if I had done drugs in the past or if I had ever been in jail. Of course, my favourite genre of music was rap and hip hop, right?

I had to decide whether I should be offended or amused by their stereotypical thinking. I decided I would use those opportunities as teachable moments. I could either avoid the elephant in the room or I could teach these students that what they'd seen on TV was not quite the reality. Not every black male ends up in jail and has a bunch of baby mamas. Not all Latinos try to smuggle drugs into the country. Not all people from India eat curry morning, noon, and night. Not all Asian women work in nail salons. Everyone has dreams and aspirations, no matter their skin colour or background.

I asked each of my students what part of the world they would visit if given the opportunity. Their responses were revealing. Many of my students had never been outside their own town, never mind Canada. And yet the world called to them and they were eager to learn about different countries and cultures.

I'd arrived with preconceived ideas about my students being narrow-minded or intolerant, but they were just like any other kids. They hadn't had many opportunities to interact with other people, so all they knew was what they'd learned from television. And my students were not only eager to learn otherwise, but to see otherwise. They wanted to travel the world and learn more. And with a little hard work, I told them, the world would be their oyster.

By the end of the school year, I was walking through the halls of the high school feeling spry, with my shoulders back and my head held high, no longer wishing to hide in the corner or fade into the background. I was different from the rest of the students and teachers, but I was happy to be so. My students knew that Ms. Duval was different, and yet she was just like everyone else. They learned that you cannot define people by their skin colour or by what you see on TV, but by their character. Not only did my students learn a valuable lesson, but I did too. I learned not only to be more confident in my own skin, but that people can be very accepting of you if you just open yourself up and give them the chance.

~J. Duval

71

Seeing Rightly

The excursion is the same when you go looking for
your sorrow as when you go looking for your joy.
~Eudora Welty

hen I first opened my art studio, I was fortunate to have a blind student. Nick and his twin brother (who was not visually impaired) started classes with me when they were seven. It was important to their mom that I accommodate, but not substitute, curriculum for Nick. At first, I was hesitant, not wanting him to feel singled out.

I soon learned that my reservations about his impairment were *my* handicap, not *his*. Nick was a remarkable child: brilliant, extroverted, and so well adjusted that I marveled at his sense of self and his extraordinary confidence. He was always willing to try new materials and tools. He kept the students around him entertained in lively conversation and imaginative musings. His enthusiasm was contagious. He participated in the same projects that the sighted students did, with minimal assistance from me. When they painted, he painted; when they sewed, he sewed.

In class, he talked openly and easily about his visual impairment and answered questions from the other students and myself about what life is like for a blind person. We talked about color, line, and form. Although three-dimensional activities were easier for him to comprehend, he engaged in drawing and painting as well. One of our favorite activities was having Nick draw lines on paper while the other students told him what they saw in his drawings. He would choose color as carefully as a sighted student, and when asked why he chose a particular color, he would always give a thoughtful and creative answer. Once, I bought him specially scented crayons, thinking that he would enjoy being able to identify them by scent.

"What are these?" he scoffed when I handed him the new pack.

"Scented crayons. Try them."

He opened the box, took a sniff, and handed them back. "I'd rather have the real crayons," he stated.

One particularly busy afternoon several years into his tenure at the studio, he asked one of his usual provocative questions. "Do you think that someday I will be able to drive?" I was preoccupied with helping another student, but being very familiar with his level of candor, I was comfortable enough to answer him honestly.

"Drive?" I asked. "Like a car? No, Nick. I don't think you will be able to drive." With a little humor, I added, "And, please, at least not while I am still on the road!"

We all laughed, but he wasn't finished. "Someday they might have a car designed especially for visually impaired people. Don't you think that can happen?"

"Yes, I do," I replied. "But Nick, someday they might have an operation or procedure that would allow blind people to see. Wouldn't you rather have that?"

He thought for a moment and then responded with a simple "No." All at once, everyone stopped working. I couldn't believe what I had heard.

"Why not?" I asked.

His reply was careful and unforgettable. "Because," he began, "what I think things look like in my head and what they really look like might not be the same. I don't want to be disappointed."

I stood there speechless. Every preconceived notion that I had about the visually impaired shattered in the wake of his genuine, honest answer. Never again would I be so arrogant as to think that my sighted world was any richer or fuller than his unsighted one.

Nick is now in his twenties and thriving as a very active and creative college student. His prophetic idea about a car for the visually impaired has come to pass thanks to the driverless cars that are starting to be marketed now. I am certain that when the cars are widely available, Nick will own one.

As a visual artist, I am wholly dependent on my sense of sight. Until I met Nick, I often pitied those who couldn't marvel at the beauty in the world around us. But through working with students like Nick and watching my own father struggle with macular degeneration, I have come to realize that it is not their world that is limited; it is mine.

I am a prisoner of reality, while their reality is limitless. I read Antoine de Saint-Exupéry's book, *The Little Prince*, years ago, but it wasn't until meeting Nick that I fully understood one of the most important lines in the book: "It is only with the heart that one can see rightly; what is essential is invisible to the eye."

~T.A. Barbella

From Mother Russia to Uncle Sam

Only one thing matters. One thing; to be able to dare.
~Fyodor Dostoevsky

"They're all recent immigrants — mostly from the Soviet Union. Nine kids altogether. Sounds like a project right up your alley, right?" said my principal.

I'd only been teaching for a few years. This was a high-school English class but I was gung-ho to take on the challenge. I announced the idea to my new, nervous students.

"So, this English class is going to be a little different. We're going to write a play and then perform it."

Vlad guffawed. "Write a play! Yes! Good idea. Let's write a play." I wasn't sure if he was being sarcastic, but I suspected it.

Irina looked at her shoes. "No," she said simply. "No." I pressed her to say more, but she shook her head, the color draining from her face. "My English," she said, by way of explanation.

"I can do it," Mika said, eager to please. "What play do we write?"

"Well, I thought you could each write about your own experiences, being new to the United States," I suggested. "We'll call it 'From Mother Russia to Uncle Sam.' What do you think?"

Clearly, these nine teenagers were still getting the hang of the change in culture, and they looked at me like I'd lost my marbles.

What kind of wacky teacher includes her students in a discussion about curriculum?

Instead of making suggestions, they nodded obediently, and I got them started. We read from plays and monologues for student actors, and slowly I could see their confidence growing.

All except for Irina, the only girl in the group. After class, she told me that she wanted to write something, but didn't know where to start. She loved nature and hoped to capture the beautiful landscapes she'd found hiking in the emerald forested hills near her new home in the suburbs of Seattle. "How about writing a poem that you could read aloud?" I suggested.

"Or a song?" she asked. "I play the guitar. But I had to leave it in Russia when we moved."

First order of business: get Irina a guitar. We found a parent at the school who had a dusty remnant of teenage optimism stashed in his closet. He happily passed on the abandoned guitar to Irina.

It so happened that the Northwest Folklife Festival was approaching in May, and I made a discreet application in the hopes that we would have a play to put on by the time spring rolled around. I received a letter saying that my class had been accepted to perform in the largest theater inside the festival, mid-afternoon on a Sunday.

Vlad laughed. "Yes! Excellent! We will be Seattle celebrities!"

The kids were understandably nervous as the day arrived and the audience filed in. Nearly 500 people filled the seats. I'd put Vlad first in the line-up. He and his friend Leo had written a humorous scene about their love for driving in the United States. The audience cracked up at their impressions of American racecar fanatics, and they applauded vigorously. Vlad high-fived me on his way off the stage. "That's how a superstar does it," he said.

The other students were received with generous support from the audience. I remember the heavy feeling of standing backstage as Mika sat alone in a chair onstage. He shared the monologue he wrote about his family's history and their departure from the Soviet Union. His father had worked at Chernobyl, and after the nuclear accident, the family left for the United States, but their dad was too ill to travel with them. The audience was absolutely silent, moved by his simply told story.

I saved Irina for last. I had been afraid she'd be too nervous to go on stage. Instead, she strode confidently into the spotlight, leaned on a stool, and pulled her guitar strap around her shoulders. Her voice was high and clear as she sang of evergreens and starfish and boulders and blank white skies.

Finally, when all the students came out for their bows, the audience rose and gave them a standing ovation. The kids beamed as they came off stage, and we all celebrated with our families as we enjoyed the rest of the day at the festival.

Many years later, I ran into Irina at our local park. She had her three small children in tow, the baby in a stroller. "Do you still sing?" I asked.

She blushed and nodded at her kids. "To my children. I sing to them. I sing that song sometimes as a lullaby. So they know how lucky they are to live here." She gestured at the pine trees towering above the path.

~Ilana Long

The Weight of Labels

Labels are for filing. Labels are for clothing.
Labels are not for people.
~Martina Navratilova

By the time he was ten years old, Sean carried the heavy, invisible weight of multiple negative labels on his small shoulders. Over the past four years, he had been described as impossible, difficult, disobedient, rude, unmotivated, and uncooperative. No one knew what to do with him because he didn't do his work in class and was a "constant disruption." Some teachers privately predicted that Sean would end up dropping out of school and going to jail. Such is the cynicism that sometimes threatens to replace the idealism that most teachers bring to their vocations.

And so, day after day over the years, Sean was sent to me because I had a tiny room with only small groups for reading instruction. Sean wasn't allowed to participate because, in theory, being banished from his classroom was intended to be a punishment. That was the intention, but *not* the reality. Over the years, my little room became a kind of refuge for him. Even though he was expected to sit quietly, it was obvious to me that he was glad to get out of the classrooms where he seemed to be stuck in a rut of bad behavior.

In my reading groups, I usually read a picture book to the students several times a week, and then a reading or writing lesson was created. While I presented my lessons, Sean wiggled around in his chair, chewing on his fingernails and occasionally looking up at the illustrations if I happened to turn my book his way. I assumed that he wasn't interested in the stories because I had chosen those books for my younger students.

I was wrong.

One day, I finished reading a magnificently illustrated picture book, *Heckedy Peg*, by Audrey Wood with pictures by Don Wood. It tells the story of a very strong mother whose children are captured by a witch, Heckedy Peg. The clever mother is able to outwit Heckedy Peg and rescue her children. When I finished reading and slowly closed the book, there was a sweet and thoughtful silence as the children digested the story. Then I heard Sean's voice from the back of the room. "Not a good ending. Really not good. I could have done better."

I spun around to look at him. He had never spoken out during one of my classes before. I had been told to ignore him, and until that moment, I had pretended he wasn't there.

"Really?" I asked. "You're disappointed in the ending?"

"I like all of the other books you've read." And then, to my great surprise, he began to list books I had read to my groups, providing a commentary about many of them. I sensed that this was a moment I needed to seize, and so I asked him to join me for lunch. While we ate our sandwiches, he continued to discuss the ending, and I had a crazy idea. I told him that if he would write down his suggested ending in a letter to Audrey and Don Wood, I would try to find an address for them and mail it. The next morning, he arrived in my room and proudly produced the letter. I found a possible address, used our school's return address, put on a stamp, and dropped it in the mail.

That happened in May. In August, I returned to school and pulled a mountain of mail from my mailbox. Nestled among the catalogs and educational flyers was a letter with the return address of Audrey Wood — but it wasn't addressed to me. Even though I was extremely curious about what she might have said, I knew the pleasure of opening that envelope was not intended for *me*. I tucked it away until the first day of school, and when the day came, I found Sean's classroom and asked his teacher if I could interrupt for a minute. Sean had a letter from a famous author. Sean walked slowly to the front of the classroom and took it from me.

"Why didn't you open it?" he asked.

"It isn't addressed to me," I replied with a conspiratorial smile.

The teacher, who knew Sean's reputation, looked surprised, but then asked if he would like to open it. Sean tore it open and then nervously passed it to me to read. My heart soared as I read aloud the carefully written words that described how pleased the author was to receive his letter and that she liked his suggestions about a different ending for her book. She hoped he would continue to be a creative thinker... and from one author to another, she was grateful for his ideas.

I slipped the letter back in the envelope and smiled at the stunned expression on Sean's face. I'm sure it was the first compliment he had ever received about his writing. The students sat in hushed awe, and then his teacher asked for a high-five. That was a life-changing moment. Over the following months, little by little, all those negative labels began to slip away. He wasn't sent to my room anymore, but we met for lunch occasionally. He shared stories he was writing. I noticed he had stopped chewing his nails.

When Audrey Wood came to Colorado for a book signing, I was able to chat with her and thank her, not only for her beautiful books, but also for changing the life of a young boy who needed to find his true voice and know that someone cared what he had to say. Her letter to him lifted the weight of all those labels and gave him new possibilities.

~Caroline S. McKinney

74

The Village

I wondered why somebody didn't do something.
Then I realized, I am somebody.
~Author Unknown

aryan's math teacher approached me a few days after school started and asked, "What is the plan to help Maryan learn math?"

"What do you mean?" This was a question I had never been asked in all of my years as a school counselor.

"Well, her lack of English is not the problem; she simply has zero math skills." He stared at me and waited for an answer. I attempted to grasp what he was saying.

I checked with our district office and got the bad news. There were no math services for ESL students. Somehow, I was now responsible for providing remedial services for math deficiencies for an ESL student.

Maryan was a refugee from Somalia. She had escaped with her sister and brother-in-law. Her mother and other siblings were still in Somalia. Maryan was the age of a high-school sophomore but had never received any formal education. She had only been taught enough language skills in her native language to read sections of the Koran.

She had never been allowed to read anything else or learn any other skills — like math. According to her teacher, she did not even know the concept of counting or how to write numerals. She could not graduate until she could pass both Algebra and Geometry. We had our work cut out for us.

If Maryan was going to have a chance at creating a promising life in America, she needed a high-school diploma. I rolled up my sleeves and went to work to make a plan.

First, I needed to meet Maryan. I invited her to my office and I was stunned when she entered. She was regal. She stood tall, covered from head to toe in the traditional Somali dress for women. Her face shone round and bright, the beautiful fabric of the headdress framing her glowing face. The smile that captured me became a symbol of Maryan's attitude, resourcefulness, and genuine excitement to be alive and allowed to learn.

This young woman displayed a self-confidence and eagerness to succeed like I had never seen before. She truly understood that learning is a great privilege. Maryan told me through broken language and gestures that she wanted to be a nurse. She was willing to do whatever she could to learn math.

My second step was to speak with her math teacher. He was a bit skeptical about Maryan catching up in math when she could not even count! However, he was willing to give it a try. Our plan was for one-on-one tutoring to work with Maryan at her level during his math class time. In other words, he would provide the materials, but I had to find the tutors.

This took me to step three of the plan — the tutors. Public schools and teachers are stretched as thin and far as possible. So, my idea was to turn to the kids! I contacted several gifted students who I knew had an interest in helping and possibly teaching, and who were available during the last period of the day. We came up with a schedule for the tutors. Within one week, we all worked together to have Maryan learning math at her level.

For most of my life, I had known the African proverb, "It takes a village to raise a child." But now I truly saw the proverb in action. The gifted students began to teach Maryan the most basic of math skills — the meaning of math symbols and how to count. One day, I slipped into the room to find Maryan and two gifted students watching *Sesame Street* DVDs. They were counting with "The Count," and laughter filled the room. Laughter truly is an international language.

The tutors began to work on addition flash cards with Maryan and before we knew it they were working on multiplication and division flash cards. Maryan was excelling. Her sharp mind and positive attitude made teaching her a joy.

By Christmas, the tutors were ready to start working basic math problems with Maryan. The math teacher provided harder and harder problems, and by the end of the school year Maryan was ready to tackle Pre-Algebra during summer school. By the beginning of the school year, she was ready to tackle Algebra — making A's for each semester. During Maryan's senior year, she took Geometry — making A's and B's for each semester. Maryan graduated on time, having learned English and math among all of the other required classes and subjects. She packed twelve years of learning into three.

As Maryan walked across the stage at graduation, I could not help but feel joy and pride. We all felt like we had been a part of something very special. Together, we helped this beautiful, poised child grow into a successful student. She was ready to go to the next level of learning, and in fact she enrolled in community college in the fall with a focus on pre-nursing.

It took a village to get her ready to soar — a team of teachers, fellow students and, yes, a school counselor. I had almost choked when I was told it would be up to me to provide Maryan with remedial math help. However, I found that by sharing the load, it was not heavy. With all of us working together, it had not been a burden at all. It had been a joy, as a village, to work with this young, motivated Somali immigrant and put her on her chosen path to helping others.

~Gwyn Schneck

75

A Hawk in a Pigeonhole

*Preconceived notions are the locks
on the door to wisdom.*
~Merry Browne

"Advisory" was my least favorite part of the day. After more than twenty years as an English teacher, how did my principal expect me to suddenly get the hang of counseling a group of fourteen-year-olds about their emotional issues? I felt totally under-qualified. Nevertheless, every Friday afternoon, I sat on the carpet in a circle with my students and listened, arranging my face in an expression of concern and caring as the kids shared complaints about too much homework and sibling rivalries.

Hannah raised her hand. "I have something important I want to say." She blew her bangs out of her eyes. Dressed in oversized jeans and a flannel shirt and sporting a close-cropped haircut, she was the epitome of grunge. Hannah was usually shy about speaking out in the group, so we all sat up and paid close attention to her soft voice. But I, for one, was totally unprepared for what she was about to say.

Her next words changed me, changed the way I relate to my students, and changed my perceptions of my world.

"Most of you know me as Hannah, but I'm asking you not to call me that anymore. That is not my name." I furrowed my brow. What was going on here? It was a Friday, the last class period of the day. Parents were already lining up in their cars outside.

"My name is Henry. I would like you to call me that from now on."

Blinking, I realized that "under-qualified" didn't even skim the surface of how poorly equipped I was to understand and support this conversation.

"I am a boy," Hannah — no, Henry — stated. "I have always felt like a boy, and now I want everyone to recognize me as a boy. I've never been comfortable being called a girl because I am not one. My parents support me, and I really hope you all will, too."

I braced myself for snickering and whispered comments. But the circle of students was dead silent.

"This moment is something that I've been dreading for years, but also looking forward to. This moment is when I finally have the courage to tell you all who I really am. I'm proud of who I am. I'm proud to be Henry."

Nobody spoke. I figured that as the teacher it was up to me to say something. I just couldn't think of what. My mouth opened and closed uselessly. Finally, the guy sitting next to Henry put an arm on his friend's shoulder. "I always knew it," he said.

Marcus, the toughest kid in eighth grade, had a funny look on his face. It almost looked like he was tearing up. He uncrossed his arms and began to applaud, and the others joined in.

Henry beamed. At fourteen, this kid had accomplished something in a few short sentences that most adults would never be brave enough to manage.

The students took Henry's declaration in stride. They patted Henry on the back, told him "good job," and wished him a relaxing weekend. His friends hugged him and told him they were proud, and the other kids looked on with a detached tolerance.

It was the adults, like me, who seemed to have the hardest time processing the information. How could Henry have suffered like that, living his whole life as a sham, and how could we possibly help him?

In time, I managed to remember to use "him" and "he" each time I spoke about Henry, but it was with growing discomfort that I looked back upon my mistakes of the past, or worse, my incapacity to see that a child who I taught every day was in conflict.

How many papers had I received already from that student where he had typed only his last name, ashamed to write down the female name he no longer wanted? How many times had I pitted the "boys against the girls" in an academic competition, and placed him at a table with a gender with which he did not identify?

I remember Henry had come to me two years earlier. He was playing one of the children in the musical I was directing, *The Sound of Music*. Henry, then Hannah, had asked me, "Would it be possible for me to wear pants? I'm not comfortable in a dress."

"Absolutely not," I answered immediately. "The show is set in the 1930s. All the girls are supposed to wear dresses."

Henry wore pants at the dress rehearsal. The next day, I brought in a dress for him and told him to wear it. I was frustrated during the performance. Every time I looked over at Henry, there he was in his dress, looking like he'd been socked in the face with a dead fish. He was miserable.

Henry's honesty taught me a lesson. True, I've had to learn a lot of newfangled concepts in my twenty-some years of teaching, like how to work an interactive whiteboard and grade lessons online. But most importantly, one student's bravery taught me the most progressive of lessons and gave me the opportunity to learn acceptance.

As teachers, we need to put aside our preconceived notions and stop putting students in boxes that we've created. It took a courageous fourteen-year-old for me to recognize that I was the one who was living the sham by deciding who was who, and contributing to the blind categorization of kids rather than admiring each individual for who she, or he, truly is.

Later, after I learned the truth, I apologized to Henry for forcing him into that dress and making him sing "Climb Every Mountain" in operatic falsetto. He shrugged. "That's okay. You didn't know." True. But today, because of Henry, I know better.

~Ilana Long

76

La Profesora de Inglés

It is better to fail in originality than
to succeed in imitation.
~Herman Melville

I was "a desperation hire" — a certified teacher brought on just days before the school year began — a warm body filling an empty slot. I, too, was desperate — desperate for a job and for work that would change my routine and be an adventure. I wanted to do something that involved risk and would let me feel passionate about my work. So, during an impetuous moment in mid-August, I resigned from a comfortable college teaching position, moved across the state of Texas, and found myself inside a high-school classroom.

The classroom was barren save for a small metal desk and a decrepit, peeling Formica bookcase. Dog-eared hardcover books were strewn in ramshackle order across one of its shelves, their dust jackets missing. Tattered paperbacks, their corners curled up and their pages crumbling, were thrown haphazardly on top of each other like a game of *Jenga*. I walked closer to read their covers; they weren't in English. Odd.

"Are you there?" Someone banged on my door. It was Penny, my department chair. "I have your literature books!" She pushed a cart toward me, parking it adjacent to my desk. "Remember, your freshmen must look at these each day; they must write in their journals twice a week and..." Penny squared her shoulders. "...one more thing. The curriculum guide's inside your desk. Follow it! *No* exceptions! It'll take them where they need to go. Understand?"

"Yes, ma'am."

Penny marched out of my room. I placed a literature book on top of each scarred and weary desk, slid into one of them, and opened the monstrous volume, captivated by its contents — classic short stories, ancient myths, *Romeo and Juliet*, and excerpts from *The Odyssey*. The morning bell sounded, jangling my nerves and jarring me from my seat. Within minutes, rambunctious freshmen clamored past me and took their seats. The tardy bell rang, and they settled down. The school year had officially begun.

During that first week, I followed the curriculum guide. Monday, I lectured on the five elements of fiction, and my students robotically copied my notes from the chalkboard into their notebooks. Tuesday, I read aloud from the literature book. When I turned a page, so did my students. When I asked questions, some students raised their hands and answered; most, though, merely nodded and smiled. During Wednesday's journal-writing activity, some students wrote; most just smiled, pretending to write. Although fidgety, my students were quiet, respectful, and compliant. Their faces, though, were full of eagerness — the kind of eagerness a teacher yearns for.

On Thursday, even after the air-conditioner in my classroom stalled, I continued reading aloud from the literature book. But the August sun that perched over the Chihuahuan Desert poured its hot oranges and reds into the sky like a pot of molten lava, making my classroom beastly hot. My freshmen squirmed in their seats, so I ushered them outside to a nearby bench where they nestled around me like eager baby ducklings. I resumed reading, but then one of my students stood up, pointed to the west, and shouted, *"El Diablo, El Diablo!"*

I shaded my eyes and peered across the desert. A trio of dust devils materialized in the distance — whirling dervishes of what looked like columns of smoke moving across the *despoblado* — the deserted land — between the high school and nearby Mexico.

"*El Diablo…*" Another student tugged on my shirt sleeve. "*…trae mala suerte!*"

"What?" I shook my head in desperation. "I don't understand!"

"*El Diablo trae mala suerte!*"

I politely nodded my head and smiled. At that moment, I realized that I'd mistaken their polite smiles, nods, and silent compliance as comprehension. The now obvious truth was that I was teaching in a border community where most of my students spoke *no* English. I spoke *no* Spanish. What a quandary! But my students' eagerness tugged on my heartstrings. I desperately wanted to teach them English, *but how?*

Later that afternoon while standing in line at the grocery store, I riffled through the magazine rack and stumbled upon a comic book. I thumbed through it, attracted to its colorful pages, action scenes, and easy-to-read dialog. I was about to return it to the rack when I noticed that it contained many fundamental literary elements. Ah-ha! I'd found a solution to my dilemma. But what about the literature book and curriculum? Abandoning them would get me in trouble with Penny and was certainly a risk, but I was excited and didn't care. So before returning to school, I purchased every comic book I could find.

I returned to my classroom and secretly took concepts from the existing curriculum and created my own using comic books as the context for teaching simple vocabulary, verbs, sentence structure, dialogue, myths, the hero archetype, and the elements of fiction. By semester's end, my students were confidently reading and constructing sentences.

But despite their progress, my freshmen still couldn't read from the ninth grade literature book — a fact that displeased Penny. "I told you to use the textbook and curriculum guide. *No* exceptions. Instead," she said, "you undermined me with your unconventional tactics. Why? What were you thinking?"

"I remember you telling me that the textbook and curriculum would take my students where they needed to go. I believed you and wanted to do as you requested. But my students spoke and read no English. Without English, I couldn't take them where they needed to go until I got them where they were supposed to be. But you're right," I tried to appease her, "I was wrong in not bringing my plan to you. Please understand, I was desperate to teach them English. I meant no harm."

"No matter your intentions, I'm not recommending you be re-hired." She stormed out of my room.

Figuring I had nothing to lose, I packed away the ninth grade literature books, replacing them with some seventh grade readers I'd unearthed in the bookroom. By year's end, my students easily read at the seventh grade level. And they were increasingly confident and performed better in their other classes. How far they'd come! Even so, at my end-of-the year review, I expected harsh words from my principal followed by termination.

"I don't agree with your unorthodox methodology," he began, "but I admire your willingness to take personal risk on your students' behalf. I'm pleased with their progress. So, I'm renewing your contract — with one condition. You agree to teach the same students until they graduate."

I agreed. During the next three years, I took my students from where they were to where they needed to be. After their graduation, I reflected upon the act of desperation that brought me to them. Since arriving, I found what I'd sought: I changed my routine and surroundings; found adventure; did the uncomfortable; risked the uncertain; and found passionate work.

But, most importantly, I discovered what matters most in a classroom is neither the curriculum nor the books. Rather, it's an impassioned teacher with the real stuff inside — one who's willing to take risks and help students discover the real stuff inside themselves. And I learned what *trae mala suerte* means in English: "it brings bad luck." The only thing that would have brought us bad luck would have been my continued use of the *ordinary* curriculum with my truly *extraordinary* students.

~Sara Etgen-Baker

77

A Good Warmer-Upper

I don't really think in terms of obstacles. My
biggest obstacle is always myself.
~Steve Earle

One late summer day, Jason appeared in the junior-high learning center to take academic assessments for the upcoming school year. Toothpick slim, with wavy dark hair and dancing blue eyes, he possessed none of the usual adolescent awkwardness. In fact, he seemed bent on charming me as I administered the tests designed to reveal grade-level performance and learning gaps. However, when I checked his work, my heart sank. In the language section, numerous gaps appeared. In fact, his grammar skills revealed major deficits.

When I went over the results with him, I wasn't sure how to explain his low scores without impairing his will to succeed. I hemmed and hawed, and finally resorted to the classic question, "How do you think you did on the language portion?"

Jason wiggled around in his chair, grinned, and said, "Well, Mrs. Johns, what I think I need is a good warmer-upper!"

Inwardly, I smiled at his optimistic confession. His cheerful attitude gave me hope, because a willing heart can overcome all sorts of obstacles, including missing language skills. I chose to believe the best for this engaging young man who wanted so badly to succeed.

At the time, I had no inkling of how he would help me in the years to come.

As the school year began, Jason made fine progress in closing the gaps, although it was never fast enough for him. He was crushed by not being on grade level, and he continually fought feelings of inadequacy and failure. Fortunately, our school had a sports program, and his natural athleticism caused him to succeed in soccer and basketball. For the next couple of years, his sports performance helped offset his dread about all things academic.

Our small, private school was an updated version of the one-room schoolhouse concept. Since the junior high and high school students were grouped together, it was possible for a teacher to have the same students for several years. By the time Jason reached high school, his learning gaps had long since disappeared. With satisfaction, I observed him plow through grade-level academic skills with grit and hard-won confidence.

Then came the dreaded required elective — speech. In spite of his quick mind and athletic ability, speech was a hurdle he would rather not jump. However, over the years, I had learned that the same people who would rather throw up than speak in public would gladly role-play in dramatic productions. With that in mind, I presented a good warmer-upper.

Dramatic competition was a popular event at our annual Student Convention, so I wrote a one-act play and offered Jason an acting option. He accepted and received a lot of positive reinforcement for his character of a grumpy walrus who, symbolically speaking, ate his problems. After that, his issues with public speaking vanished. In the following years, he gave speeches, recited poetry, wrote essays, and won several awards. His innate leadership skills flourished with platform time. He was a bright light, a star performer in our school.

Then, a huge setback occurred. At least, it seemed that way at the time. Jason and his girlfriend married when he was a junior in high school. His future threatened to derail with the challenges of being a teenage husband with a baby on the way. Nevertheless, we rallied and provided the support he and his wife needed. They graduated with honor and dignity.

My contact with Jason diminished after graduation. Occasionally, I would see him at a basketball game, and once he called me with a random question about poetry. His confidence in my knowledge of language-related topics warmed my heart.

Three years later, enrollment at the school had decreased to the point where we were unable to operate in the students' best interests. Nevertheless, closing the school was a heart-rending decision for me. For thirteen years, the school had been my life. I had the privilege of working at a place where people loved and respected me. Now that those doors were closed, what would I do?

The next fall, I enrolled at the local university. Although I pursued a long-time dream of obtaining a master's degree, it proved difficult. I was a nobody at the college, a lowly graduate assistant who performed grunt work for professors. When I made copies, ran errands, and graded papers for someone else, it felt like I had taken several steps backward.

One especially discouraging day, I wandered through the basement of the university library, attempting to do a professor's irksome chore. The tomb-like atmosphere pressed down on me. I felt buried alive, overwhelmed with graduate studies, wasting my time on a fool's errand. I couldn't find my destination and there was no one to ask for directions. The room I was looking for seemed to have floated away like a ghost.

Then I heard someone speaking. I doubted the speaker had anything to do with the missing room, but the sound might lead me to people who could help. Soon, I glimpsed college kids leaning against a building wall at one end of a nearby courtyard, collectively paying attention to the unseen voice. Rays of sunlight permeated this patch of basement, an odd anomaly.

I waded through students and peeked into the crowded room. To my utter surprise and joy, I saw that Jason was the speaker. His blue eyes flashed warmly as he addressed the audience; the listeners seemed enthralled.

I slipped away after a few minutes, but my heart soared. In spite of the odds, Jason was in his element, achieving his dreams. Before I left the scene, I asked a student about the meeting. He explained that the president was outlining the year's goals for the Student Council.

I smiled. That sounded just like Jason.

In a moment, my personal perspective shifted from despair to a can-do attitude. Seeing a former student flourish gave me what I needed to push through the challenges of graduate school. With perfect timing, Jason provided what I needed most to get me back on track — a good warmer-upper.

~Mary Pat Johns

78

I Can Hear You Now

You have brains in your head. You have feet in
your shoes. You can steer yourself
any direction you choose.
~Dr. Seuss, Oh, the Places You'll Go!

fter recess one day, I realized Christopher hadn't returned to class. I sent a couple of boys to check in the restroom for him. They returned almost instantly. "He's in the bathroom crying and he has locked himself in the stall," they reported.

Of course, I needed to retrieve him. As I approached the restroom, I could hear his sobs. "Chris, it's Mrs. Boyer. What's the matter? I know you're in there. Why are you crying?"

"Dhose boys kweep making fun of me at weecess. Dhey cawed me Dummy and said I tok stwange."

"Okay, Christopher, I will talk to those boys who are making fun of you. It's time for you to come back to class."

Reluctantly, he opened the stall door. Tears streamed down his face.

"Teacer, I don't want to come to skool. It's too hard, and nobowdy yikes me."

I needed to learn more about Christopher so I could help him. I talked to his mom. She told me her son didn't start talking until he was almost two. She had her hands full as a single mom, raising Chris and his sister while working two jobs. She also didn't speak English well, so helping him with homework would be difficult.

I felt bad for Christopher. Yes, he *did* talk funny. He had repeated first grade and struggled with academics. He worked with the speech teacher daily. Frequently, he would stutter and mispronounce words, making it difficult to understand him.

Many of Christopher's assignments were turned in with pictures drawn around the margins. Chris did have a gift. He was a talented artist. So, I asked him if he could tell stories with his artwork. Aha! Maybe this was what he needed to bolster his self-esteem. He came alive when he was drawing.

One day, during reading group, I noticed Christopher staring at the other students while they read. He kept watching their lips. I asked the speech teacher to observe Chris during reading time.

"It looks like he's lip reading," she said.

So, we decided to have his hearing checked. The hearing test indicated that Christopher had substantial hearing loss in both ears! No wonder he couldn't *talk*; he couldn't *hear*. He qualified for hearing aids through an assistance program.

The first time Chris came to class wearing his hearing aids, he had a baseball cap pulled down over his ears, but I could see how excited he was to be able to hear. During story time, he sat mesmerized as I read a Dr. Seuss book. After hearing the story, he came up to me.

"Thank you, Mrs. Boyer, for helping me. Now I can hear you read *Oh, the Places You'll Go!* I like that story!"

What a difference the hearing aids made for Christopher! His speech started improving, too.

For the first time, he wanted to participate in class discussions. He told me by the end of second grade that reading was his favorite subject.

I was switching to third grade the next year, so I requested that Christopher be in my class again. I wanted to make sure that he had every opportunity to succeed. My class became involved in a wonderful project where they wrote and illustrated books to be given to doctors' offices for their waiting rooms. The children were so excited to write their own stories, and everyone wanted Chris to draw the illustrations to go with the stories.

Beaming with pride, he announced he wanted to be an illustrator of children's books when he grew up.

I was blown away when Christopher volunteered to speak at an event to thank teachers, principals, and local business owners who had given him a computer to use at home for his schoolwork. He now had the courage to speak in front of a group to express his gratitude for what he had been given.

As Christopher stood at the podium, speaking with confidence and appreciation, tears streamed down my face. Christopher had blossomed and grown into a confident and happy boy. He had come a long way. He just needed the tools to have a chance.

I was a teacher for twenty-five years, and Christopher was one of those students who taught me more than I could ever teach him. Thank you, Christopher, for teaching me to never give up and always have hope, no matter how difficult things get. I can hear you now.

~Patricia Boyer

79

Seeing Us

You can observe a lot by just watching.
~Yogi Berra

Sometimes, I ask my students what they see. My senior creative-writing students, especially, have fun with this exercise. I teach them that a writer is a person on whom nothing is lost (thank you, Henry James) and then assign an exercise in which they must describe one of their teachers in detail as though he or she were a character on the page. Their peers then guess the teacher. I learn a lot about my colleagues through this exercise. About myself even.

This year, after my students had shared their work aloud and guessed the name of each other's subjects, my student Niko said, "I wanted to write about you, Ms. Flaherty."

I chuckled. "You could've."

"Really?" he asked, his face — and several faces in the class — suddenly alight with refreshed interest.

"Yeah, it's okay," I said. "We all have our things, and there's no judgment in that. You look at me every day. Tell me what details make my character."

A beat passed. Then Natalie raised her hand. "You sit like that all the time."

I looked down. I was seated in my office chair at the front of the room. One leg was tucked under me, and the other was crossed over the tucked knee.

"Ugh! I was gonna say that," Niko said from the back.

Rachael raised her hand. "You change your shoes according to your mood. I've, like, seen you go behind your desk and change them during class."

I nodded. True. Sometimes I tired of high heels and changed to flats while no one was looking — or so I thought.

"No, but it isn't just that," Natalie said. "You, like — your outfits are always coordinated. Everything goes together in, like, a specific way."

Rachael nodded.

They were just warming up.

"But it seems like your outfits reflect your mood for the day," Natalie continued. "It's like you wake up and say, 'Today, I feel sassy,' and then dress to fit that."

As she said that, I was wearing a black skirt with a cropped jean jacket and my tall black boots that looked more rugged than formal. Silver bangles clanked at my left wrist, and a honking garnet ring popped from my right knuckle. My hair was pulled back into an extended ponytail that definitely had some Mohawk DNA to it. I laughed. Sassy, huh?

Devin popped up in his seat. "No offense, but you're very…" He paused as he searched for the right phrase. "…hard on us. You expect a lot. Which is good. And we all know that you're doing it because you want us to be better. And we are better."

"Aw…" Seriously, *awww*.

"But you're mean, too," a boy named Tom countered.

Natalie championed me with, "Nuh-uh," but I hadn't felt offended.

"How so?" I asked Tom.

"I don't know. You're, like, mean to us."

"No, Tom." I shook my head. "I'm mean to *you*."

He spread his hands. "See?"

The class smiled. They had witnessed our repartee before.

"But I do that with you on purpose," I said. "You like to be teased. You like sarcasm. It's like affection for you." Tom's face showed that he conceded the point. "Now, if I did that to her — " I gestured across the room to Kelly, a student I knew to be sensitive. " — I would make her cry."

"That's just it," Natalie jumped in. "You read us. You know the second we stop paying attention. I don't even know that I've zoned out, but you're already telling me to come back. You, like, know us."

I shrugged. "A teacher's trick."

She shook her head. "I don't know. You see it, like, way more and way faster than other teachers."

"And you do this thing when you lose your train of thought," Erin, a girl near the front, started. She lifted her hand and acted it out as she explained in a softening voice, "You touch your hair while you try to remember."

"I do?" I thought back. "Yeah, I do. See, Natalie? You all know me, too."

"You never noticed that before?" Erin said.

"No. Points for originality, Erin. You're definitely paying attention." I re-directed to serve the characterization lesson. "What about other things? What kinds of things do I say?"

"Oh," Rachael made her goofball face. "I got this. You say 'good chat' at the end of things. It isn't always even a conversation. It's just how you end one thing and move to the next."

It was also my response to student non sequiturs.

"Or you, like, drum your fingers," she added.

That was a new observation, too.

"Your voice changes when you read your own writing to us," Natalie added. "Your voice gets — I don't know — more expressive or something."

It made sense. I am most familiar and connected with my own pieces, after all.

"Those were strong observations. You were detailed. Nice work," I said. Some faces said they weren't done teaching me about myself, but it was time to wrap up the lesson. "Keep those sorts of things in mind when you're creating characters. How do they sit? Do they have go-to phrases particular to them? How do they dress, and how does that reflect who they are?"

They nodded, taking it in, but the fun of the exercise had yet to leave their bodies. They were still alert, maybe wondering if I was going to let them go at it again, but the bell rang and their daily, reluctant shift to packing up began. I stayed in my chair, wishing them good days and fist-bumping Devin as he passed to the door.

Overall, I like that exercise. The kids overflow with excitement as they try to guess each other's teacher pick, and it's great for character work. But it also serves to bond the class, which is particularly important in a writing class. I ask my students to be vulnerable when I ask them to share their writing with each other. Something that they created is being thrust forward for criticism, so they have to build that trust. They have to build an *Us*.

Once, a former creative-writing class challenged me to describe them. They really seemed to think they had stumped me. Didn't they know by now that I was a writer? Nothing was lost on me.

"Sure," I agreed. "But let's keep it focused on one thing since there are so many of you. Say, how you move when you read aloud in class." They agreed.

"Okay." I started on one side of the room and moved across. "Danielle always thrusts her notebook onto her knees before she reads aloud." Surprise. Gasps.

"Zach always scoots forward to the edge of his seat as he reads. Brittany fidgets with her fingers and rings." Accuracy. Gasps.

"Bobby pulls at his chin when he's concentrating. Sierra flips her hair to one side and over her shoulder." Wonder. Gasps.

"Should I go on?"

"How do you even see all that?" Bobby asked.

I answered what all teachers know: "I see my students. Every day, I see my students."

~Margaret M. Flaherty

Chapter 9

Inspiration for Teachers

Learning from the Students

Get over the idea that only children should spend their time in study. Be a student so long as you still have something to learn, and this will mean all your life.
~Henry L. Doherty

80

The Shoelaces

I feel the capacity to care is the thing which
gives life its deepest significance.
~Pablo Casals

It was a typical holiday season at school — scraps of ribbon everywhere, candy canes stuck to shoes, and kids as hyper as popcorn kernels in the microwave. How were we — the teachers — ever going to make it to Break?

As a way of promoting service learning, and for students to better understand the reason for the season, my class adopted a thirteen-year-old boy to support. I invited students to contribute a small amount of money or to create handmade gifts. We raised enough to purchase a new pair of sneakers for our adoptee.

One day, after school, I invited volunteers to join me at the local sporting-goods store. When my elves arrived, we walked up and down the aisles, assessing various styles that might appeal to our giftee. We knew the correct size, but no other specifications were provided. My helpers eventually narrowed down the choices to two pairs of Adidas and one pair of Nikes, which caught my eye because of their neon laces. The students giggled at my choice, stating that the laces were just too "out there." I feigned a sad, puppy-dog face, but smiled inside at the camaraderie we had built as a class during this project.

"Laces don't matter if the shoe is good," a voice added. We turned to see Terence standing nearby.

"Hey, T," one friend called.

"When did you sneak in?" another added.

"We're debating the choices. What do you think?" I asked.

He studied the options. He explained how Nikes were designed to support jumpers, specifically basketball players. As an athlete, Terence was respected by his peers, so it was no surprise when a unanimous decision was made.

When school resumed in January, our team received a "Mahalo Letter" from the local charity, which I hung on the bulletin board for all to see. And though the identity of the recipient remained anonymous, the students were happy to know their efforts had made a difference.

One day, Terence approached my desk and asked to borrow a Sharpie. Due to graffiti on campus, the pens were considered contraband, prompting me to ask, "So, what do you need it for?"

He hesitated. "Never mind. I can use a regular one," he said, and walked away. Surprised, but unable to pursue the conversation, I let him go.

Another day passed, and I found Terence elbow deep in a tub of markers. I inquired, "Need some help?"

Shaking his head, he pulled one pen out at a time, drawing a line on scratch paper. "Just cleaning out the dried-up ones," he said.

"Well, thanks. That's a job I always dread," I said.

When he finished, Terence asked, "Can I take these home to work on a project?" I hesitated for fear the supplies might not return. However, I also knew Terence's family probably didn't have many resources, and he had never proved to be untrustworthy, so I agreed.

As he headed out, I caught a glimpse of a long neon string, and what appeared to be the outline of shoes inside a bag. I paused. It was the same neon color as the laces on the shoes we purchased for the holiday donation. Did Terence receive the shoes but was too embarrassed to wear them? Was he using pens to alter their appearance? Was Terence our class's adoptee?

I asked the agency and I was assured that Terence wasn't the recipient of our gift. Still, I was confused and curious about his actions. Pondering the situation while at the drugstore checkout line, I spotted a rack of shoelaces in plain colors. My mind raced to Terence, and

I wondered if new laces would spare him the time it would take to blacken the neon set. I grabbed a black-and-white pair and completed my transaction.

The following day, I asked Terence to wait after class. "Thanks for cleaning out the old markers," I started.

"Yep," he replied, eyeing me suspiciously.

I paused and added, "By the way, I couldn't help but notice the shoes you were carrying last week…" I pulled out a small plastic bag and extended my hand. "Not sure if you could use these or not?"

Terence looked at the black-and-white laces and froze. Had I crossed a line? Was this an insensitive move on my part? I started to retract my hand, but stopped as Terence reached out. He never looked up or spoke, but he accepted the small bag and slid it into his pocket, then left the classroom silently.

The next day, Terence seemed unfazed. He smiled at friends, volunteered to take a note to another classroom, and completed tasks as he had done all year. As students were dismissed, I took special notice of his shoes, expecting to see new Nikes with even newer laces, but was disappointed to spot his normal Converse shoes. *Hmmm*, I thought. *Maybe the laces weren't such a good idea.* Another week went by, but no new shoes appeared. I resigned myself to the fact that perhaps he was using them at home. At least, I thought, our school-based relationship hadn't been compromised.

In late January, a new student enrolled at school. The counselor matched current students with new ones as buddies to show them around campus. Unbeknownst to me, Terence volunteered to be Mitchell's buddy. At recess, the boys stopped by my room. I welcomed Mitchell to our team and thanked Terence for being such a great ambassador. He smiled and shared, "Ms. C always has supplies if you need them." His mention of supplies reminded me of the black markers, hence reminding me of the shoes. Absentmindedly, I looked toward the floor as the boys exited. Terence was still wearing his Converse sneakers, but Mitchell was sporting a new pair of Nikes—with black-and-white laces!

The light bulb went on. Terence wasn't trying to "save face" for himself, but for a friend! Later, I learned that Mitchell's father had been unemployed, but recently moved the family to our town when he secured a job. Terence and Mitchell's families attended the same church, and the boys played ball together. Coincidentally, the church worked in partnership with the charitable organization that solicited donations during the holidays for struggling families. The pieces fell into place. Mitchell settled into our school seamlessly, and no one was the wiser about the shoes, which had been conveniently semi-scuffed. Neither Terence nor I said a word to each other about the laces, but we seemed to share this charitable secret together.

On the last day of school, several students brought goodies for the teachers as tokens of appreciation. I had my fill of cookies, hand-made cards, and coffee gift certificates, but it was the anonymous braided keychain made from bright neon shoelaces that was my most memorable gift of all!

~Sandy Cameli

81

The Perfect Age

*Be on the alert to recognize your prime at whatever
time of your life it may occur.*
~Muriel Spark

The assignment was up on the board for my sixth grade, inner-city students in East Los Angeles: "What is the perfect age, and why would you like to be that age?" As a new, twenty-three-year-old teacher, I spent hours each night reading the latest teaching journals, magazines, and books about helping students reach their potential. I hoped this assignment would be fun but help them think about their futures and what they hoped to achieve in life. I could tell by their expressions that maybe, just maybe, this would do the trick!

They had a half-hour to write this assignment. They did not need to worry about spelling or punctuation at this point. We would revise their stories later after they had written their rough drafts. After a half-hour, I collected their papers. I was excited to see their ideas. I soon found, like all assignments, that some were great, some students did the absolute minimum, but all thought quite a bit about the perfect age!

Billy thought the perfect age was eighteen because he wanted to join the Army. He wanted to see the world and be stationed in Hawaii to see the "hot babes" on the beach. Never mind that this was at the height of the Vietnam War, and I doubt if he would have had the chance to relax on the beaches of Hawaii for long before being deployed to the jungles of Vietnam.

Hilda asked me how old I was. When I told her I was twenty-three, she wrote that she wanted to be the same age. She said she would like to be a sixth grade teacher, wear nice clothes, have long pretty hair, and have fun with her students like I always seemed to do. I am glad it looked like fun to her! She did not realize that since she only read at a third grade level at that time, I was very stressed out to see all of the work I needed to do with her that year so she could become a teacher at twenty-three.

Next was rambunctious Alfonso. He wanted to be twenty-one years old so he could become a famous boxer like he saw on TV. As you know, boxing can be a very bloody battle and many times one of the fighters is knocked unconscious. The thought of sweet Alfonso boxing made me shudder. I hoped that he either became a really great boxer or changed goals before he reached twenty-one.

Several boys wanted to be professional football players to make lots of money. The ages they thought were perfect differed, but the outcomes were the same. They saw professional sports as their way out of the barrio, with lots of money coming their way. Jorge said he would use the money to buy his mom a new home with a bedroom for each member of the family. That would be eight bedrooms!

Polly Maria wanted to be twenty-five. She thought that would be fun because she hoped by then she would be a mom and she loved taking care of children. She helped take care of her brothers and sisters, and her mom said she did a great job. She wanted to have four children, and she would name them Maria Luisa, Maria Ana, Maria Lucia, and Maria Patricia. I guess boys were not in her plan.

Serious Michael wanted to be thirty. He thought by then he would have a business degree from the University of Southern California, his own business, and a beautiful wife. I am sure he has done that and is enjoying a wonderful career with a lovely family.

Quinceañera was a concern for two girls. This is the age when many girls from Latino families have a big coming of age birthday party. So Amelia and Sophia felt this was the best age to be as they were already dreaming about this big event in their lives. At recess, they would sit and talk about their dresses, how they would wear their hair, who they might invite, and which cute boys they might dance with at the reception.

But I will always remember Victoria's story. She was a shy, bright, thoughtful child. She never said much, but you could see her thinking deeply. For this assignment, she sat and thought for ten minutes, then picked up her pencil and wrote something that has stayed with me my whole life. In that assignment, she became the teacher, and I was the student learning from a wise eleven-year-old.

Victoria wrote that every age was the perfect age. She wrote that God designed life that way so we could experience each stage of life. She said that every person deserves to be a beloved baby who is the center of the family's attention. Victoria then said that it is wonderful how we get to experience our first day of school in kindergarten, making friends throughout our school experience, graduating from high school, hopefully getting married, having children, and perhaps living long enough to have grandchildren or even great-grandchildren.

Her paper brought tears to my eyes then and still does now. As a sixty-seven-year-old retired teacher, mom, and grandmother, I have thought of Victoria and her wise words throughout my life. When I am weary or wish I were younger, I remember Victoria's wisdom. God did plan every age to be the perfect age for each of us. He wanted us to have the opportunity to experience every stage of life. Amazingly, Victoria saw that as an eleven-year-old!

~Ginny Huff Conahan

82

Straight from the Heart

Encourage, lift and strengthen one another. For the
positive energy spread to one will be felt by us all.
~Deborah Day

I came back into my classroom after our usual Wednesday afternoon staff meeting and dropped a stack of handouts on my desk. I was tired, but looking forward to our Valentine's party the next day.

Valentine's Day was one of my favorite holidays at school. It was a nice break from the routine of a long New Hampshire winter, and the theme of love came at a time when my fourth graders were most susceptible to its influences. Sure, love from parents and adults was still important. But somewhere around the month of February, the increasing need for peer acceptance and a burgeoning awareness of the opposite sex developed, creating the perfect setting for embarrassed giggles and demure thank-yous as syrupy love notes and prefabricated Valentine puns were torn from their envelopes.

I imagined the students sorting their cards into categories and popping the attached red lollipops into their mouths, feigning indifference to the faded white "Be Mine" messages stamped on them. I knew they would secretly reread the cards and the names on the backs, hoping that at least one of the love notes stamped on the store-bought cards were real sentiments meant specifically for them.

Thinking of this, I smiled and looked around the classroom. Our bulletin boards and walls were decorated with white streamers and pink and red hearts. Heart folders were taped to the fronts of everyone's desk, ready for tomorrow's "mail." Even the digital clock was decorated with paper hearts.

With a start, I noticed the time. My son would be waiting for me at daycare. Time to go. As I picked up my briefcase, I remembered that I had Valentine pencils for everyone in my desk drawer. Things would be hectic tomorrow. Might as well put them in the folders tonight. Tearing off the cardboard seal, I quickly placed one in each person's folder. Finally, I flicked the light switch and locked the door. Little did I know that Valentine's Day would have a whole different meaning in the morning.

I got the call sometime after midnight. I listened to my brother's voice and tried to clear the fog of sleep from my brain. My sister had been in a terrible car accident. She had been going too fast and slammed her car into a highway sign. A passing EMT worker had stopped to help and, noticing that she had a faint pulse, called an ambulance. But the internal bleeding and blow to her head were too much. She died shortly after her arrival at the hospital. My sister, who was only thirty-eight years old — a year younger than me — was gone.

A couple of days later, when the funeral arrangements had been made and reality had penetrated the shock, an assistant with whom I worked closely brought me papers to look through. Among the papers was the Valentine's Day folder I had made for myself. It was filled with cards and small gifts from my students. The simple innocence of the children and their paper cards brought me comfort. Among the Valentine's cards were notes and sympathy cards from the children expressing their feelings about my sister's death. One note touched my heart in particular:

Mrs. Arnault,

I am sorry about what happened to your sister. We are all sad for you. I hope you will get happier soon, but it is okay to cry and be sad. I know I would cry forever if my sister had died.

I hope you will be okay when you are teaching. If you start to cry in school, we will not mind.

I wish life was not so difficult. Maybe you will see your sister in heaven some day long from now. I really hope she is okay, and I hope you are okay. I am sure you and your family are very sad. I wish she could have lived until Valentine's Day, but at least you still have family.

I wish you were here on Valentine's Day at school so we could spend time with you, but I understand how you feel. I hope you had a good Valentine's Day even though it is difficult to go through. I care for you a lot, and I feel so hurt for you. Deep down this is coming from my own heart. I wish I could make you happy, but there is nothing I can do except comfort you. When Mrs. M. told me, my mouth fell down to the ground. Happy Valentine's Day, Mrs. Arnault!

Love, Lauren

I cried when I read this note because it brought back the innocence of my own childhood, a time when I wanted the adults I cared for to be happy. I cried because this one nine-year-old's sincere compassion erased some of my pain. I cried because Lauren's note connected my soul to hers and changed the nature of our relationship.

Lauren was the teacher, and I was the student that Valentine's Day. Her note, typed on a small piece of paper, taught me that love truly can heal all wounds. She taught me the importance of carrying on because there were people in my life who cared for me and depended on me. And every Valentine's Day after that, through fifth grade, sixth grade, seventh grade, and eighth, until Lauren went on to high school, I sought her out to thank her for making paper cards and heart-shaped treats meaningful to me again.

Fourteen years later, her sweet words still reside in a cherished scrapbook dedicated to my sister.

~Catherine J. Arnault

Learning My Lesson

Forgiveness does not change the past,
but it does enlarge the future.
~Paul Boese

I had just received my first long-term teaching assignment days earlier. It was November, and a teacher in an inner-city school had to take an early maternity leave. I was offered the position teaching Core French and Art to Grade Seven and Eight pupils, but I was warned it was a tough assignment. I knew it was in a "rough" part of town. But at twenty-one, I was fresh out of teachers college and full of enthusiasm. I accepted.

I had four classes with over a hundred students to deal with. Some were friendly, and some were quiet and observant, but it seemed that most of the students were loud and disrespectful. All my wonderful lesson plans seemed to go awry as discipline became my number-one priority. My head spun as I tried to identify the "class clowns" with their snickering, inappropriate language and rude body noises. I'm sure it became a challenge to some of them to bring the new teacher down. Needless to say, at one point, I felt they had succeeded, when I found myself weeping in the principal's office, telling her that I couldn't take it anymore.

The principal, a Sister, was very supportive and marched into the classroom, ready to issue suspensions. I was simply to tell her who the culprits were. The class settled down and she left, advising me to send her anyone who was being disrespectful.

I began reviewing French vocabulary and was asking simple questions relating to Christmas. "What will you give your mother for Christmas?" My eyes scanned the classroom. Several pupils (the ones who had never given me any trouble) had their hands up. Others had bored looks and were doodling in their notebooks. Others simply had their heads down. I decided to single out one of the pupils with his head down, Robert.

"*Robert, qu'est-ce que tu vas donner à ta mère pour Noël?*"

The pupils with their heads down looked up. The others stopped doodling and stared at me. *Progress,* I thought with satisfaction. I finally had their undivided attention. I turned to Robert.

Robert had looked up, but his face, unlike the others, had contorted into a mask of pain. "I hate you!" he cried, and ran from the room.

What had I done? Stunned, I met the sea of frozen, unbelieving faces in the room.

"His mother committed suicide, Miss," one of the girls near me said softly.

I wanted to cry. "I didn't know," I murmured in shock. "I didn't know."

Why, of all the pupils in the class, did I have to call on Robert? If I had known about his mother, I would never have used that question as an example. I felt heartbroken and battered, crushed and alone. *Poor Robert,* I wept inwardly. *How must he be feeling?*

The next few moments were a blur. Robert ran to the principal's office, and she came back to the classroom, allowing me to speak to him privately in her office. His body was slumped in sorrow. I did the only thing I could do: I spoke to him from my heart. I told him how sorry I was, that I hadn't known, and that I would never have wanted to hurt him or anybody in that way. I asked him for forgiveness.

Over the years, I have learned that when you speak from the heart, pupils listen. Robert believed me. I think he saw his pain reflected in my eyes. He sensed my sincerity and genuine sorrow. Robert taught me that you can't assume that everyone in your class has a mother and father; that you should find out as much as you can about the students you will have in your care; that pupils have histories that are filled with pain and loss; and that you have to remember that you are not teaching "subjects," but human beings with feelings and vulnerabilities.

As I struggled with the challenges and the shifting personalities of many students that first year, I realized that teaching was always going to be a learning and shifting experience, with successes and mistakes, triumphs and tribulations. Lessons to teach and lessons to learn.

Robert gave me my first gift as a teacher: the gift of forgiveness. And a lesson I'll never forget.

~Rosanna Micelotta Battigelli

84

Practicing What I Teach

*You gain strength, courage and confidence by
every experience in which you really
stop to look fear in the face.*
~Eleanor Roosevelt

ast fall, I accepted a position as an English instructor at a high school for students who are gifted in the arts and technology. During freshman orientation, my department chair, Dr. Cunningham, introduced members of the English and Literary Arts faculty to the parents of entering students. She introduced us individually, by first and last name, and emphasized our published work in the genres of poetry, fiction, and creative nonfiction.

"As you can see," said Dr. Cunningham, "our faculty members are out in the publishing world pursuing their own writing goals. Here at this school, we practice what we teach."

I loved her introduction and the concept of "practicing what we teach." I felt like this job was going to be a great fit for me personally and professionally.

Switching schools can be difficult for even the most seasoned educators, but overall my transition was smooth. I quickly learned my students' names and focus areas, prepared my lesson plans for the first few weeks, and introduced myself to other members of the faculty.

My students and I got into our routine of reading some classics, studying vocabulary, and analyzing nonfiction articles. After each unit, I assigned a paper, test, or project that allowed students to incorporate their art. Additionally, I required my students to read some of their work aloud. I felt that it was a great experience, preparing them for college and the workforce.

One day, a sophomore named Amber was reading her vignette for the class. I was jotting down a few notes as she spoke, in order to provide her with accurate and timely feedback. But as she continued, I was so captivated by her words that I could no longer take notes. She had my full attention.

"For some of you, this won't make the tiniest bit of sense," Amber read. "For others, this could quite possibly be the most relatable thing you've ever heard. I struggle to find the words to explain to you why I am the way that I am. I'm not even sure those words exist. I am stuck in an eternal in-between, sandwiched between the loud mouths and the loud minds."

She definitely had my attention as she continued reading.

"I am desperate. Desperate to get away from the feeling, the constant suffocation, the never-ending fear. Yet I stay. I stay fighting to get out of the eternal in-between. I stay, perfecting the words I will probably never have the nerve to say."

Amber concluded her piece, entitled "Social Anxiety," and returned to her seat. For the rest of the day, I thought about her vignette, how difficult she found it to speak in public and the fact that she did it anyway. I was impressed with her ability to convey her feelings, and I felt a bit guilty for not treating public speaking with more care.

About a month later, I received an e-mail from my department chair asking me if I would like to participate in the upcoming faculty readings. The readings are an annual, school-wide assembly in which instructors of the English and Literary Arts department read their original work.

"Would you like to read one of your essays?" Dr. Cunningham asked. "It's optional, but most people in the department participate. It's a great way to promote our upcoming Writer's Fest."

I asked her if I could think about it for a while. I thought about how much I despise public speaking (yes, even though I am a teacher) and that I had never read my own work in front of a crowd. For this particular reading, my audience would be the entire student body and members of the faculty: a total of about 400 people. The thought was horrifying. I envisioned myself sharing my raw, original thoughts and words with everyone and realized... it was exactly what I require of my students — all the time.

At that moment, I thought about Amber and her piece on social anxiety, and I e-mailed my department chair to tell her that I was going to participate, even though I felt a little queasy about it. I knew it was the perfect opportunity to show my students that I was willing to take on challenges similar to the ones I asked of them.

On the day of the readings, I shared an essay about my son and my lack of artistic abilities. My students and colleagues laughed at my punch lines and clapped when I was finished. Overall, it was a successful experience.

It reminded me that my job is so much bigger than lecturing, testing, and imparting knowledge. It's about connecting with my students, serving as a positive role model for them, and learning with them. And one of the best ways to do that is to practice what I teach.

~Melissa Face

85

Lighting the Way to Tomorrow

Life is a circle. The end of one journey
is the beginning of the next.
~Joseph M. Marshall III,
The Journey of Crazy Horse: A Lakota History

It has been many years since I locked the door to my fifth grade classroom for the last time. My students are adults now and have gone on with their lives, as I have gone on with mine. But every now and then, I have the privilege of running into one of my former students. Sometimes I have to look closely to recognize them. They are not ten years old anymore.

One afternoon I stopped by the district office for a meeting and I was sure the young woman sitting behind the desk was one of my former students. I glanced at her nameplate and recognized the name immediately. Carol. Yes, of course.

"Do you remember me, Mrs. De Maci?" she asked.

"Denim blue is the color of my favorite jeans," I replied, reciting a line from one of the color poems she had written in class.

"How did you remember that?" she exclaimed, quite surprised.

"Just lucky, I guess," I responded, with a teacher-remembers-all grin.

For some reason, after all these years, I can still remember some of the poems that my students wrote. I treasure them.

I could also recall Carol sitting in the front row of the classroom, in a seat nearest the window, her pencil moving across the page in sync with the other students in class. This was always a special time for me, observing the beauty of young scholars at work and wondering where their lives would take them.

I ran into another student one morning, standing next to her in line at the pharmacy. Margaret had loved to write.

She was now a junior in college, having exchanged her navy-blue-and-white school uniform for a colorful skirt and sweater. "Are you still writing?" I asked her.

"No," she countered. "I think term papers have taken a lot of that out of me."

"Promise me you'll find a few minutes here and there to write a poem or short story just for fun," I urged. Margaret had such a flair for words. A true gift.

Another time I was waiting in a doctor's exam room and there was something familiar about the nurse: the way she moved and talked and… smiled.

"It's me, Mrs. De Maci. Sara."

"Sara? How are you? I see you're doing well," I said, smiling back.

I didn't remember her mentioning that she wanted to be a nurse. But here she was, clearly at home in her chosen profession. I thought about Sara all the way home. I was so happy that she was happy.

At Mass one Sunday morning I was sitting in the second pew behind a broad-shouldered Marine in uniform. His presence was palpable. I felt a surge of pride wash over me.

There's a part of the Mass where we stand and offer one another a sign of peace — usually a handshake or a hug. This beautiful young man in front of me turned around and offered me his hand.

"Do you remember me, Mrs. De Maci?" he asked.

"Tell me your name," I whispered, holding his hand in mine.

"Joseph."

My eyes filled with tears, my heart full of admiration and awe for this brave young man who stood before me in the uniform of our country. He had come home early from his tour of duty because he had fallen ill. I hugged him tightly, seeing him sitting in his blue-and-white school uniform in the third row right behind Jennifer.

"I'm so proud of you, Joseph," I said, not wanting to let go of his hand. And for a moment we were both back in that fifth grade classroom where life seemed simpler, and there was almost always peace.

I have never forgotten that special day. And I have never forgotten him. He has seeded himself somewhere down deep in my soul, touching that place in my heart reserved "For Teachers Only."

I have come to realize that once upon a time I was taking care of them — these students who sat before me every day with questioning faces. I had graham crackers in my desk drawer in case they hadn't had time for breakfast. I made sure they put on their sweaters at recess because it was chilly outside. I walked them across the playground to the campus library, assuring them that reading was a path to freedom and a better life.

And at the end of the day, I said goodbye to them. "See you in the morning. Take care of yourself."

And now these young men and women were taking care of me. Helping me fill out forms so I could continue on my road to retirement. Taking my blood pressure and temperature so I could remain well. Fighting for my freedom in a faraway land so I could live in a country that has given all of us so much.

I would have liked to thank Joseph, Carol, Margaret, and Sara — as well as each and every one of my students over the years. Thank you for coming into my life and teaching me how to love... and thank you for giving me hope for a better world.

You were all special.

~Lola Di Giulio De Maci

86

Preschool Peer Mentoring

Perseverance is failing nineteen times
and succeeding the twentieth.
~Julie Andrews

I heard my name being called and turned just as the young boy crashed into me. With a big bear hug and a smiling face, he said once more, "Whhhhhhhen-D!"

"Michael, how are you?"

Before he could answer, another voice spoke. "Michael, why are you in the hallway?"

Then she turned to me. "May I help you?"

I introduced myself. I was from the childcare center down the street and had an appointment with the kindergarten teacher. Michael had been in my preschool and then Junior Kindergarten three years ago.

She visibly relaxed. I was about to say goodbye when she asked, "Do you have time to visit our classroom?" I accepted the invitation.

The second grade children were busy at various tables. "In the afternoon, they do group work."

"Whhhhhhen-d, look, look!" Michael grabbed my hand and pulled me over to his group's table.

I spent a few minutes with him, viewed all of the students' projects, shared one last bear hug, and then thanked his teacher before leaving. I couldn't help but smile — he'd come such a long way.

Before Michael came to us, his assigned specialist advised us that Michael's long-term prognosis was still uncertain. Michael was six months old when an accident had occurred. The resulting injuries caused significant brain damage.

There were delays in all areas of development, but the most significant one was that he could not walk. He scooted around by crawling. The specialist felt that although there was no certainty of success, Michael should aim to stand independently and then move on to walking. She also specified that he should wear a white helmet during the days to protect him from any further head injury.

By the end of his first year with us, Michael showed improvement in all developmental areas, the most dramatic one being able to walk independently. He had an uneven gait, but it was improving.

The following spring, it was suggested that we encourage him to pedal a tricycle. This would strengthen his legs and help him with his walking. Initially, Michael resisted our attempts to encourage him to use the pedals on the tricycle. He preferred to use his feet to propel himself forward. By mid-June, though, he started to use the tricycle pedals.

Unfortunately, one of the other children crashed into Michael. His tricycle tipped over, and although he was not hurt, he refused to go near the tricycle after that. Michael became interested in something else.

The playground slide had steps that led up to a twelve-foot walkway and then to the slide itself. Michael wanted to make it up those steps. Each day, he returned to the steps to practice. Then one day, it happened. First step, second step, third, fourth, and up he went. The girl who had been in front of him and was now at the top of the steps looked back at him and said, "Come on, it's easy!" There were claps and cheers when he made it to the top.

Then, as Michael faltered and considered whether he should try the slide as well, the little girl said, "Here, let me go first. I'll sit down, and you sit behind me. That's what we do with my little brother."

She sat down, spread her legs so they each touched the inside edge of the slide, and held onto the slide's edge. With Michael sitting behind her, they went very slowly down the slide. When they reached the bottom, Michael turned around with the biggest smile that could ever be on a child's face, looked at me, and said, "WHHHHHHHEN-D, I did it!"

Although this story is about Michael, it is also about that little girl named Shelby. Michael's determination to succeed did propel him forward on that day, but it also happened because Shelby recognized his hesitation, encouraged him, and competently used her own past experience to support him as he successfully achieved his goal. She had stepped into the role of mentor and, in doing so, reminded me that we are all teachers — and we are all learners.

~Wendy Poole

87

A Student's Student

Every great achiever is inspired by a great mentor.
~Lailah Gifty Akita

I attended a small Catholic school in north Seattle, and as early as middle school I knew that I wanted to be a fiction writer when I grew up. Instead, I became a teacher, and seven years into my teaching career at a small Catholic school in West Seattle, I finally decided to give up my writing dream.

It didn't mean I stopped writing altogether, but it meant giving up on my first novel, which I had barely started, unless writing the first chapter eighteen times counts for something. Then one spring, four years later, my seventh graders and I had the privilege of meeting bestselling author Jamie Ford. After hearing his advice about writing award-winning stories, I revisited my old dream.

I created a novel-writing project the following September when my seventh grade students became my eighth graders. Each week, during language-arts class, my students spent an hour writing stories and sharing their work in small groups. During that hour, I told them that I, their teacher, would be doing the same assignment. They were excited to have me working alongside them in solidarity.

Little did they know that during this hour, I ended up writing e-mails to parents and staff. I planned the next day's lesson, graded papers, and shopped online — for academic products, of course.

Enter Kellen, an energetic eighth grader full of encouragement, which he employed to push himself and his classmates to be the best they could be. He loved sports, and as much as he was an athlete, he was also a coach.

During a story-writing period, he approached me with a question about his book and caught me doing teacher work. He called me out immediately.

"Hey! You're not writing!" he exclaimed, both excited and disappointed he'd caught the teacher off task.

I admitted it and switched my screen back to my novel.

All was well until he caught me a second time during a different writing session. Again, I had no excuse. I went back to work, and this time I wrote wholeheartedly, truly working on my novel — the one that had been on the back burner for the last four years. Then it hit me — plot direction, a core theme and, most importantly, an idea for a second chapter. And a third. In fact, a blur of rising action came into focus, and I was rapidly imagining my story unfolding. I felt like I had just crossed that threshold when a book goes from an idea to a full vision that just needs to be written and modified instead of created from scratch.

What struck me even more in that moment, however, was the realization that I needed someone to push me to write. Why not Kellen?

I've had many voices in my life tell me to keep writing, but it became clear that I needed a new voice — someone other than my family and friends. I never thought that voice would come from a student of mine, but who better to own my accountability than someone for whom I'm supposed to be an example of studiousness and turning in work on time?

In my class, as in many others, each student has a job, whether it's erasing the whiteboard, washing lunchroom tables, or putting up chairs at the end of the day. Thinking out loud right in front of Kellen, I said, "Maybe I should add a new class job where someone assigns me writing homework."

"Can that be my job?" he requested with wide-eyed eagerness.

"I think you'd be the right person," I said.

Thus, the "professor" job was born.

At first, my fourteen-year-old professor started me off at two pages a week. Then over Christmas break, he assigned me ten pages — a goal I failed to meet during the two-week hiatus. But Kellen wouldn't let me quit. He gave me assignment after assignment, all the while speaking encouraging words: "Quitting is not an option." "Find a way, like you always do."

One time, I asked him how he found the professor job, and of course he said he loved it. Then I asked, "Do you love it because you get to give your teacher homework or for some other reason?"

He looked at me in all sincerity and said, "You should write. You need to write."

At that moment, I took his belief in me and made it my own. A slew of accomplishments followed in the next few months. Once struggling to write ten pages in two weeks, I knocked out eight in a single night. I frequented coffee shops around Seattle as an incentive to get my assignments done. Before I knew it, I had fifty pages completed, then seventy-five, and finally, five months after becoming my student's student, I realized an old dream — completing a first draft of 109 pages, nearly 65,000 words.

I had always considered myself a writer, but thanks to Kellen, I finally consider myself a novelist. Since he became my professor, my dormant idea developed into a complete rough draft. Since he became my professor, I went from writing barely once a month to writing not only every day, but craving time and coffee to do it. Most significantly, since he became my professor, I believe that I can climb the arduous mountain that is writing a book.

After completing the draft, I was ready to take a break, but Kellen wouldn't hear of it. He generously gave me a week off, and then promptly began assigning me work for my next book. As the school year grew intensely busy in the spring, he still encouraged me to write. But like a good teacher, he recognized my need to focus on schoolwork and adapted to that need.

Writing can be a lonely journey. I count myself so blessed and fortunate to have had Kellen's guidance and mentorship throughout the process of writing my first book. He even continued his class job after graduating. He wants to see one of his former teachers become a published author. I will always be grateful for his unyielding faith in me.

One of the most powerful lessons I've learned as a teacher is that students can inspire teachers to do some amazing things.

~JC Santos

88

You Don't Know if You Don't Ask

Ask the right questions if you're going
to find the right answers.
~Vanessa Redgrave

I t was a Monday morning. The first bell had rung, and the classroom buzzed with second graders preparing to start the day. Pencil sharpeners whirred. Backpacks flew onto hooks. Conversation hummed about Little League games, birthday parties, and all the fun from the weekend.

I glanced over my lesson plans for the day. Objectives spelled out. Questions prepared to inspire critical thinking. Assessments in place to make sure my students learned what they needed to know. I was ready.

Alex stomped into the room and shoved his binder into his desk before making a beeline for me. He furrowed his brow and planted his feet in front of mine.

"Mrs. Jolley, are we taking a math fact quiz today?" His angry tone let me know that this was not the time for a cute or clever reply.

"Well, yes, of course. We always take a math fact quiz on Mondays," I replied. "I know you've been studying. I'm sure you will do well."

Thinking I had eased his tension about the test, I was unprepared for what happened next. Alex let out a loud grunt, "UGHH!" The next thing I knew, this usually good-natured second grader thrust his hand toward my face — middle finger extended!

Gasping under my breath, my mind raced with myriad thoughts, all likely unsuitable for me to say: "How dare you do that to me?" "Do you know how much trouble you're in right now?" "What do you think the principal will say when she hears what you've done?"

Then my mind switched to more appropriate teacher language: "Were you thinking that was an okay choice for you to make?" "Do you understand what that means?" "What could you have done differently to express your feelings?"

Thankfully, though not really knowing why, I had the presence of mind to stop and ask a question before saying anything about that finger: "Alex, are you having a rough morning?"

He glared at me, his finger still on display. "Yes! Don't you understand? I slammed this finger in the door on my way to school, and I won't be able to write very well for my math quiz!"

The right question. Sometimes it's the most important part of the whole day.

~Cindy Jolley

89

My Kindergarten Hero

Growing up is losing some illusions,
in order to acquire others.
~Virginia Woolf

 e had just completed a unit on community heroes, and I had given my kindergarten class an assignment to write or draw about their favorite hero. Each child was busy creating colorful masterpieces adorned with fire helmets and shiny police badges. Several students had chosen to draw larger-than-life brothers and sisters or moms and dads. I even had a family pet barking at me from one table in the back of the room.

However, one little boy was having difficulty with the assignment. Cameron had touched my heart early in the school year. He had dark brown hair and wore his thick-rimmed glasses just a little crooked. He resembled a younger version of Harry Potter at best. He often snorted when he laughed, and the rest of the class would laugh along with him.

Cameron was on the autism spectrum, but that didn't matter to me or his classmates. We all loved him just the way he was. He was full of wonderful stories and brought a special feeling to our classroom. I sat and watched as Austin, a precocious little boy with freckles, worked with Cameron. Austin had a wonderful way of interacting with Cameron, and he helped him find his hero. Within a few minutes, Cameron quickly began scribbling blue lines and curves on his paper — he was particularly fond of the color blue.

Finally, it was time for everybody to share their hero pictures. I listened as each student proudly stood in front of the class, picture held high, and described his or her hero. Maddie's daddy was a policeman with the K-9 unit. She shared how her daddy and his dog helped catch bad guys. Cory's dad was a football coach, and he helped kids get big and strong and win lots of games. Even Mark, who was very shy, held up a larger-than-life picture of his mom and spoke just above a whisper as he shared how she was his hero because she always took care of him. Next, Amanda shared how her dad was brave because he checked inside her closet and under her bed every night to make sure there were no monsters.

I listened intently to each student's description of his or her hero. Several students even elaborated by giving their heroes superhuman strength, but I learned early in my career you don't mess with creativity.

It was finally Cameron's turn to share his hero. Cameron stood up and anxiously placed his large blue stick-figured drawing in front of his face. He then quickly blurted out it was a picture of me. He added that I helped him learn things and then quickly sat back down. Tears began to form in the corner of my eyes, but nothing could have prepared me for what happened next.

When Austin stood up to share his picture, I was certain it would be a policeman, but he surprised me when he proudly held up a picture of his friend Cameron. He shared that Cameron was his hero because he had this sickness that made it really hard to learn, but he was like Superman and was really smart. He had drawn a red cape on his cartoon-like picture of Cameron and embellished the costume with a large red "C" on Cameron's chest.

The tears were now making their way down my checks, but were suddenly cut off in mid-stream. Cameron abruptly stood up, and put his arms up in the air as if he were going to take off and fly. He gleefully yelled out, "I'm Superman!" The entire class stood up and began striking Superman poses, too. Within minutes, we were all laughing as though we had each truly discovered the secret of becoming superheroes.

If only adults could see the world through the eyes of a child. What had started out as a simple lesson on community heroes had turned into a moment that changed my understanding of what it truly means to be a teacher. Teachers are tasked with a very important job, leading their children in discovering their own amazing qualities and helping them find their inner superhero.

If you should ever visit my classroom, you may find the corner of a red cape peeking out from the locker in the corner of the room. Hey, you never know when the next superhero may learn how to fly in my classroom.

~Melissa Monteith

Feeling Ohana

*We cannot always build the future for our youth, but
we can build our youth for the future.*
~Franklin Delano Roosevelt

As a new high school teacher struggling to fit in, I became a "yes man." Yes, I would chaperone Homecoming. Yes, I would tutor in the library after school. Yes, I would join the committee that the seasoned teachers avoided. If I continued to say yes, maybe I'd be granted tenure.

By my fourth year I knew better. A former student asked me to be the advisor for KIWIN'S, which is a community service club within Kiwanis International, which also sponsors Key Club. I had over seventy essays analyzing *Oedipus Rex* to grade and I wanted to say "no."

The girl sensed my reluctance. "We've asked other teachers. No one can."

"What would I have to do?" I didn't mean to sound uninterested, but I knew I'd be stabbing my eyes after reading those essays and, time-wise, being an advisor for another club seemed out of the question.

"We'd need your room for lunch meetings. And… maybe you would chaperone a few events?"

Like Oedipus, I couldn't escape my destiny. My classroom filled with students on Thursdays yelling "Awooga, Awooga," a strange club cheer, while I graded papers. They'd bait me to join in, but I was too busy. And too embarrassed.

But I did participate. I joined a jog-a-thon, supervised bake sales, and stuck roses on floats for the New Year. A few years passed and I remained the advisor to the KIWIN'S club, but I was determined to remain just a chaperone. I let the kids do the work. After all, they were learning how to be leaders.

Then Christine Chau, a short girl with long black hair and dark-rimmed glasses, came along.

It soon became evident why Christine's peers elected her club president. She lived by their motto: "One Family. One Mission. One word: KIWIN'S." Though seemingly quiet, I'd watch her personally invite students to club events. She'd strike up conversations with new people who came into the room. She especially believed in the Hawaiian concept of *ohana*, the feeling that family extends beyond the classic definition. She wouldn't leave anyone behind, including me.

During one lunch meeting, the classroom was filled wall to wall with students. The cacophony of chatter made it chaotic. Christine stood up, adjusted her dark-rimmed glasses, and prepared to speak. *Uh-oh,* I thought. *This could be bad.* But she spoke, and they quietly listened. She had their attention and respect. I remember sitting at my desk, watching in awe. Here was a student leading a room full of teenagers better than some teachers. Better than me.

I felt guilty. I had been just an observer for too long. She was a senior who managed AP classes in addition to weekly KIWIN'S meetings, district meetings, and community service events. Certainly, I could do more.

Like a true leader, Christine sensed this and invited me to fulfill a more active role. We worked together by adding two video-game tournaments to support local, struggling families. We invited other clubs, like Red Cross and Make-a-Wish, to participate in some of our events. It was clear that Christine believed that *ohana* extended beyond our club and embraced the school as a whole.

The year sped by and DCON, the district convention and final hurrah, was upon us. Students from schools from all over California stayed at a hotel for a weekend of teenage leadership conferences and seminars. But the event was also used for Kiwanis to recognize the clubs that were most inspiring in giving back to their schools

| Learning from the Students

and communities. There were several awards and scholarships to be earned. There was one, however, that I had my eye on: Distinguished President, for Christine Chau.

Saturday night, as we finished dinner in a banquet room with hundreds of students, advisors, and educators, my students huddled together in anticipation. I checked items off my program with my pen as the evening progressed to the award for which Christine was nominated.

The tension had me shredding the corner of my fabric napkin underneath the table. Sorry, Marriott. My hands were restless.

Suddenly, it was time. Two other schools earned third and second place for Distinguished President. As the student who earned second place took pictures on the stage, I watched the large projection screen. Christine's name would either appear on the top slot or it would be a bust.

I closed my eyes. Opened them. Took a long breath.

The announcer finished taking photos with the student on the stage and was back at the microphone.

Our students were on the edges of their seats, phones ready. What would I say to the club if she didn't win? But I knew that the sense of *ohana* she helped create over the course of the school year would soften any loss. We tried. Award or no award, we did our best to serve those in need. Though it's good to be recognized, whether it's a teacher earning tenure or a club president winning a plaque, putting heart into helping others is the real award. Our club achieved that. But I so wanted her to win.

The announcer cleared his throat.

"And in first place… from Marina High School… Christine Chau!"

Her friends embraced her. Chaperones stood, clapping. My knees wobbled, but I stood. Tears streamed down my cheeks. It was the first time in my life that I had ever cried with such admiration and pride for another human being. I clapped loudly until my hands were red and sore.

That year, our KIWIN'S club left DCON with fifteen trophies, ten of them first-place victories, a true testament to Christine's leadership and an amazing year of service for our members. Since graduating, Christine has visited on multiple occasions. She always returns with a smile and gives hugs to current members. She currently studies business at California State Fullerton.

As for me, I'm still trying to balance my regular duties with adjunct duties, grad school, and life. But if KIWIN'S has taught me anything, it's that by creating that spirit of *ohana,* I've also created a network of people for guidance and support.

And though I now have tenure, I'm still a "yes man" — by choice. Christine taught me that even busy people can make time to give back to others. Now, when my KIWIN'S students ask me, "How do you feel?" I don't wave them off and continue to grade papers during their club meeting. I stand with pride and shout at the top of my lungs, "I feel good! Oh, I feel so good! I feel fine, all of the time! Awooga! Awooga! Awooga-Awooga-Awooga!"

~Cory Rasmussen

91

Expect the Unexpected

A characteristic of the normal child is
he doesn't act that way very often.
~Author Unknown

Working as an elementary-school teacher and a librarian taught me that children say funny things. On the first day of kindergarten, a boy told me, "I'm just trying this out for today. I don't think I'll be back tomorrow." I guess that's how his mother convinced him to board the bus. I don't know how she managed to get him to attend school the rest of the year, but whatever she did worked.

Another kindergartner got off the bus and couldn't remember where he had to go. When asked if he knew the name of his teacher, he replied, "Yes, it's Mrs."

I once taught a second grader who believed his mother knew everyone from George Washington to Abraham Lincoln. Whenever I mentioned a historical figure, he'd say, "My mother knows him." She must have been 300 years old.

No matter how many times I reminded one particular boy to return his library book, he ignored me. I assumed he either loved it and couldn't bear to part with it, or he'd lost it. Finally, at the end of the school year, he brought back the book with an excuse. "I'm sorry it took so long," he said, "but I needed the book to prop up my gerbil cage." Judging from the gnawed cover, his pet had enjoyed the book in more ways than one. I hope the gerbil learned to read.

Children are full of surprises. One day after lunch, I returned to my classroom and discovered the linoleum floor was wet and slippery. During recess, a student had entered the room, stopped up the sink and left the water running so it would overflow. He was the same boy who threw weekly temper tantrums and frequently announced he was quitting school, although he never followed up on that promise. His attitude made me wonder what I was doing wrong. However, my confidence was restored at the end of the year when he smiled, hugged me and said, "You're the best teacher I ever had!" I can only imagine what would have happened if he *hadn't* liked me.

Expect the unexpected when you work in an elementary school. One day in the library, a group of third graders jumped up from their chairs, screaming. A few minutes later, they calmed down and read quietly. Their silence didn't last long. Soon, they leaped up again, shrieking as if they were actors in a thriller movie. It didn't take long to discover the cause of their unpredictable behavior: The culprit was a lost chipmunk. The animal would scurry past their feet, hide for a while, then emerge and scamper around the room, causing chaos. Two hours passed before the confused creature found his way back outside. I was just as relieved as he was. Maybe more.

My favorite memory occurred just before I left teaching. I was standing in the hallway of the administration office, waiting for an appointment, when someone called my name. A young man hurried to my side. He towered over me, but at one time, he had been in my second grade class. He told me what he was doing, and I was thrilled. Is there any better news than hearing a former student say he's applying for a teaching job? I don't think so!

~Laura Boldin-Fournier

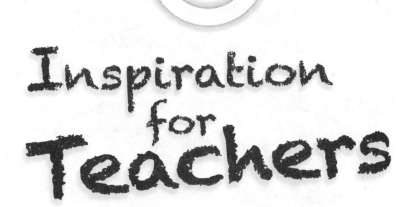

Chapter 10

Inspiration for Teachers

The Quiet Ones

In teaching you cannot see the fruit of a day's work. It is invisible and remains so, maybe for twenty years.
~Jacques Barzun

92

Ode to the Quiet Wheel

Quiet people have the loudest minds.
~Stephen Hawking

Here's to the quiet student,
the one who remembers her pencil,
the one who remembers his book.
Here's to Melanie
who always has a smile,
and to Justin,
who knows that names can hurt
along with sticks and stones.
Here's to the students who have their homework,
every day,
who raise their hands,
who risk being wrong and speak their opinion,
when their opinion isn't popular.
Thank you for your bravery.
John, thank you for sticking up for the underdog,
and befriending that new student.
And thanks to Katelyn for helping the substitute
that day I was out.
Here's to the student who comes to school,
every day

hungry for an education, breakfast, or both,
who wants to learn
and listens well,
who respects his friends and teachers,
who respects the janitor sweeping the hall, the bus driver,
the cafeteria worker serving a hot lunch and cold milk,
not because he will get in trouble if he doesn't,
but because he realizes even at this tender age
that everyone deserves respect.
Here's to the students who know that
please and thank you go a long way.
Here's to Amy, Rachel, Jen,
Adam, Brendan, and Joe,
Chelsea, Alanna,
Michael and DJ,
and the ones whose name you do not hear.
You know who you are.
Thank you for not taking the easy way out.
Finally,
here's to your parents.
Thank you for doing your job,
for instilling the value of an education in your child,
for modeling respect and tolerance.
Thank you for holding up your end of the bargain
when you decided to bring this
beautiful, complex human being
into this beautiful, complex world.
Thank you
for your time,
for your love,
your patience and discipline.
These are gifts your children will open —
for the rest of their lives,
pass on to their children,
their children's children.

These are the quiet wheels,
the students who often go unnoticed—
until now.

~Mary Ellen Redmond

She Looked at Me

*There are only two types of speakers in the
world. 1. The nervous and 2. liars.*
~Mark Twain

rs. Rhodes spoke as she walked to the front of the class. "Today, you need to select one of the topics from the board for an oral report."

I groaned internally. *An oral report! She might as well
line me up in front of a firing squad,* I thought.

I took a deep breath and scanned the list of names and inventions on the smaller chalkboard located on the wall to our right. One name in the center of the board captured my attention. *Who's that person?* I wondered. I didn't know, but that was going to be my choice.

Seated in the middle of the classroom, I fixated on that name. As Mrs. Rhodes called on students to announce their selections, the only thought I had was, *Please don't pick that one. Please don't take mine.*

Finally, it was my turn. I breathed a sigh of relief. "Johannes Brahms," I said as I tried to act nonchalant. Once I vocalized his name, panic washed over me. *How am I going to do this? I have to get up in front of these people and say something about some person I know nothing about.*

Later in the day, I sat in my living room and flipped through my parents' album collection. "Oh, thank goodness!" I exclaimed as I found an album of symphonic compositions that included one of his pieces.

I pulled the vinyl disk from the dust jacket, placed it on the record player, dropped the needle in place, and cranked up the stereo.

Classical music flowed throughout the house. "This is perfect," I said as I headed to my bedroom to grab my tape player and find an empty cassette. Collecting those items, I headed back to the living room to set up my makeshift recording studio. After a few playbacks, I had the music transferred from record to tape. With that task completed, I set out in search of the other items I needed for my report — a dowel rod, a suit jacket, and a music stand. With reports due the following week, I used every spare second to prepare.

When the big day came, my nerves were jittery as I slipped into my seat and waited for my turn to present. Eventually, Mrs. Rhodes called my name. "Jill, you're next."

Sweat beaded on my palms as I forced myself to walk to the front of the classroom. I set up my music stand and pulled the cassette player from my bag and placed it on the table. I felt faint as I donned my dad's suit jacket, grabbed the wooden dowel, and clicked the Play button. When I glanced at my teacher, she smiled.

Before speaking, I blinked a few times, trying to calm my labored breathing. "Johannes Brahms," I announced, then turned my back on the classroom, banged the dowel rod on the music stand three times, and raised my arms. As the music swelled and my legs wobbled, I flung my arms to and fro like a crazed conductor guiding the symphonic sounds of the invisible orchestra that billowed from the cassette speakers. All the while, sweat rolled down my neck and collected underneath the suit jacket.

After the music ceased, I turned around and proceeded to tell the class about Mr. Brahms. For a finale, a classmate played a short tune on the dulcimer. Finally, my time was up, and I returned to my seat, sweat-soaked and emotionally spent.

The next day, my teacher handed me a piece of paper. At the top in red was my grade for my report on Brahms. For a few seconds, I stared at my score, and then I glanced at Mrs. Rhodes. Her eyes locked onto mine, and she smiled. I wanted to hug her. Me, the shy kid who had little self-confidence and was uncomfortable with the world, had just received a 100 for a project that forced me out of my comfort zone. I had never seen myself as a student capable of earning 100% for any type of project, yet there it was in bright red at the top of my paper.

Not only did that grade boost my confidence, but Mrs. Rhodes helped me see my potential. From the nonverbal communication of a smile and eye-to-eye contact, she looked beyond my shyness — and saw me.

Although three decades have passed since that class, I have never forgotten Mrs. Rhodes or that assignment. As a teacher myself, with every class and every student, I try to emulate my former teacher's communication technique of looking students in the eyes and letting them know that I see them — truly see them and their potential. It's one way I can pay tribute to the teacher who influenced my life the most through one project, one grade, a couple of smiles, and eye-to-eye contact indicating that she looked beyond the shy mask I wore — and saw *me*.

~Jill Printzenhoff

Just One Note

From a small seed a mighty trunk may grow.
~Aeschylus

I endured middle school. I agonized through almost every moment. I pulled myself through every day hoping to stay invisible, and yet somehow wondering why it was impossible for anyone else to see me.

It wasn't that my lot was worse than that of any other seventh grader. Of course, students shoved past me in the hallways, boys made crude comments on the stairs, and old friends dropped me for someone new. But those things happened to all of us. I knew the rules. I was simply supposed to blend in with the giant mass around me.

My teachers were competent, and most would never have been mean, but my invisibility was never stronger than in the classroom. They just didn't see me. I was not the most intelligent, beautiful, or interesting. Therefore, I attracted no attention.

The few times a teacher did notice me, I desperately wished I could disappear again. There was the math teacher who turned my name, Maya, into a Meow Mix commercial when he took roll every day. Then there was the science teacher who threw a dried corncob at a misbehaving student but missed. The flying missile misfired and smacked me hard on the top of my head. It hurt, but I was too afraid to say a word. The teacher looked at me, assessed that I was not dying, and continued the lesson without an apology. After one second in the limelight, I gladly retreated back into the shadows for the rest of year.

The one class in which I felt fairly safe was concert band. Sixth period became my sanctuary. It wasn't that anyone noticed me there. I was one of a long row of flute players. And because I didn't want to make anyone angry, I never challenged for a higher position, I sat unnoticed in last chair. Still, I was somewhat happy.

In band, every instrument had a voice, and every voice had to perform, or the entire band suffered. As small as my part was, at least I had a part. I didn't need to speak to my peers. It was enough to add my voice to theirs and make something more beautiful than any of us could create on our own.

Even though we were all needed, I quickly learned that did not make us all equal. One of the prettiest girls in seventh grade sat next to me. Compared to my own wild mop, her hair was always straight and smooth. I wondered if my hair would behave better with different hair products. After several days, I finally summoned enough courage to ask, "Kaley, what shampoo do you use?"

She raised her eyebrows in surprise that I could speak, yet she was nice when she answered me. Almost immediately, though, the girl on her left leaned over and smothered a laugh. "What in the world did she have to say?"

"She asked me what shampoo I used!" Kaley laughed softly. "What a strange thing to ask!"

Now, I have to laugh when I realize the truth in Kaley's answer. She was not trying to be mean. It really was a strange question! But I probably don't need to state that it was a long time before I spoke to any of them again.

Then, one day, a simple comment from a teacher changed my life.

Although we had an award-winning band program in our district, we still had a lot to learn in middle school. One of the things we needed to work on was our tone. One day, our band director, Mr. Curtis, curtly waved his hand to cut us off in the middle of a song. "You are not in tune!" he exclaimed. "We must learn to play in tune!"

He played a B-flat pitch and pointed to our first-chair flute. "Tune your instrument!" Then, as he went down the line of flute players, he expressed his dissatisfaction with each tone. No one escaped.

The realization slowly dawned on me that my turn was coming soon, and I was horrified. In just one small moment, I would lose my invisible cloak and have to play all by myself while my peers sat and listened. I felt frozen in my chair.

"Maya." Mr. Curtis had to call my name twice. "Maya! It's your turn. Play!"

It was only a note. A few seconds of music heard in a school full of jumbled voices, class bells, footsteps, and slammed locker doors. But it was enough. I sat up, held my flute to my lips, closed my eyes, and took my turn. I played my single note quietly, with vibrato, and with all the feelings I had felt that year. I poured my heart into that one moment of music, and the sound echoed softly through the room. I was right on pitch, and I knew it, but I didn't expect Mr. Curtis's reaction.

He looked at me as if for the first time and smiled. "Band," he stated. "That is what I have been waiting for! That was a perfect note, with perfect vibrato, and perfect pitch!" And then he said something I have never forgotten. "Maya, that one note has earned you an 'A' this year. Keep it up."

I would like to say that I was brave enough to challenge my peers and earn first chair that year, but I wasn't. Instead, I was grateful to sit under my teacher's leadership in a place where I belonged. And as I learned to trust him more, I learned to trust myself. I stayed the course through high school and finally earned a coveted place in our band.

One comment, one moment, one ray of light into the shadow of my middle-school life, and a seed started to sprout. I was firmly planted, and my roots took hold. Thanks to one teacher who shed light on one small voice, I had found a place to grow.

~Amellia Pinson

Editor's Note: After Amellia's story became a finalist for this book, she sent us this note:

I wrote this story as a response to a challenge from my students. They stated if they had to submit "painfully honest" journal entries to me, I should have to submit my writing, too. As they implied three journal entries a week might be impossible, I wrote four stories in the same amount of time to show them it could be done. That week, I sent the stories off, one by one, never daring to hope one might actually make it this far in the selection process. I haven't shared "Just One Note" with my students yet; I think I'll wait just a bit longer now. The suspense would not be good for them or for me!

Then, after Amellia learned that her story was chosen to be one of the 101, she wrote this:

After I received your e-mail, I actually forgot to eat my lunch! When my 5th period students came into my room, they asked why my food was still sitting on my desk. Because these are the students who challenged me to write, I told them "our" story had made it to the final selection round.

I was not prepared for their response. My most cynical class, full of brilliant but streetwise students, suddenly broke into loud cheers and applause. In fact, they were so happy, it took me a bit to settle them down. As excited as I am, I think this might mean as much to them as it does to me. Several immediately asked if they could write stories, too. Of course, I said, "Yes!" Thank you for giving me such a moment to share with my students. It is not one I am likely to forget!

95

A Child's Wisdom

We are all different, which is great because we are all
unique. Without diversity, life would be very boring.
~Catherine Pulsifer

hat was I going to do? School was going to be out soon, and one quiet little girl in my class still had not earned an octopus. I made them from bright-colored yarn and gave them to my students as awards for doing something special.

I had introduced the octopus award early in the school year. My first winner was a little boy. The class was curious as I called him forward. I was holding a paper in one hand and an octopus in the other.

I said, "You did very well on this math test. For showing so much improvement, you've earned the very first octopus award. But there's one more thing."

Not being sure what this was all about, he asked, "What?"

I held out his paper and added, "Are you willing to let me keep this test?" The trade-off was no paper to take home to show his parents. Instead, he would have the admiration of his classmates as the first winner of this award.

I knew not every child could be an "A" student, but I believed each child could show improvement. To me, that was worth rewarding.

My personal reward was to watch each winner's face. A smile would light up their eyes as they stood to proudly receive their prize. But these public commendations had an unexpected result.

A winner would sometimes keep the colorful octopus on his or her desk for days. I noticed that other children looked at it, but did not try to grab it or knock it off. Instead, there was a kind of respect. I felt this silent motivator was more powerful than any general reminder to the class about earning one. I waited to see what would happen.

By the end of the year, only the quiet little girl had not won an octopus. I knew I couldn't make up a reason to reward her. My second graders were too smart for that.

One Friday afternoon, I gave a simple assignment. "Draw any picture of your choice. Write a few words to tell me about it." I collected their papers and took them home to review. When I saw the little girl's paper, I got excited. She had drawn a simple blue sky and green grass by a pond. On a path nearby were three people side by side. One was using crutches, one was in a wheelchair, and one had no obvious physical need.

Above her drawing she had written: "The sky is blue. The grass is green. And all the people are different." Bingo! I couldn't wait to get to class to make a trade — an octopus for this drawing. The look of joy when I called her forward was worth the wait.

I'm retired now and her paper is long gone, lost in one of my many moves. What has remained is her simple wisdom, treasured in my heart. It helped me develop a variety of relationships that I enjoy, just because "all the people are different."

~Darlis Sailors

96

The Smallest Sign

Hope is faith holding out its hand in the dark.
~George Iles

I had been teaching for sixteen years, and as anyone can tell you, sixteen years of doing anything, even something you love, can wear you down. I had seen many students come and go in the elementary classrooms where I had taught, and though my passion for teaching hadn't waned, I often wondered if I was doing any good as a teacher. Was I really inspiring them to pursue and achieve their dreams?

That's a difficult question for any teacher to answer. I teach at an inner-city school where the students come with many challenges in their lives: economic, social, and emotional. But they are still children, and when I see them at the beginning of each year, the hope in their faces and that which I feel in my heart make me think that maybe there's something I can do to help them to see the possibilities in their future.

During my first year of teaching, I was filled with that hope, and I took time to learn what every student was interested in, what their favorite subjects were, and what they dreamed of becoming when they grew up. I was determined to inspire each and every one of them, and ignite a desire within each of them to know, question, and understand.

For most of my students, that seemed to be the case. Many were enthusiastic coming in, and that enthusiasm just grew as the year went by. By finding out what they loved and connecting it to our lessons, I got them interested in all the wonders the world had to offer. I felt I was teaching not just to their minds, but to their hearts.

But there was one little girl in my class who didn't respond the way the others did. She was a quiet, shy child named Ashley who sat at her desk and did her work, finished all her homework, and was well behaved. However, she didn't seem interested in being engaged in the class conversations. She was helpful and kind to everyone, but there wasn't a great deal of enthusiasm in her eyes.

Getting Ashley to find that love of learning became my goal for that year. I wanted to figure out what she was interested in, what sparked her desire to learn, what would light up her face with the joy of discovery. She liked to read and write, so I encouraged her, reading her stories and essays and letting her know how much I liked them. I showed her books in the library I thought she might enjoy. Ashley liked to draw, so I asked her to draw pictures for any assignment she felt needed them. She drew dozens of wonderful pictures, but nothing seemed to bring a smile to her face.

In fact, as the year progressed, Ashley withdrew more and more. She completed every project, but there didn't seem any joy in the doing of it. She remained kind, but her friendships with others grew more distant. There didn't seem to be the smallest sign she enjoyed school at all. By the time the end of the year came around, I felt I'd failed this little girl.

On the last day of school, the students and I were having our going-away class party, and everyone seemed happy that summer was just around the corner. Many of the students told me they'd had a great year in third grade, and some were even sorry that school was finally over. I should have felt happy.

But I didn't. Ashley seemed ready to begin summer also, but there was no happiness on her part. She sat quietly at her desk, grinned a little when someone laughed and smiled at her, and silently packed up her supplies when the three o'clock bell rang. She didn't even look at me as the children began to leave the room.

I was on my way out the door when I spied a book I'd bought earlier that week. It was a children's book about a little girl who went on all kinds of wonderful adventures. I hadn't known then why I'd bought it, but now, staring at it in my hands, I knew. I opened the first page, grabbed a pen, and wrote an inscription to Ashley. I told her I hoped she had a wonderful summer, and that I knew she'd have all kinds of great adventures in her life, too. Then I put the book in her hands, and the wave of students exiting classes pulled us all to the front of the school. Book in hand, Ashley disappeared onto a bus and was gone.

Sixteen years later, I was sitting in another classroom, ready to start another year, hoping I could still find a way to inspire the new class of children I was about to meet. I was checking my e-mail and came across one that said the following:

Hi Mr. Buentello,

You were my third grade teacher. I'm all grown now, but I'll never forget when you gave me a book on the last day of school. You wrote a note on the inside. While it probably was a small gesture to you, it really meant a lot to me. At the time my life was very unstable. Reading has always been an inspiration for me. The gift you gave me was the first book I ever owned, and I will never forget the moment you gave it to me. I just wanted you to know how thankful I am.

Ashley

I sat there reading and re-reading that e-mail. Then the morning bell rang. I rose up out of my chair, felt a fresh wave of hope wash over me, and went to greet my new class.

~John P. Buentello

The Quiet Ones | 341

97

The Teacher Who Believed in Me

It takes a big heart to help shape little minds.
~Author Unknown

I remember those days as a young child as if they were yesterday. The alarm clock would go off in the morning, and I would lie in bed dreading school. My mother knew the routine all too well. She'd come into my room and coax me out of bed. With much debate and a million excuses why I couldn't go to school, I would reluctantly crawl out of bed with a sick feeling in my stomach thinking about the day ahead of me.

In the early 1970s, I went to Public School 95 in the heart of Brooklyn, New York. My classes were overcrowded, and I felt lost among the many students. In grade school, I was painfully shy. I didn't raise my hand because I was terrified I would stutter or say the wrong answer. It had happened in the past, and I replayed the moments in my mind when the kids laughed at my awkwardness.

To make matters worse, I was extremely tall and lanky. At 5'6", I towered over my classmates. I would slump to make myself appear shorter until my back and legs ached. Every day, I was taunted. "How's the weather up there?" they'd say with a giggle. I was also called the "Jolly Green Giant." I was anything but jolly.

I kept everything bottled up because I was too ashamed to tell my parents that I was being teased in school. My grades were dropping, and I was failing many subjects. My teacher had warned me that if my grades didn't improve, she would have no choice but to have me repeat fourth grade. I was devastated. *Now I'll feel even more stupid, and I'll be even taller than the rest of the younger kids,* I thought to myself. Just the idea of getting left back made matters worse.

It was January, just after winter break, and I was giving my mother a particularly hard time while getting ready for school. I begged, "Please let me stay home just one day. I promise I'll help you clean up the apartment!" I tried to bribe her, but my pleas fell on deaf ears. She was having none of it. Off to school I went.

I was sitting at my desk when a tall, willowy woman walked into our classroom. She had a kind face and a warm smile. "Good morning!" She seemed to light up the room. "My name is Mrs. Gustafson. I will be your teacher for the remaining part of the school year." She went on to tell us that our teacher had to take a sudden leave of absence for a family emergency. I wasn't too sure what that meant back then, but from the moment I saw Mrs. Gustafson, I had a good feeling about her.

Mrs. Gustafson told us that she would learn everybody's name by the end of her first day. When it was my turn to tell her my name, I mumbled "Dorann" softly. She looked me straight in the eyes and said equally as quietly, "Can you say your name a little louder?" After I repeated my name a bit louder, Mrs. Gustafson smiled broadly. "What a pretty name. So different and unique," she said. For the first time in school, I felt special.

Later in the day, when we were lined up for recess, Mrs. Gustafson came over to me and bent down to whisper in my ear, "Stand up straight and tall. Be proud of your height." As I looked up at her, she winked. She understood! In my young eyes, she had to be at least ten feet tall!

The next morning, when my alarm clock went off, I got out of bed on my own, without prompting from my mom. I ran to the bathroom to brush my teeth as my mom sprinted behind me. Quite puzzled, she asked me if I was feeling okay. "Mom, Mrs. Gustafson said we're going to do something that is a lot of fun today in school!" To this day, I'll never forget the shocked expression on my mom's face.

That day, our math lesson turned into a bubblegum contest. We were divided into three teams. Each student was given a piece of bubblegum. The goal was to see which team blew the biggest bubbles! Mrs. Gustafson assigned a few students to measure the height of the bubbles with a ruler. After all of the bubbles were measured and documented, it was up to each team to tally all the measurements to see which team had the highest score. I was eager to add up our score, even though math was my weakest subject. To my delight, our team came in second place. We all got colorful stickers that said "Good Job!" I couldn't have felt more excited or proud.

I started to like school more each day. In just a few short weeks, I loved school! I looked forward to seeing what Mrs. Gustafson had in store for us. She made learning fun, with games and small incentives. But, most of all, she believed in me, so I started to believe in myself. I learned to stand up tall and be proud of my height. I participated and raised my hand when I knew the answer. I spoke louder. I wasn't afraid to make a mistake for fear of being laughed at.

Although I was sad to see the school year end, I left fourth grade with the confidence and tools I needed to face fifth grade in the fall. Not only was I promoted, but I passed all my subjects with B's and even an A. I will never forget Mrs. Gustafson. She made a shy, gawky young girl believe in herself.

~Dorann Weber

98

The Child
I Didn't Want

I don't know if you've ever noticed this, but first
impressions are often entirely wrong.
~Lemony Snicket

I already hated dealing with Victor's parents, their lack of cooperation and disconnected phone numbers. He was the youngest in a family that contained many children with behavior problems. I'd had a couple of his siblings in previous years and dreaded having this child in my class.

I taught first grade in a low-budget charter school that was quickly becoming known in our town for accepting unruly students, often those who'd been kicked out of another school for behavior problems. Teachers were not given the choice on their class rosters, and Victor would be my student whether I wanted him or not.

I didn't mind that he came to school with no backpack, no lunch, filthy clothes, and was not quite potty-trained. I could loan him a Spiderman backpack and offer him granola bars. I was even willing to deal with the potty accidents. "No worries, Victor, that happens to everyone."

But Victor was not like his siblings.

It was clear from the first day that he wanted to read books, not throw them. He didn't yell. He didn't break crayons on purpose. In fact, he paid attention, practiced reading when he was done with other subjects, and attended my after-school tutoring group of his own volition. He loved sitting cross-legged in a reading circle with a simple version of *Little Red Riding Hood* or *Hansel and Gretel*. He quickly became a confident reader.

Instead of dreading Victor, I now looked forward to having him in class each day. He was an old soul, a gentleman's gentleman with a delightful wit behind his dirty face and snot-smeared sleeves. And now that he was reading well, our next job together was writing. He often stayed in with me during recess, grumbling a little to save face with the other students. He diligently practiced the letters, shape by shape, mouthing the sounds each made. His pencil grip and letter size needed work, but we were making progress. As always, Victor was pleased with himself.

"Look what I can do!" was his battle cry when he made a perfectly formed letter A.

Unfortunately, Victor's siblings were still having behavioral problems in school. His parents grew tired of the consequences the children earned and the regular phone calls from school administrators. One day, when I was home sick with the flu, Victor's mother came to school to get all of her children, and she didn't bring them back. Not even Victor. I was heartbroken. To take him away when I was out sick seemed cruel.

Although I knew it wasn't about me, I felt punished by his mother's choice. Victor was my responsibility. I was his teacher, and he was my student. We had stories to read and write, and now that would not happen. Not in my classroom, anyway.

His empty desk with a pile of playground sand underneath was all I had to remember him by. I felt guilty that he would go to a new teacher unable to write at grade level. We just hadn't had enough time. And I didn't even get to say goodbye.

It weighed on me the rest of the school year. As the other students progressed from writing sentences to paragraphs and then stories, I thought of Victor. He would have enjoyed writing a list of pets or a letter to a friend. As the reading curriculum grew more difficult, I thought, *Victor was a strong reader. He would have been reading this, too.* Occasionally, another student would say, "Remember Victor?" *Yes, of course I did.*

As the school year came to a close, I was doing playground duty on a hot, dusty afternoon. Students and teachers alike were sweaty, tired, and looking forward to drippy cherry Popsicles and summer days off. A woman walked up to our playground fence and said, "Are you Mrs. M?"

"Yes," I said. "Do I know you?"

"No, but you were Victor's teacher earlier this year, right? I work at Lake View School with Mrs. Kaye. She's Victor's teacher now, and she wants you to have this." The woman handed me an envelope. I thanked her and opened it.

It was a hand-printed letter from Victor.

Dear Mrs. M,
I can write now. My favorite color is green. I miss you.
Love, Victor

The letter included a drawing, all in green, and a large smudge of dirt that proved it was Victor's!

I did not know this teacher, Mrs. Kaye, but only a person who loved little Victor would bother to send his previous teacher a letter. She must have realized I would worry about him: his grubby self, his learner's soul. Instead of feeling that my time with Victor had been cut short, I began to feel that Mrs. Kaye and I had the privilege of sharing him. Although I did not get to be the teacher who taught Victor to write, at least I had taught him to read. I'd had the joy of spending a few months of his life with him, of feeling he was mine.

Funny how, at the beginning of the year, he was the child I hadn't wanted.

~Carrie Malinowski

99

The Book Fair

*I know every book of mine by its smell, and I have
but to put my nose between the pages to be
reminded of all sorts of things.*
~George Robert Gissing

It was the week of the Book Fair, and our fifth grade class was scheduled to go to the library on Friday. I thought the library was an amazing place. It was filled with so many books that could transport you to wonderful and interesting new places, real and pretend. In my eyes, the library ladies had the best job in the whole school. I wondered if they secretly sat in a comfy chair in the corner of the library and read stacks of books when classes were not scheduled to be in there.

I loved reading. I loved all books, even encyclopedias. I had developed a habit of opening a book and smelling it before I started reading it. Sometimes, I even read the last page first.

Mr. Acree, my math teacher and favorite teacher that year, pulled me aside after class one day. "Vickie, the library ladies were telling me they needed a little extra help this week," he said. "They are busy with the Book Fair. Would you be interested in helping them out?"

I couldn't believe it! My face flushed with excitement as I thought about being a helper in the library. I grinned as the words came out of my mouth. "Yes, I would," I told him.

I hoped I had said it loud enough. I was so shy, and Mr. Acree was older than our other teachers. He walked around the class as he asked questions so he could hear the students' answers.

"Great!" he said. "Now, they can't pay you for working, but you can pick out a book at the Book Fair, any book you want."

I thought I would pass out from happiness right then and there! My large family didn't have extra money for me to buy books at the Book Fair. But now, not only did I get to be a helper in the library, but I would be rewarded by picking any book I wanted!

I would say that was the best day of my fifth grade school year, except the best day had already happened and would be pretty hard to beat.

The best day of fifth grade had been at the start of the school year on September 9, 1976. My mama had gone to the hospital to have my fifth sibling. I was the oldest. I was so nervous and worried about my mama that I was having a hard time concentrating. Mr. Acree, being a good teacher, recognized when something was not quite right with one of his students.

He set his chalk on the metal ledge and slapped the white dust from his hands. He walked around to the front of his metal desk and braced himself against it with the palms of his hands. The midday sunlight made his white hair glow.

"I'll tell you what," he said to the whole class in his firm teacher's voice. "Let's do something a little different today. Let's just talk about what's going on in our world."

The whole class cheered. I was so relieved; I closed my eyes for a moment. I knew I couldn't focus on learning math with so much on my mind. I had already begun to wander mentally back to the long hospital hallways that smelled of disinfectant. My mama was sweating and breathing heavily when my aunt had picked us up. I barely heard bits and pieces of what the other students were talking about... the parade last weekend, the new rides at the fair, the beauty pageants and who would be going on what night...

"Vickie." Mr. Acree tried to get my attention back to the classroom. "What about you? What's going on with you?"

There was still plenty of chatter going on in small groups all over the room, so he hadn't drawn anyone's attention in my direction. I hated being the center of attention. I blinked as I looked at him, and he restated his question, "What's on your mind?"

My brain raced to find something interesting to say. There was only one topic to be found, and I blurted out, "My mama's in the hospital having a baby, and I'm worried about her!"

The room fell silent, followed by the sound of students shifting in their seats. Tiny white particles floated downward in the sunbeams cutting across the desktops in the front row. Within moments, several students had volunteered their own experiences with a newborn sibling coming home from the hospital. I listened intently as the stories unfolded, each one a gift of peace to me. By the end of class that day, I was no longer a worried, nervous fifth grader, but a confident, excited big sister. I didn't feel alone in my situation. I felt connected to my classmates and grateful to my teacher — my favorite teacher.

As I dusted the shelves in the library, I recalled that special day back in September. I had already processed all the returned library books by inserting new date cards in the pockets on the inside covers and placed them in the appropriate location on the shelves. The baby, my little sister, was healthy. She and my mama had returned home in just a few days. I smiled as I thought about that happy day, my new baby sister, and all the fun stories that had been shared by my classmates.

"I've never seen anyone smile so much while they worked," exclaimed one of the library ladies. I just smiled up at her and continued to dust.

"Well, you've cleaned enough," she said. "Thank you for all your help today. Go on over there and pick out a book."

My smile got even bigger, and my full attention was now on the rows and rows of brand-new books. I walked slowly toward the first shelf with respect and awe. It was a difficult decision, one that couldn't be rushed. I took my time and picked up book after book, smelled each one, read the title, and glanced at the illustrations. Then I saw it... the perfect book, *The Country Bunny and the Little Gold Shoes* by DuBose Heyward, with pictures by Marjorie Flack. The salmon-colored linen cover portrayed a mother rabbit with a string of little bunnies lined up on each side. The book begged to go home with me. My heart raced as I reached to claim it as my own.

I presented my choice to the library lady, received her approval and endorsement, and strode straight to Mr. Acree's classroom to share my selection with him. His face beamed when I walked through the open door, holding the book close to my heart with the cover facing out.

"Thank you," I said proudly. "I'm going to read it to my new sister."

A smile spread across his face. I noticed wrinkles in his expression I hadn't noticed before. I thought I saw him wipe his eyes. The sun shone through the window at his desk. His white hair glowed. For a moment, I thought I saw an angel.

Then he chuckled and said, "Good."

~Vickie McEntire

Breaking the Ice

*To exist is to change, to change is to mature, to mature
is to go on creating oneself endlessly.*
~Henri-Louis Bergson

I will always remember the day that Josh walked into my fifth grade classroom. The scowl on his face made me realize I was in for a long year with this boy. Josh was brilliant. He was doing seventh grade math with ease. He was an incredible artist, a beautiful writer and a great athlete.

Josh was also failing every single class. He would not do what he did not *want* to do. Telling him to do something multiple times made the scowl appear and his obstinacy grow deeper. Even when I went to put my hand on his shoulder, he would recoil like I had burned him.

Our first few months together were a constant cycle of me encouraging him to do better, Josh getting angry, and me getting frustrated and feeling helpless. One day, when I was walking by his desk, I noticed that Josh was drawing instead of writing. As I was about to redirect this behavior, I noticed how beautiful the drawing was. It was better art than I had seen some professionals do. I told him how beautiful it was and kept walking around the classroom.

At the end of the day, all the children packed up, and we walked out to the parking lot together. After they left, I went back to my classroom and sat at my desk. The picture that I had complimented was there. My eyes began to tear up as I realized that this was the first sign of the ice breaking between us.

The next day, knowing very well that he would not want any public acknowledgement, I privately thanked Josh for his artwork. For the first time all year, I saw a smile. I noticed as the day progressed that Josh would strike up a conversation with me, even though it was brief. This from the boy who had avoided me from day one. These small conversations escalated to jokes and real talks about life.

I soon learned that Josh's life was not easy. He, like many of his peers at the school, had been forced to grow up too fast. He was doing his best to stay out of trouble and make sure his older brother stayed out of trouble, too.

Josh liked a challenge. To motivate him to write an essay, I challenged him to a race. If he completed the essay, I would have a foot race with him. He accepted the challenge and completed the essay. As promised, I brought my running shoes the next day. I had another teacher watch my class while we went outside to race. I knew I was going to lose, but went through with it anyway.

He beat me… terribly. He felt so bad about how easily he had beaten me that he asked if I wanted a redo. I did not want to be embarrassed twice, so I politely declined. When we arrived back in the classroom, all of the students wanted to know who won. I was fully ready to publicly accept my defeat, but Josh announced to the classroom, "That is between Ms. Blake and myself. You do not need to know." I was stunned by his kindness and mature attitude.

At the end of the day, while I was walking the kids out to the parking lot, Josh's stepsister ran up and gave me a hug as usual. Shortly after, I felt another pair of arms wrap around my waist. I turned to see Josh, the boy who did not want me to touch his shoulder, giving me a hug. He looked at me and said, "Thank you for getting me," and then ran off to get into his car. That was when the final barrier between us fell.

To this day, I keep in regular contact with Josh to make sure he is doing well at his new school. I am also the proud owner of several of his original works of art. I had them framed, and they hang in my home. He is one of the many students who taught me to never give up on a child. They all want to succeed, and they all want love; all it takes is a little patience.

~Jessica Blake

Discovering My True Self

If you hear a voice within you say "you cannot
paint," then by all means paint, and
that voice will be silenced.
~Vincent Van Gogh

I looked out at the smiling faces packed into the school auditorium. Flashes from cameras lit up in all directions. The applause filled my ears. I had done it, I had really done it.

Just a few months earlier, I would never have pictured myself acting in a play in front of two hundred people. "Not for a million dollars," I would have said. But when the time came, I got up on stage and faced one of my greatest fears — and discovered I could do more than I ever gave myself credit for. I found a new person inside me, a much more daring, outgoing person who had been hidden all along, just waiting for the opportunity to emerge.

If not for my teacher, Mrs. Sather, I might never have found that opportunity.

In the first and second grade, I was extremely shy. I had friends, but it just wasn't in my personality to be very outgoing, even when I knew someone well. I was even quieter with strangers, and so I wasn't very good at meeting new people. I was afraid I would do or say something wrong, so usually I just smiled and listened to other people's conversations.

I did well in school, though, and I loved to write. I would escape in my writing, where I could be myself and never have to worry about what other people thought of me. In my stories, I was never shy.

My second grade teacher, Mrs. Sather, always encouraged me to write more. She told our class to go after our dreams and dig in with both hands. I think she was one of the first people to see my inner strength.

One day, she announced that our class was going to perform a play she had written, a take off on *The Wizard of Oz*.

"I'll begin to cast everyone tomorrow," she said. "I need someone who is not afraid to be on stage in front of a lot of people to play the lead part of Dorothy. Anybody want to try?"

A few excited hands shot up — mine, of course, was not one of them — and Mrs. Sather smiled. "We'll talk more about it tomorrow," she said.

The three o'clock bell rang, and my classmates slowly filed out with their *Beauty and the Beast* backpacks and *Lion King* lunch boxes, chattering about the play.

I lingered at my desk, loading up my backpack, and was one of the last to leave. "Dallas," Mrs. Sather called to me. "Will you come here for a minute, please?" Confused, I nodded and hurried to join her at her desk. *Was I in trouble?* I grew even more worried when she said, "Maybe we should wait for your dad to come pick you up. He might want to hear this, too."

As if on cue, my dad walked in, his tall, lean frame filling the doorway. "Hi, Dal, how was your day?" he asked as he helped me slip my backpack over my shoulders.

"Um, fine," I managed to croak out through my dry throat.

"I was just telling the class about the play we'll be performing in the spring," Mrs. Sather related. "It's going to be a take off on *The Wizard of Oz*, and Dallas, I was thinking you would be perfect for Dorothy. But I was surprised you didn't raise your hand when I asked who was interested in the part."

Me, the lead? Was she crazy? I was terrified just thinking of standing on stage in front of all those people. I hoped to grab a small part where I could sit in the background and watch everyone else sweat over lines in front of all those pairs of eyes.

"W-well," I stammered, "um, I thought it seemed really hard, and I was never very good at talking in front of lots of people."

"Oh, Dallas, you're great at memorizing things, and you have such a sweet personality. Perfect for Dorothy!" She paused. "Of course, plenty of girls would love the role, and I could get somebody else…"

Mrs. Sather gazed into my eyes as if seeing my inner self locked away inside. "But I'd love for you to give this a try for me. I had you in mind for Dorothy while writing the play! If you really don't want to, though, I won't make you. It's your choice."

My mind was spinning faster than the merry-go-round on the school playground. Mrs. Sather, whom I loved and admired, wanted *me* in this role. She believed in *me*. My gaze shifted across the room and stopped on a poster I had never noticed before. It showed a shooting star and read, "If you reach for the stars, you might at least grab a piece of the moon."

I realized it was time to throw off my shy cloak and show the world who I really was. I looked Mrs. Sather right in her sparkling blue eyes and said, "Okay, I'll try."

Fast-forward through five months of practicing, set building, line memorizing, and costume creating. We were ready. I knew my lines, blocking, songs — and the rest of the cast's lines, blocking, and songs. Still, I was as nervous as I had ever been. My knees shook. My heart pounded like I had just run a mile. I proved to myself that I could do it in practice, but could I prove it to everyone else when it really mattered?

"It doesn't matter how you do tonight," said Mrs. Sather, as if reading my thoughts when she came backstage for a final check. "You have already shown yourself how wonderful you are. That is the most important thing."

I smiled because I knew she was right. I proved I could take chances, be daring, and have fun doing it! At the end of the play, when the audience stood and applauded, I knew they were not just cheering for my performance that night, but for the performances they knew would come in later years because of my newfound confidence.

~Dallas Woodburn

Meet Our Contributors

Beverly Anderson received a BA in Elementary Education and an MA in Teaching Theory and Practice from California State University, Fresno. She is retired after thirty-four years of teaching and is the President of the Western Neuropathy Association, which she co-founded in 1998. She enjoys helping people learn about neuropathy.

Catherine Arnault received her Bachelor of Science in Elementary Education in 1984 and her Master's of Education in Curriculum Development and Instruction in 1991. She taught third and fourth grade in southeastern New Hampshire for twenty-six years before retiring to explore her interest in writing.

T.A. Barbella is a writer and artist living in San Jose, CA. Retired from thirty years in education, she currently provides independent instruction and consultation services to families of special needs students. She holds both bachelor and master's degrees, is an avid reader and animal lover, and enjoys all creative endeavors.

Rosanna Micelotta Battigelli has received four Ontario English Catholic Teachers' Association Best Practice Awards for her unique strategies in early literacy, promoting positive pupil interactions and self-esteem, and helping pupils who grieve. Her novel *La Brigantessa* will be published by Inanna Publications in 2018.

Jessica Marie Baumgartner's motto is "Adventure first, then write!" She has authored the *Embracing Entropy* series, and *My Family Is Different*. Her stories and articles have been featured in *Outposts of Beyond*, *Circle Magazine*, and many more. She's a member of Missouri Writers' Guild and Society of Children's Book Writers and Illustrators.

Pamela Berardino has "found her place in the world" as a Library Media Specialist in a K–2 school in Connecticut. Whether teaching in the classroom or the library, she has always shared her passions for flying, music, sailing, technology, and writing with her students. She lives with her husband and two spoiled cats.

Sandy Kelly Bexon is a communications specialist in Alberta, Canada, where she has enjoyed a successful career as a reporter and nonfiction writer for over twenty years. She enjoys fiction — both to read and to write — and is currently working on her second novel. Learn more at sandykellyauthor.com.

Jessica Blake received her Bachelor of the Arts in education from Metropolitan State University of Denver. She currently teaches fifth grade in Denver, CO. In her free time, she enjoys baking, cooking, writing, and creating. In the future, she would like to get into education policy as well as write novels.

Laura Boldin-Fournier is a retired teacher who lives in Florida. She is a previous contributor to the *Chicken Soup for the Soul* series. She is the author of *Orangutan's Night Before Christmas*, a humorous children's book. She is also the winner of a short story contest sponsored by wordsandbrushes.com.

Jackie Boor began her freelance writing career in 1968. She went on to raise three children and build a distinguished career as a large group facilitator, mediator, civic engagement specialist, speaker and award-winning author. Besides gardening and golf, Jackie enjoys educational adventures with colleagues and family.

Helen Boulos received her Master's in Education at the University of Virginia in 2000. She currently lives with her husband, three children, two dogs, and four cats in Wilmington, DE. She has been featured at *BlogHer* and *Scary Mommy*. She likes to think she sees the humor in a life well lived.

Patricia Boyer is a retired teacher who has written articles for children's magazines. She volunteers with her husband and therapy dog, visiting hospitals and reading with children. Patricia enjoys traveling, reading, and plans to continue writing motivational stories about children and her dog's experiences.

Affectionately know as "Jim Carrey with a Ph.D.," **Dr. Danny Brassell** is a best-selling author of fifteen books, including *The Reading Makeover*, based on his popular TEDx talk. He is a highly sought-after speaker and consultant on leadership development, reading, motivation, and communication skills. Learn more at DannyBrassell.com.

John P. Buentello is the author of books, essays, fiction, nonfiction, poetry and articles. He is the co-author of the novel *Reproduction Rights* and the anthologies *Binary Tales* and *The Night Rose of the Mountain*. He is completing a mystery novel and a collection of short stories. E-mail him at jakkhakk@yahoo.com.

Dr. Sandy Cameli, EdD, has worked with middle level learners and educators for nearly thirty years. Currently she serves as an Education Specialist for the Hawaii Department of Education supporting teacher leaders statewide. Writing stories about her teaching and learning experiences makes her heart smile.

Linda Carol Cobb taught English electives at the same high school in Virginia Beach, VA for thirty-seven years. She sponsored an award-winning newspaper and forensic team. Unwilling to retire, she teaches seminars, copyedits and coaches public speaking. She writes true stories about her Tennessee family and personal experiences.

Ginny Huff Conahan taught for fourteen years in Los Angeles Unified Schools and sixteen years in Fort Collins, CO for kindergarten through college-level students. She has a doctorate in Education from USC. Now retired and a grandma, Ginny loves crafts and volunteering. E-mail her at gcona@comcast.net.

Harriet Cooper writes essays, humor, creative nonfiction and health articles for newspapers, newsletters, anthologies and magazines. She's a frequent contributor to the *Chicken Soup for the Soul* series. She writes about family, relationships, health, food, cats, writing and daily life. E-mail her at shewrites@live.ca.

Katie Coppens lives in Maine with her husband and two children. She is a middle school English and science teacher. She has published two books: *Creative Writing in Science: Activities that Inspire* and *Geology Is a Piece of Cake*. Learn more at katiecoppens.com.

Tracy Crump enjoys storytelling and has published numerous stories in the *Chicken Soup for the Soul* series. She encourages others through her Write Life Workshops and webinars, speaks at conferences, and edits a popular writers' newsletter, "The Write Life." But her most important job is Grandma. Visit her at TracyCrump.com.

Brie Dalliant has since overcome her depression. She wishes for everyone out there to know that one life can change the world. One life can make a difference, and you are one life. Though she hopes to pursue a medical career when she is older, she plans on writing as a side job or hobby.

Lola Di Giulio De Maci is an essayist and children's author. Her stories appear in numerous *Chicken Soup for the Soul* books, the *Los Angeles Times*, *Reminisce* and *Sasee* magazines. Lola is a retired teacher with a Master of Arts in education and English. She writes overlooking the San Bernardino Mountains.

Stephanie Delorme taught fourth grade before deciding to stay home with her two miracle daughters, Evelyn and Abigail. She shares their stories on her blog thankyouinfertility.wordpress.com. In 2016, she opened an Etsy shop, Mommy's Heart Prints, where she strives to bless others through her artwork and writing.

J. Duval is a fourth year teacher who loves reading, writing, art, music, and mathematics. She loves working with young people and inspiring them to make a difference.

Deborah Elaine received her Bachelor of Arts from Ball State University in 2010. She enjoys traveling, writing, and spending time with her many nieces and nephews.

Marie Ellen is a very proud single mother of three talented children; her love for her children will often show in her passion for writing and poetry. She is a traveler and loves to explore new places and meet new people. Marie Ellen loves animals, reading, music, dancing and being close to the ocean.

Jerome Elmore received his bachelor's degree in Special Education and Masters of English and American Literature from Southern Illinois University Edwardsville. He is married to his wife Karen. Jerome enjoys trout fishing, traveling and gardening. He retired in 2015.

Tanya Estes has both a bachelor's and a master's degree from The University of Texas. She spent many years in education, mostly as a librarian. She now writes full-time while raising her son with her loving husband in Georgetown, TX.

Sara Etgen-Baker's teaching experience at Fabens High School provided her with both her greatest teaching challenges and her greatest rewards. Her story is a recap of her initial experience and her desperate desire to connect with and teach the students whose eagerness to learn captured her heart.

Melissa Face lives in Virginia with her husband and two children. She teaches English 11 and 12 at the Appomattox Regional Governor's School for the arts and technology. Melissa enjoys traveling, reading, and writing nonfiction when she is not busy grading student work. E-mail her at writermsface@yahoo.com.

Margaret Flaherty won the Teacher of the Year Award her first year of teaching high school English. Her essay "The Power of Character in the Classroom" is available on NEA.org and she is currently working on a memoir about surviving the first year of teaching.

George M. Flynn is a husband, father of three, freelance writer and a retired English teacher. He is also an avid gardener and the author of *Twilight Journey and Other Stories*, a collection of heartwarming short stories. The book is available by contacting him at georgeflynn46@hotmail.com.

Lynne Daroff Foosaner is a political activist, freelance writer, painter and grandmother… not necessarily in that order. Read her blog at WisdomoftheAged.wordpresss.com.

Daisy Franco is a writer, performer, and former teacher. She has been published in *Chicken Soup for the Soul: Dreams and Premonitions*, among other publications. Daisy holds a BA degree from the University of Illinois at Chicago and an MA degree from DePaul University. She is working on several writing projects.

Stephanie Gates is an educator by day, and writer by night. When she's not teaching or writing, she enjoys spending time with people she loves, dining out, traveling, dancing and anything else that nurtures her spirit.

Patricia Gordon taught general music in elementary classrooms, and now teaches music education courses at Grand Valley State University. She and her husband live in West Michigan near their five children, nine grandchildren, and two great-grandchildren. She writes romantic fiction under the name Patricia Kiyono.

Yvonne Evie Green taught Outdoor Environmental Ed. grades 1–12 in USD 501 Public Schools, Topeka, KS for twenty-four years, and first grade for thirteen. She also taught adult and children's zoology at the Topeka Zoo and has led a writing group since 2001. She enjoys her three children and four grandchildren. She's a true nature lover!

Lonnie D. Groendes is a U.S. Army veteran with a Master of Fine Arts degree in Creative Writing for the Media from the University of North Carolina at Greensboro. He is the author of two "cozy mystery" novels: *The Blue Ridge Murders* and *Deadly Reading,* and the inspirational book *Enchanted Summer* for all ages.

Bradley Hall was a substitute teacher in Jacksonville, FL for ten years. While he is no longer in the classroom, he still finds time to teach wayward students.

A native of Oklahoma, **Elizabeth Ann Harsany** has been teaching English for almost nine years. She has taught in public, private, and charter schools. She currently lives in Michigan with her loving and supportive husband, Joshua; their son, Zachary; and their dog, Logan. Her story is dedicated to the staff and students of Peterson-Warren Academy.

Miriam Hill is a frequent contributor to the *Chicken Soup for the Soul* series and has been published in *Writer's Digest*, *The Christian Science Monitor*, *Grit*, *St. Petersburg Times*, *The Sacramento Bee*, and Poynter online. Miriam's submission received Honorable Mention for Inspirational Writing in a Writer's Digest Writing Competition.

Jennie Ivey lives and writes in Tennessee. She is the author of numerous works of fiction and nonfiction, including stories in dozens of *Chicken Soup for the Soul* books. Learn more at jennieivey.com.

Mary Pat Johns is a Bible teacher at Faith Family Church in Victoria, TX. This is her second story published in the *Chicken Soup for the Soul* series. She writes devotionals, short stories, and is currently at work on her first book-length novel. Learn more at marypatjohns.com or e-mail her at johnsmarypat@yahoo.com.

Cindy Jolley is a former teacher who loves not only teaching, but also learning from her students and others around her. Inspired by her experiences in the classroom, Cindy is now following her heart to write and illustrate stories for children. She lives in Grapevine, TX.

Megan Pincus Kajitani is a writer, editor and educator. She's written for publications such as *The Chronicle of Higher Education* and *Mothering* magazine, and books such as *Mama, PhD*. She's edited books including The New York Times bestseller *The Daring Book for Girls*, and she has taught in various classrooms from kindergarten to adult ed.

Jeaninne Escallier Kato has several teaching credentials and a master's degree. She taught for thirty-six years in the California public school system and is author of the children's book *Manuel's Murals*. Jeaninne continues to write for online journals. She lives with her husband and three furry children in Northern California.

Wendy Keppley, a Florida native, counseled troubled teens and taught college courses for high school honor students. She enjoys family, playing with her grandsons, and living in the woods near Tampa, FL. Wendy also loves writing, kayaking, reading, yoga, exploring waterfalls, and oneirology. E-mail her at wendykep@gmail.com.

Catherine Kopp received her BS from Framingham State and her Master of Education from Lesley University. She has been teaching elementary school since 1973. She currently teaches fourth grade in Denver, CO, where she lives with her husband, Jim. During her free time, she enjoys reading, yoga, and gardening.

Jeanne Kraus is a retired elementary teacher with thirty-eight years of experience. She is a public speaker and author of children's books. Her three children's books deal with issues related to ADD in children. Currently, Jeanne is a private tutor and volunteer in a local elementary school.

Tom Krause, an Inspirational Educational Speaker, speaks to educational audiences nationwide. Tom has been published in the *Chicken Soup for the Soul* series more than twenty times. Learn more at coachkrause. com or e-mail him at justmetrk@aol.com.

Sandra J. Lansing received a Master of Arts in English Composition from California State University, San Bernardino in 1997. She has worked as a freelance and staff writer and is the author of three published books. Recently she completed a book of encouraging poetry. Sandra is a guest teacher with two daughters.

Carolyn Lee received a BS in Middle Grades Education from Mercer University and her MEd in TESOL from Grand Canyon University. She lives in Georgia with her husband, Gary. They have five adult children and nine grandchildren. Carolyn enjoys writing, traveling, researching her family tree, and doing faith-based ministry.

Genein Letford received her Bachelor of Arts from UCLA and a Master of Education from Cal State University. She has been awarded numerous teaching awards and is a sought-after speaker focusing on creative and financial literacy. She is working on her first book on these important topics.

Kristie Betts Letter has won several teaching awards in Colorado for forcing *Hamlet* on high school seniors, and loves playing pub trivia with her husband. Editorial L'Aleph publishes her poetry book *Under-Worldly*, available on Amazon. Learn more at kristiebettsletter.com.

Nancy Lewis is a retired public school educator who now works part-time as a pet sitter. In addition to writing, she enjoys playing bridge, visiting family, singing in the church choir, and coordinating a volunteer storytelling group. Nancy has one daughter, six grandchildren and a cat named Fred.

Barbara LoMonaco has worked for Chicken Soup for the Soul as an editor since 1998. She has co-authored two *Chicken Soup for the Soul* book titles and has had stories published in numerous other titles. Barbara is a graduate of the University of Southern California and has a teaching credential.

Ilana Long is a writer, actress, stand-up comic, English teacher and mom of teen twins. She is the author of *Ziggy's Big Idea*, published by Kar-Ben Publishing in 2014 and is seeking representation for her surreal, comic novel about teaching, titled *How I Married a Gelatinous Sea Blob: A Plagiarized Love Story*.

Katherine Mabb's hero is her daughter who is an artist, designer, and home renovation consultant/builder. Although retired, Katherine enjoys teaching at a public school, as well as facilitating a literacy course at her area library. She has a special place in her heart for all of her nieces and nephews.

Bridget Magee is a writer, poet, speaker, teacher, and mom — not always in that order. When not writing, Bridget can be found reading. She lives in Tucson, AZ with her husband, two daughters, and crazy dog, Smidgey.

Carrie Malinowski was a first grade teacher and reading tutor for many years. She now enjoys working with anxiety sufferers in the mental health field. Carrie is the author of *Tattletale: A Teacher's Memoir*, *Hand-Me-Down Bear*, and is a previous contributor to the *Chicken Soup for the Soul* series.

Mike McCrobie taught high school English for thirty-three years in Oswego, NY. He's now a contributing columnist for *The Palladium-Times*. His self-published memoir, *Our Oswego*, is available at amazon.com. He's proud to follow the lead of his daughter Sarah, who has had several stories published in the *Chicken Soup for the Soul* series.

Vickie McEntire writes about things that are important to her: literacy, community and family. She has been published in *Telling Stories*, a Calhoun Area Writers anthology, local magazines, and on her blog at aliteratelife.blogspot.com. Her first children's book, *Baby Birds*, inspired by her children and grandson, is available on Amazon.

Jessica McIntosh-Brockinton received several degrees from the University of Central Arkansas and is a Schedler Honors College and Sigma Sigma Sigma alumna. Recently married, she loves biking, kayaking, and traveling with her husband, Gary. Currently, she works for the Arkansas Department of Education.

Caroline S. McKinney recently retired from the School of Education at the University of Colorado where she was an adjunct, teaching graduate courses in children's literature, reading and writing for over twenty-five years. During many of those years she was a literacy teacher and staff developer for Boulder Valley Schools.

Melissa Monteith holds a BA from Warner University and a M.Ed. from Antioch University. She has a passion for inspiring others to find the silver lining in each day. She is a teacher, writer, and motivational speaker. She resides in Pennsylvania with her beautiful daughter who has autism. E-mail her monteitm@gmail.com.

Linda Morel publishes personal essays and is a food columnist at the *Jewish Exponent*. She teaches writing through Teachers & Writers Collaborative. Linda is writing a family memoir. She lives in Manhattan with her husband and enjoys cooking and baking with her grand-daughters. E-mail her at lindamorel2@gmail.com.

Marya Morin is a freelance writer. Her stories have appeared in publications such as *Woman's World* and Hallmark. Marya also penned a weekly humorous column for an online newsletter, and writes custom poetry on request. She lives in the country with her husband. E-mail her at Akushla514@hotmail.com.

Nicole L.V. Mullis is the author of the novel *A Teacher Named Faith*. Her work has appeared in newspapers, magazines and anthologies, including the *Chicken Soup for the Soul* series. Her plays have been produced in New York, California and Michigan. She lives in Michigan with her husband and children.

Katie O'Connell writes from the heart. A former teacher and mother of two, she is passionate about living an authentic and meaningful life. Her writing has been featured in *Reader's Digest*, *Sasee*, *Patheos*, and several *Chicken Soup for the Soul* books. Follow her work at blog. heartwiredwriting.com.

Amellia Pinson has been teaching middle and high school students for the past ten years. She has learned that one word in her English classroom can be just as powerful to her students as one note in the band room was to her. She still plays her flute in church each week, and Mr. Curtis will always be her favorite teacher.

Wendy Poole is now a retired Early Childhood Educator. She worked in both staff and management positions within the ECE field as well as teaching part-time at a community college. Wendy also wrote/piloted a literacy program for preschoolers and also wrote/piloted a parenting information program for newcomers to Canada.

Jill Printzenhoff teaches high school science in the southern tier of New York, and counts it a privilege to work with teens. When she's not in the classroom, she spends as much time as possible on family adventures, biking rail trails, kayaking local waterways, fishing, and writing nonfiction and inspirational stories.

Laura Raicu was born in Bucharest, Romania and currently resides in Illinois where she teaches high school English. She has a Master of Arts in Teaching from National Louis University and a BA from the University of Wisconsin–Madison. She has been writing and telling stories since she was a child.

Cory Rasmussen teaches tenth grade world literature in Huntington Beach, CA and is an MFA student at Chapman University. He is an advisor for ASB, KIWIN'S, and *Runes Literary Magazine*. There's no other career he'd rather be in, and he feels grateful to be involved with such a great school.

Michele L. Rausch is an educator and coach in St. Louis, MO. She wears many hats in her life and believes in the power of a good hug. "In my twenties, I spent most of my time trying to make people love me. In my thirties, I learned to love myself. Now, in my forties, I'm sharing that love with the rest of the world."

This is **Mary Ellen Redmond's** twenty-third year teaching English to students in the Dennis-Yarmouth School District on Cape Cod, MA. *The Ocean Effect*, her second chapbook, was published in 2011, but the publication she is most proud of is the poem tattooed on her son's rib cage.

Virginia Reeder lives in East Texas and is a retired teacher. She spent fifteen years as a cross-country truck driver, among the many occupations she considers "life experiences" prior to becoming a teacher. Since retiring, she has joined a local artist consortium, taking art and writing lessons while enjoying many grandchildren and great-grandchildren.

Sharika Reeves was born in the city of Pahokee, FL where she and her siblings were raised by their grandmother. She's the youngest of five and works as an administrative assistant. Sharika enjoys traveling, journaling, writing poetry, and spending time with her family. Her goal is to become a children's book author.

Martin Reisert, a California State Teacher of the Year, teaches sixth grade at Oak Valley Middle School in the Poway Unified School District. He has traveled to nearly sixty countries, and together he and his wife Heidi have two boys. He has a tennis academy. Learn more at ReisertTennis.com.

Julie Rine holds degrees from Ohio State University and Marygrove College. She has one daughter and teaches high school English in northeastern Ohio. She enjoys yoga, writing, reading, and geocaching. She is a frequent blogger for the Ohio Education Association's blog, *Voices of Change*.

Ellen Rosenberg is a retired teacher who now spends her time riding horses, caring for wildlife, and writing.

Darlis Sailors graduated from Vanguard University in Costa Mesa, CA with a Bachelor of Arts degree. She was a California certified classroom teacher for several years before opening a private music studio in her home. Now in Arizona, she enjoys local walkabouts, photography, reading, and writing for children and adults.

JC Santos teaches humanities to adolescents by day; by night, he writes, reads and revises what he hopes will be a published novel. He loves playing basketball — as long as his joints cooperate — and a good fish fry. Despite aspiring to author novels, he'll always be a teacher. E-mail him at mr.jsantos@gmail.com.

Anne Cavanaugh Sawan lives with her husband, five children, two dogs, three cats, chickens and assorted fish in the suburbs of Boston, MA. She has written for *Scary Mommy*, *BLUNTMoms*, *Adoptive Families*, *MeeGenius*, *Brain, Child*, and recently published her first picture book, *What Can Your Grandma Do?*

As a retired educator, **Gwyn Schneck** celebrates the diversity of our world. She currently writes, speaks, and loves to bring life lessons and humor to any audience. Learn more at mykidscounselor.com.

Eloise Elaine Ernst Schneider is an artist, author, and teacher. After many years in the classroom, Eloise now spends most of her time creating in her art studio. Her paintings can be found at fineartamerica. com/profiles/eloise-elaine-schneider.html?tab=artwork.

Jackie Sinclair graduated with a BA in Elementary Education from Spring Arbor College. She and her husband, Gary, have two grown children and six grandsons. Together they enjoy hiking, traveling, reading and exploring new places. Jackie is especially thankful for Gary's help in writing her story.

E.M. Slone is a dedicated wife, mother, educator, artist, writer and cancer survivor. She has completed a dual BA in Art Studio and Art Education at the University of Kentucky and an MA in School Counseling. She enjoys all things creative and finds solace in nature, books, and yoga.

Ariela Solomon is a social work student at Salem State University. She currently interns at an elementary school and finds it extremely rewarding. Ariela enjoys traveling, playing music, being outdoors, writing, yoga and spending time with friends and family. E-mail her at aa12sponge@verizon.net.

Mara Somerset is a product manager in the automotive industry. She has two daughters, two stepchildren and four lively grandchildren. When she isn't running, crafting, reading or traveling with her husband, she loves to write inspirational short stories.

Naomi Townsend is a teacher, new mother, and writer based in Portland, OR. She is currently working on her first children's book.

Award-winning author **Susan Traugh's** stories have appeared in several

Chicken Soup for the Soul books. Her YA novel, *The Edge of Brilliance*, about the heroism of a teen with bipolar is on her website at www. susantraugh.com. Susan lives with her family in the San Diego area where she reads, writes, and walks in the California sunshine.

Jude Walsh writes memoir, essays, and fiction. A teacher for thirty-three years, she focused on literacy, children with learning disorders, language development and, with a group of visionary teachers, founded a school. Her writing is published in literary magazines and anthologies, including *The Magic of Memoir* (She Writes Press, 2016).

Dorann Weber is a freelance photographer and newfound writer living in the Pinelands of southern New Jersey. Her photos have been featured in ads through Getty Images, and on several Hallmark cards. Her love for *Chicken Soup for the Soul* books inspired her to write. Dorann likes hiking with her family and exploring new towns.

Kate Wells received her Bachelor of Arts in Anthropology from The University of Texas at Austin. She is an English teacher at Charter University Prep in California. She volunteers at the local animal shelter and is a volunteer violinist at the American River College in Sacramento.

After eleven years of teaching, **Patricia Wood** is now a stay-at-home mom to her two toddler girls. Happily married and pursuing her dream of being a writer, her daughters and educational experiences inspire her writing.

Dallas Woodburn is a writer, editor, teacher and literacy advocate living in the San Francisco Bay Area. To date, she has been a proud contributor to more than two dozen titles in the *Chicken Soup for the Soul* series. She regularly blogs about simple, joyful, healthy living at DaybyDayMasterpiece.com.

Jenine Zimmers is the author of the novel *Fatty* as well as several cookbooks and children's books. She is also a graphic designer and former reporter, whose work has appeared in *The Washington Times*, *New York Post* and *Daily Racing Form*. Jenine is a graduate of Mary Washington College and lives in Brooklyn, NY.

Meet Amy Newmark

Amy Newmark is the bestselling author, editor-in-chief, and publisher of the *Chicken Soup for the Soul* book series. Since 2008, she has published 140 new books, most of them national bestsellers in the U.S. and Canada, more than doubling the number of Chicken Soup for the Soul titles in print today. She is also the author of *Simply Happy*, a crash course in Chicken Soup for the Soul advice and wisdom that is filled with easy-to-implement, practical tips for having a better life.

Amy is credited with revitalizing the Chicken Soup for the Soul brand, which has been a publishing industry phenomenon since the first book came out in 1993. By compiling inspirational and aspirational true stories curated from ordinary people who have had extraordinary experiences, Amy has kept the twenty-four-year-old Chicken Soup for the Soul brand fresh and relevant.

Amy graduated *magna cum laude* from Harvard University where she majored in Portuguese and minored in French. She then embarked on a three-decade career as a Wall Street analyst, a hedge fund manager, and a corporate executive in the technology field. She is a Chartered Financial Analyst.

Her return to literary pursuits was inevitable, as her honors thesis in college involved traveling throughout Brazil's impoverished northeast region, collecting stories from regular people. She is delighted to have come full circle in her writing career — from collecting stories "from the people" in Brazil as a twenty-year-old to, three decades later, collecting stories "from the people" for Chicken Soup for the Soul.

When Amy and her husband Bill, the CEO of Chicken Soup for the Soul, are not working, they are visiting their four grown children.

Follow Amy on Twitter @amynewmark. Listen to her free daily podcast, The Chicken Soup for the Soul Podcast, at www.chickensoup. podbean.com, or find it on iTunes, the Podcasts app on iPhone, or on your favorite podcast app on other devices.

Meet Alex Kajitani

Fifteen years ago, Alex Kajitani was a struggling new teacher in one of California's poorest neighborhoods. His students seemed unmotivated, unengaged and uninterested in what he was teaching. Demoralized and desperate, he set out on a journey to turn his class, and his life, around.

Today, Alex holds the title of California Teacher of the Year and a Top-4 Finalist for National Teacher of the Year, 2009, and is lauded for his innovation and "real talk" as a teacher. He's also known as "The Rappin' Mathematician," and the creator of MultiplicationNation. com, the first-of-its-kind, interactive, online program devoted to getting *every* kid to master their times tables, so they can be confident in math, and in life.

A highly sought-after speaker, Alex's journey — from frustrated new teacher to being honored at The White House Rose Garden — is one he now shares with educators and business leaders across the country, to inspire them to new heights and fresh ways of thinking.

Alex is also the author of *Owning It: Proven Strategies for Success in ALL of Your Roles as a Teacher Today,* named "Recommended Reading" by the U.S. Department of Education, has a popular TEDx Talk, and was featured on the *CBS Evening News*, with Katie Couric exclaiming, "I LOVE that guy!"

In his free time, you can find Alex hanging out with his family, or at the beach surfing (or both!).

For more inspiration, or to book Alex to speak to your school, district or organization, visit AlexKajitani.com.

Chicken Soup for the Soul

Thank You

We have been so inspired by these stories, not just the 101 that you have read in this volume, but the thousands that were submitted. We read them all, and they make us admire all the teachers out there even more than we already did. We hope that you will find them as inspiring as we did.

We owe special thanks to our editor Susan Heim, who not only read thousands of submissions, but also did the first round of editing and picking out the quotes that add so much value at the beginning of each story. We are also grateful to Ronelle Frankel, Mary Fisher, Barbara LoMonaco, and D'ette Corona for reading hundreds of submissions each.

D'ette Corona, our Associate Publisher, was Amy and Alex's fearless leader in creating the final manuscript and working with all our wonderful writers. Barbara LoMonaco and Kristiana Pastir, along with outside proofreader Elaine Kimbler, jumped in at the end to proof, proof, proof. And yes, there will always be typos anyway, so feel free to let us know about them at webmaster@chickensoupforthesoul.com and we will correct them in future printings.

We also want to thank Alex's wife, Megan Pincus Kajitani, for helping with story selection and preliminary editing behind the scenes. She shared a story with us in this collection as well.

The whole publishing team deserves a hand, including Senior Director of Marketing Maureen Peltier, Senior Director of Production Victor Cataldo, and graphic designer Daniel Zaccari, who turned our manuscript into this beautiful book.

Chicken Soup for the Soul

Sharing Happiness, Inspiration, and Hope

R eal people sharing real stories, every day, all over the world. In 2007, *USA Today* named *Chicken Soup for the Soul* one of the five most memorable books in the last quarter-century. With over 100 million books sold to date in the U.S. and Canada alone, more than 200 titles in print, and translations into more than forty languages, "chicken soup for the soul" is one of the world's best-known phrases.

Today, twenty-four years after we first began sharing happiness, inspiration and hope through our books, we continue to delight our readers with new titles, but have also evolved beyond the bookstore with super premium pet food, television shows, podcasts, positive journalism from aplus.com, and licensed products, all revolving around true stories, as we continue "changing the world one story at a time®." Thanks for reading!

Chicken Soup for the Soul

Share with Us

We all have had Chicken Soup for the Soul moments in our lives. If you would like to share your story or poem with millions of people around the world, go to chickensoup.com and click on "Submit Your Story." You may be able to help another reader and become a published author at the same time. Some of our past contributors have launched writing and speaking careers from the publication of their stories in our books!

We only accept story submissions via our website. They are no longer accepted via mail or fax.

To contact us regarding other matters, please send us an e-mail through webmaster@chickensoupforthesoul.com, or fax or write us at:

Chicken Soup for the Soul
P.O. Box 700
Cos Cob, CT 06807-0700
Fax: 203-861-7194

One more note from your friends at Chicken Soup for the Soul: Occasionally, we receive an unsolicited book manuscript from one of our readers, and we would like to respectfully inform you that we do not accept unsolicited manuscripts and we must discard the ones that appear.

Announcing...

a literacy-based anti-bullying program

- a literacy-based, proactive anti-bullying program
- Grades 1–12
- http://www.chickensoup.com/hallwayheroes

This book shines a bright light on the widespread goodwill in our world as everyday heroes demonstrate acts of kindness, compassion and commitment to others. These stories will uplift you, inspire you, and brighten your day.

978-1-61159-961-9

It's always better to look on the bright side. The 101 personal stories in *Chicken Soup for the Soul: Think Possible* will inspire you to follow your heart and make your dreams reality. The book is filled with stories about optimism, perseverance and strength from people who have reached higher and accomplished more than anyone thought they could. You'll be inspired!

978-1-61159-952-7

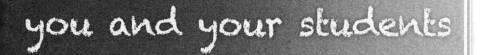

you and your students

Give a child gifts that will last a lifetime—self-esteem, tolerance, values, and inner strength. This book is filled with inspirational stories for children and their families to share, all about kids making good choices and doing the right thing.

978-1-61159-927-5

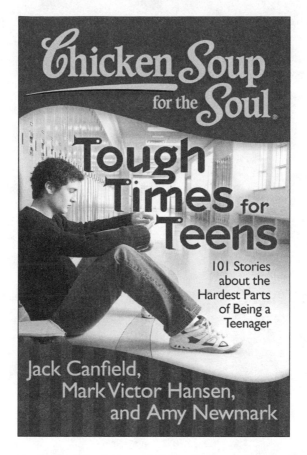

Chicken Soup for the Soul: Tough Times for Teens supports and inspires teenagers during their most challenging times, reminding them they are not alone as they read stories from teens just like them with the same struggles.

978-1-935096-80-1

helping kids grow up

Chicken Soup for the Soul

Changing lives one story at a time ®
www.chickensoup.com